Networks and Places

Networks and Places

Social Relations in the Urban Setting

Claude S. Fischer

Robert Max Jackson
C. Ann Stueve
Kathleen Gerson
Lynne McCallister Jones
with
Mark Baldassare

THE FREE PRESS
A Division of Macmillan Publishing Co., Inc.
NEW YORK

Collier Macmillan Publishers
LONDON

The Free Press
A Division of Macmillan Publishing Co., Inc.
866 Third Avenue, New York, N. Y. 10022

Collier Macmillan Canada, Ltd.

Library of Congress Catalog Card Number: 76–55101

Printed in the United States of America

printing number

1   2   3   4   5   6   7   8   9   10

Library of Congress Cataloging in Publication Data

Main entry under title:

Networks and places.

    Includes index.
    1. Sociology, Urban. 2. Community.
3. Social structure. 4. Social interaction.
5. Interpersonal relations. I. Fischer, Claude S.

HT153.N47   301.36'3   76-55101
ISBN 0-02-910240-5

Contents

List of Tables

Preface

Individuals are linked to their society primarily through relations with other individuals: with kin, friends, coworkers, fellow club members, and so on. We are each the center of a web of social bonds that radiates outward to the people whom we know intimately, those whom we know well, those whom we know casually, and to the wider society beyond. These are our personal *social networks*. Society affects us largely through tugs on the strands of our networks—shaping our attitudes, providing opportunities, making demands on us, and so forth. And it is by tugging at those same strands that we make our individual impacts on society—influencing other people's opinions, obtaining favors from "insiders," forming action groups. Even the most seemingly formal of institutions, such as bureaucracies, are in many ways, to the people who know them well, frames around networks of personal ties. In sum, to understand the individual in society, we need to understand the fine mesh of social relations between the person and society; that is, we must understand social networks.

This book is one of a growing number on social networks; it is particularly concerned with networks from the individual's perspective. It presents several empirical studies addressed largely to the question of how people's structural situations affect the social relations they form, and the character of those relations. We examine several structural circumstances, but focus most closely on individuals' physical locations in the urban setting. We examine, first, how aspects of social relations (for example, frequency of contact and intimacy) are associated with one another, and how people's social, economic, and life-cycle positions shape those bonds. Second, we examine whether and how living in different neighborhoods affects personal relations, what leads people to form attachments to their neighborhoods, and what happens to those attachments when people move between locations. We pursue these studies by analyzing two large surveys and reviewing previously published research. The concern throughout is to understand how the structural circumstances that individuals face influence the formation and maintenance of social ties.

Our studies are joined by more than a common concern with social networks. Two general themes run throughout the book. One is a specific theoretical perspective on human behavior and, particularly, on how people form personal networks. We stress that individuals create their networks but must build them within limits. People are constantly choosing which of several possible relations to pursue and how to behave in them, but they are choosing from among a small set of socially structured alternatives. As individuals' social positions differ, so do their alternatives, and thus, so do their networks and social behavior.

In the second theme we explore a familiar topic in social philosophy and sociology: the idea that modern society has brought a "decline of community," a weakening of intimate and supportive social bonds. The study of personal networks, by clearly articulating the components of "community" and by providing a precise way of analyzing social relations, allows us to examine the topic in an exact and empirical way. We certainly do not answer the question of whether "community" has declined in modern society, but we do have several observations, both analytical and empirical, to make about the argument.

Division of Labor.   It is difficult to disentangle the separate contributions of six authors to a work that has been collective in many ways. We have collaborated in several of its chapters, commented fully on each other's work, discussed at length our ideas, and striven to write a coherent book. Nonetheless, some account can be given that differentiates our respective contributions.

Fischer began this work as a pilot study on the relationship between aspects of urban location and features of personal networks. As others successively joined the project, it broadened to reflect their interests as well. Given our common concern with networks and urbanism, it made sense to combine our work into a single book. Members of the group, solely or in various combinations, prepared the separate chapters; the authors' names are placed below each chapter title. As well as generally supervising the work, Fischer rewrote (and Jones edited) all of the chapters, so that the book is thematically and stylistically the product of one hand.

The order of authorship on the title page reflects the amounts of research and writing and the general intellectual contribution of each author. In addition, Jackson developed the operational definitions of network variables and prepared the Detroit survey data file; Stueve prepared the National survey data-set that we also used; and Jones edited drafts of the book for substance and style. Baldassare's responsibilities were limited to preparation of Chapter 6.

Acknowledgments.   There were two basic sources of support for this research. One was a small grant from the Center for Studies of Metropolitan Problems, National Institute of Mental Health (grant number

1–R03–MH25406; 1974–5). The other was continuing aid over more than three years from the Institute of Urban and Regional Development, University of California, Berkeley. We are grateful to Melvin M. Webber, Director of the Institute, for his unflagging support. In addition, Jackson, Stueve, and Baldassare were supported in part by fellowships from the National Institute of Mental Health's Training Program in Social Structure and Personality at Berkeley. We appreciate the generosity of the Detroit Area Study and the National Opinion Research Center in making their surveys available to us.

Various people have commented on parts of the manuscript and we thank them: Ron Breiger, Paul Burstein, Roger Friedland, Mark Granovetter, Jane Grant, Barbara Heyns, Robert Mayer, Ann Swidler, and Erik Wright. We thank the staff at the Institute of Urban and Regional Development for typing the manuscript. And, for helping turn manuscript into book, we thank Robert K. Merton, Charles Kadushin, and, at The Free Press, Charles Smith, Gladys Topkis, and Bob Harrington.

Berkeley, California   C.S.F.
March 1977

1. Perspectives on Community and Personal Relations

Claude S. Fischer

"DECLINE OF COMMUNITY" has become a powerful catch-phrase in the twentieth century. It connotes a widespread set of beliefs about the direction of modern society and the quality of individuals' social relations: that changes in technology and society have, over the last few generations, broken down many of the barriers around small and autonomous groups; that individuals have eagerly left those groups, be they family, church, or village, to seek adventure and personal advantage beyond the crumbling walls; and, most important, that individuals have in the end found themselves alone, bereft of the intimate social ties that were woven in the confines of those small, largely bygone worlds. Thus, in the words of a recent best-selling book, "Great numbers of [Americans] feel unconnected to either people [or] places and through much of the nation there is a breakdown in community living. . . . There is a general shattering of small-group life. . . . We are becoming a nation of strangers" (Packard, 1972: 1–2).

The decline-of-community thesis is more than a general outlook on contemporary life. It also encompasses a set of assumptions and inferences about historical change, social structure, and social psychology. Such elements of the "decline" thesis have motivated us to closely examine the processes by which personal relations are established, the factors that influence their development, and especially the connections between the nature of those relations and the places in which people live.

Running through much of this volume is a concern with—indeed, an argument with—two general propositions drawn from the decline-of-community analysis: first, that limitations on the choices individuals have in forming social relations promote intimacy and commitment in those relations; and, second, that the local territorial group, the village or

1

neighborhood, is a "natural community," involvement in which is critical to social and psychological well-being. These are not historical propositions about decline; rather, they are social-psychological assumptions implicit in the historical argument. We cannot test the historical theory (although we do review some evidence on it in the last chapter); instead, we examine the social psychology assumed in the historical theory.

Overview

Part I of the book introduces network analysis and explores the nature of social networks. In Chapter 2, we define network analysis, review its development and current status, and try to demonstrate its utility as a way of understanding both personal relations and social structure, particularly in the urban setting. In Chapter 3, we examine the empirical coherence of several attributes of links (such as the intimacy of a friendship) and of networks (such as the homogeneity of a set of friends), contrasting a choice-constraint to a mechanistic perspective in making sense of the pattern of results. In Chapter 4, we examine some of the structural constraints on the formation of social networks, in particular, looking at the development of class-, ethnic-, and age-segregated ties. In Chapter 5, we focus on the consequences of individual movement through the life-cycle, exploring the changes in social networks that occur as men marry, have children, and see their children leave home.

In Part II, we analyze the interaction between social networks and attributes of the places people live. In Chapter 6, we challenge the widespread assumption that population density inhibits or distorts social relations. In Chapter 7, we argue that suburbanism generates local social ties and local activity by altering the opportunities for, and the costs of, alternative social relations. In Chapter 8, we ask what factors promote individuals' social and psychological connections to their places of residence and discover that "attachment" is a multifaceted phenomenon, each facet a consequence of somewhat different contingencies which people face and choices which they make. In Chapter 9, we challenge directly the thesis that attachment to place is vital for "healthy" social relations, in a review of the literature on residential mobility and an examination of our own data on local and extralocal relations. In the concluding chapter, we return to the decline-of-community thesis, reviewing the historical evidence and assessing the implications of our studies for that thesis.

We have approached the studies presented here from a specific perspective on human behavior, different from that which seems to lie behind the theory of decline. This perspective, which we have labeled a "choice-constraint" model, views human behavior, including the formation and maintenance of social relations, as *choices* made with limited alternatives and limited resources. Individuals' choices vary with both their preferences *and* their options. We will argue, for example, that geographical mobility and population density have no simple, direct effects on people but that their effects instead depend on the various opportunities and constraints that different people face.

The purpose of the first two parts of this chapter is to discuss in detail our choice-constraint perspective and the relationship of our studies to the decline-of-community thesis. The final section introduces our empirical method, describes the survey data we used, and specifies our analytical techniques.

Perspective

A distinction can be drawn between social-psychological models that depict human behavior as mechanistically determined and those that depict it as involving "choice between socially structured alternatives" (Stinchcombe, 1975: 12). James Coleman describes the two perspectives in this fashion:

> There are two quite different streams of work in the study of social action. . . . The first conception explains man's behavior as response to his environment; the second explains his behavior as pursuit of a goal. The first searches for causal processes and determinants of behavior, and often uses a mechanistic explanatory frame, which employs concepts of "forces" and "resultant action." . . . The second conception sees man's action as goal-directed . . . [and is] based on a conception of rational economic man (1974: 1).

Our perspective on social relations is nearer to the second conception, seeing personal bonds as the consequences of structured choices. People are constantly choosing whom they will begin, continue, or cease to interact with, approaching these relations in an essentially rational manner.[1] People seek and keep associates whom they find more rewarding than others. And they form relations that are exchanges of goods, services, and emotional support (Simmel, 1907; Thibaut and Kelley, 1959; Homans, 1974).

Stated so baldly, it might seem that we espouse a raw form of philosophical individualism; we do not. Individuals must select from the options provided by their society and their immediate milieus, and individuals learn from their society what is rewarding and what is costly about those op-

---

[1] "Rational" is here used in Simon's (1957) sense of "bounded rationality"—maximizing one's returns under conditions of incomplete options and incomplete information. It does not necessarily imply an abstract "free will."

tions.[2] It is in this sense that we focus on processes of individual will and choice, and how they are structured by a set of physical and social constraints.

Social philosophy has long been divided between these two perspectives which, respectively, assign analytical priority to the individual actor and to society. The philosophical individualism of the eighteenth century, as expressed in the doctrines of utilitarianism and the social contract, was strongly attacked by most of the early sociologists in the nineteenth century. Tönnies, Durkheim, and others assigned priority instead to society and revealed the inadequacy of philosophical individualism's concept of the social order. (After all, individuals do not vote on or negotiate their society's norms, values, languages, and customs.) However, in emphasizing this societal perspective, the importance of the individual and individual choice was relatively neglected. Perhaps the emphasis has swung too far in the other direction. It is now often difficult to find any meaningful sense of individual actors in many sociological models.

Instead, many sociologists have adopted simple mechanistic models of human behavior. In these (usually implicit) models, one "variable" is thought to "cause" another, much as one billiard ball strikes another—to use David Hume's (1748: 43) example.[3] One usually cannot find an individual decision-maker in these formulations. For example, individuals are seen as frustrated by society and therefore reacting violently, in an almost automatic manner, like a dam bursting under pressure; or they are seen as being "caused" to achieve certain occupational positions because of their family backgrounds; or they are seen as being moved to certain political behaviors by their locations in the economic structure. These formulations depict a passive individual, pushed by forces external to him- or herself.

This mechanistic view is particularly common, for example, in the study of the interaction between people and places. This has not always been so. The Chicago School, where the study of urban ecology began, interpreted ecological factors as structural circumstances to which individuals and social institutions must adjust. (For instance, retail merchants make their locational decisions on the basis of existing patterns of population distribution.) Certain contemporary urban sociologists—Herbert Gans and William Michelson, for example—continue in this tradition. They describe people as making decisions among the alternatives that the eco-

---

[2] This view is similar to that of Marx—hardly a philosophical individualist:

> What is society . . . ? The product of men's reciprocal activity. Are men free to choose this or that form of society for themselves? By no means. . . .
> The productive forces are therefore the result of practical human energy, but this energy is itself conditioned by the circumstances in which men find themselves . . . by the social form which exists before they do (Marx, 1846: 3).

[3] O'Brien and Sterne (1974) call this a "point-vector" model; see also Coleman (1974) and Stinchcombe (1975).

logical structure has provided and adapting their lives to the limitations of their places.

However, another point of view has emerged, albeit without any explicit formulation. Many sociologists and others concerned with ecological factors have treated them as if they were simple and mechanical "causal forces." They imply that these "forces"—density, city size, building design, and so on—impinge on human relations and psyches in some direct (or at least unexplicated) way. As Janet Abu-Lughod has commented, researchers have taken "a rather simple-minded approach to causality, tending to view ecological factors, such as building type, site plan, and community size, as independent variables or causes which had predictable effects on the quality of life" (1968: 157).[4]

One sees this mechanistic approach in many essays on people and space, especially in essays on population density. Oft-quoted researchers interpret density as a direct causal force on individuals, usually as a force that creates "pathologies." A choice-constraint approach focuses instead on how density affects the alternatives people face. Density can mean, for example, less space within which to work, or more people with whom to talk. Thus, the effects of density are contingent on the goals individuals have and the resources they can apply to goal-seeking. To the resident of a Park Avenue penthouse, the density of Manhattan may mean just that much more of life to choose from.

Perhaps we have drawn the distinction between "simple mechanistic" models and a choice-constraint model too sharply in this example and in general. Sociologists in the former tradition could, if asked, describe the actors in their models: the individuals who select ways of coping with crowding, choose which object of anger to attack, decide which occupation to pursue (given the opportunities provided by their family background), and select the political stance appropriate to their self-interest. The point, however, is that individuals as actors are relatively unimportant in these formulations; the focus is, rather, on social forces, causal mechanisms impinging on individuals. We intend to focus our analysis on the person, to place the impetus of social action within a perceiving and

---

[4] Louis Wirth (1945: 177) made a similar observation:

> In the ecological studies . . . it has sometimes been naively assumed that once the spatial distribution of people, institutions, functions, and problems has been traced and their concentration and dispersion noted, there remains nothing for the ecologists to do but to relate these phenomena to other ecological data to arrive at valid explanations. . . . In view of our present-day knowledge concerning social causation, we might well be predisposed to follow the general principle that physical factors, while by no means negligible in their influence upon social life and psychological phenomena, are at best conditioning factors offering the possibilities and setting the limits for social and psychological existence and development. In other words, they set the stage for man, the actor.

choosing individual, and to interpret social causes as structural limitations on individual choice and behavior.[5]

This difference in analytical emphasis is quite abstract, but it has consequences. Focusing on the individual as actor or the individual as acted upon leads to seeing theoretical problems in different ways, much like seeing figure or ground in an optical illusion. And thus it leads to different theoretical answers. We will see in Chapter 3, for example, the differing implications of interpreting social networks as products of individual selection or as *a priori* structures impinging on the individual.

One programmatic implication of this perspective is that the well-being of individuals is not necessarily maximized by directly manipulating social variables such as local involvement, density, or mobility. We may be more likely to maximize it by expanding the *choices*—that is, options, resources, and autonomy—individuals have with respect to the places they live in and the relations they form. At the same time, it must be recognized that expanding the choices and increasing the well-being of separate *individuals* may not guarantee the well-being of the *society;* it may, in fact, do the opposite. (See further discussion in Chapter 10).

Decline of Community

Our research does not test the theory that modern society has undergone a decline of community—a theory expounded in various forms by classical scholars such as Tönnies, Durkheim, Weber, and Park, and their

---

[5] This perspective is in some ways similar to Parsons' theory of action (Parsons, 1968), particularly in its voluntarism. Parsons' voluntarism and our own both stand in the middle ground between a raw individualism in which actors are totally self-directed and self-propelled and a crude determinism in which actors are pushed about by external biological and material forces. However, there are crucial differences of emphasis between the two positions, particularly with respect to where in the middle ground they stand. Parsons stresses internalized values and norms as they key influences on action; he takes external "conditions to action" largely for granted. Consequently, variation in individual behavior is primarily explained by variations in internalized norms (for example, subcultural differences, or variations in socialization). In this book, we stress those conditions to action, opportunities and constraints, as the key influences on action, and take values and norms largely for granted. (Structurally conditioned needs, such as space for a growing family, we consider in the category of "conditions.") Consequently, variation in individual behavior is explained primarily by variations in the circumstances of individual choice. While Parsons' attention is focused on the structure of values and norms, ours is focused on the structure of opportunities and constraints. Thus, our position, while certainly compatible with Parsons' voluntarism, is closer to that of Homans and Coleman, in which subjective aspects of social action are represented by a relatively simple and universal model (rational economic man) and external circumstances of rewards and costs determine variations and change (see discussions by Coser [1976: 147] and Wallace [1975]). We do not claim that this perspective is always preferable, but that it is more satisfactory for the problems at hand.

contemporary heirs such as Nisbet, Stein, Mills, Kenniston, and Fromm. It is a theory of such scope that it may be beyond any direct empirical test. In some of our analyses, we do, however, assess what appear to be underlying propositions about the social psychology of personal relations. The key proposition of this sort is, we shall argue, that *limitation on the number of potential social relations available to individuals leads to more communal social relations. Communal* refers to relations of intimacy and moral commitment, the sort of relations sociologists generally assume to be important for psychological well-being. A proposition derivative from this one states that spatial limitations in particular promote communal ties, and thus implies that local social relations are more communal than extralocal ones. (The reader will recognize these propositions as elements of the traditional conservative critique of modern society, in which expanding freedom for the individual is considered to be ultimately self- and socially destructive.)

These propositions are, of course, not manifest on the surface of decline theory. We must show how they can be abstracted from the relevant texts, a demonstration that involves at least four steps. First, we examine the concept of "community" and argue that it contains an implicit proposition of its own, that communal relations develop only in corporate groups. Second, we argue that this proposition can be satisfactorily explained only if one assumes that limitations on the choice of social relations promote communal relations. Third, we try to show how this assumption lies behind ideas about *local* community. And fourth, we try to show that the assumption does lie behind the historical thesis that community has declined.

THE CONCEPT OF "COMMUNITY"

"The concept of community has been the concern of sociologists for more than two hundred years, but even a satisfactory definition of it in sociological terms appears as remote as ever" (Bell and Newby, 1974: xliii; see also Hillery, 1955).[6] Robert Nisbet, the most forceful contemporary proponent of the theory, never quite defines community even as he calls it "the most fundamental and far-reaching of sociology's unit ideas." Instead, he describes its aspects: it "encompasses" relations of "personal intimacy, emotional depth, moral commitment, social cohesion, and continuity in time"; it is founded on man conceived in his wholeness"; it "draws its psychological strength" from "deep levels of motivation"; it "achieves fulfillment in a submergence of individual will"; and so on

---

[6] For present purposes, we can set aside two commonplace usages of "community": as a place of settlement (for example, the community of Berkeley), and as a group of people who share some other trait (for example, the community of scholars).

(Nisbet, 1966: 47–48; Tönnies' [1887] discussion is similar).[7] The community, whatever it is exactly, is contrasted to "non-communal relations of competition or conflict, utility or contractual assent" (Nisbet, 1966: 48), relations in which individuals exchange or cooperate for each one's personal ends. In Durkheim's (1889: 4) words, no one in these non-communal settings "will do anything for anyone unless it be in exchange for a similar service or a recompense which he judges to be the equivalent of what he gives." While the traditional family is depicted as the archetype community, the market serves as the archetype non-community.

Examinations of descriptions of community and similar ideas (for example, "mechanical solidarity") suggests that they contain two more specific concepts—"corporate group" and "communal relations"—and a proposition joining the two. *Corporate* refers to a group in which needs and wills of individuals are subordinate to the needs and collective will of the whole.[8] These descriptions usually refer to traditional corporate groups, those based on what Geertz (1963: 109) has called *primordial* attachments: "By a primordial attachment is meant one that stems from the . . . assumed 'givens' of social existence: immediate contiguity and kin connection mainly." Families, self-enclosed villages, and traditional lineages are examples of such corporate groups. *Communal* refers to relations that are "characterized by personal intimacy, emotional depth, moral commitment, social cohesion, and continuity in time" (Nisbet, 1966: 47).[9] These two concepts are linked by an essentially unexamined assumption, the proposition that communal relations arise in primordial corporate groups, that they usually cannot arise outside of such corporate groups, and so the weakening of these corporate groups reduces the communal quality of personal relations. It is because Nisbet believes that primordial corporate groups have declined historically that he also believes that although "interpersonal relationships doubtless exist as abundantly in our age as in any other . . . it is becoming apparent that for more and more people such relationships are morally empty and psychologically baffling" (Nisbet, 1969: 52).

The global use of the word "community" obscures these distinctions precisely because its users assume the proposition to be firmly true. Thus,

---

[7] In a later essay, Nisbet comes closer to defining community as "relationships among individuals that are characterized by personal intimacy, . . . social cohesion," and so on (Nisbet, 1973: 1).

[8] This is a more general definition of "corporate group" than Weber's, but is not inconsistent with his: "A social relationship . . . will be called a 'corporate group' (*Verbrand*) so far as its order is enforced by the action of specific individuals whose regular function that is" (1947: 145–46). This issue of authority will come up immediately.

[9] Cf. Weber (1947: 136): "A social relationship will be called 'communal' if and so far as the orientation of social action . . . is based on a subjective feeling of the parties, whether affectual or traditional, that they belong together."

corporate groups and communal relations are fused by the proposition into one concept: community.

Explaining Community

How might we explain, in terms of the decline theory, the proposition that corporate groups produce communal relations? To answer this question, we must ask a logically prior one: Why do individuals participate in corporate groups, in which they submit to the collective will? From our own rational-choice perspective, there is a simple reply: People join or remain members because it is in their self-interest to do so. But from the perspective of those who use the concept of community, this answer would be unsatisfactory because it describes groups that are voluntary associations, existing at the whim of individuals, and the products of selective and selfish "egoism." Such voluntary groups are the antithesis of traditional corporate groups in which collective will subsumes individual will—indeed, the antithesis of community. (Nisbet [1969], for example, considers purposeful efforts to create community as desperate, futile, and dangerous— witness fascism.) Furthermore, the traditional corporate groups—family, church, and village—were not freely chosen or easily abandoned.

One answer the classical theorists gave to the question of why individuals participate in corporate groups is that there is a duality in human nature, both an egoistic and a social consciousness (Durkheim, 1914). Egoistic selves direct individuals' actions outside the corporate group. In the marketplace and with strangers, people are rationally self-interested (*Zweckrational;* Weber, 1947: 117). Inside the corporate group, this grasping individualism does not exist; there, individuals are directed by their social selves and act in concert with the collective will. "Only the whole exists; it alone has a sphere of action that is all its own. The individual parts have none. . . . It is a silent and spontaneous accord of many consciousnesses which feel and think the same" (Durkheim, 1889).[10]

This account of why individuals participate in corporate groups is, however, not very useful to modern sociology. First, it begs the question by

---

[10] Tönnies assumed that there exists, in addition to individual "rational will," a "perfect unity of human wills as an original or natural condition" (1887: 37), and that this "natural will is inborn in the human being in the same way as in any species a specific form of body and soul is natural" (p. 105). Thus, community is achieved when people forego their rational will and permit their inborn "natural will" to join them harmoniously with others: "The gemeinschaft, which is best understood as a metaphysical union of bodies or blood, possesses by nature a will and a force of its own" (p. 177). Durkheim (1914: 161) wrote: "Man feels himself to be double: he actually is double. There are in him two classes of states of consciousness that differ from each other in origin and nature, and in the ends which they forward [egotistic consciousness and social consciousness]."

asserting that what must be explained, the submission of individual desires to group goals, is simply "natural." Second, it is not parsimonious, positing two human natures where one might well suffice. And, third, it is based on an archaic image of premodern societies. Contemporary anthropology has found that members of "primitive" societies are not ego-less. (However, to reject this dualism of *consciousness* is not to reject a parallel dualism of *relations*. Quite the contrary, it raises the issue of how there can be variations in the communal quality of relations if there is a single human nature. Simmel seems to approach the problem in precisely this manner.[11])

Nevertheless, people are, or at least were, members of traditional corporate groups. If we cannot explain that fact in community theorists' terms, perhaps we can explain it in terms of choices and constraints. To be sure, we cannot explain it by simple choice. As we noted above, people do not select their birthplaces or families of origin. But we can explain it by constraints on the choice of whether to leave those groups and places or to stay. This involves two reinforcing limitations in corporate groups. First, there are limitations on the range and number of possible social relations. Individuals' personal interests are submerged to those of the group when they are unable, because of spatial or social barriers, to form ties outside of it. Second, the limitation of social relations to the group forces the members to be functionally dependent on it. In such binding circumstances, the entirety of individuals' needs is met by the small set of persons in the corporate group. In the traditional village, for example, the people in the immediate vicinity supply one another's employment, material aid, sociability, political allegiance, spiritual uplift, and the like. This, in turn, makes it even more difficult for individuals to go outside the group for social relations, be they commercial or companionable, because they risk forfeiting the services they need. Their choices are all the more limited to the corporate group. In the end, full participation in the collective enterprise is the individual's most rational choice.[12]

Although we cannot prove that this analysis explains individual involvement in traditional corporate groups, we can find illustrations of the process, the limiting of individuals' choices so as to produce community, in contemporary efforts to create corporate groups. "Intentional communities" typically construct walls in order to build communal ties. Kanter

---

[11] See various essays edited by Levine (1971: 6–35, 43–69, 217–26, 251–93).

[12] One could certainly devise yet other explanations for individual involvement in corporate groups, but the two discussed here seem most applicable. For example, one alternative is that people are socialized to value the group and its members. While no doubt true, this explanation does not suffice here. From the community theorists' perspective, it is another statement that membership is a result of individual will. In addition, this explanation would not account for the historical weakening of corporate groups.

(1972) observed that a utopian commune "builds commitment to the extent that it clearly cuts off other possible objects of commitment" (p. 71). It "discourages relationships both outside the group and with internal subunits" and "regulates loyalties that might conflict with members' group obligations," even controlling two-person intimacies that might threaten group cohesion (pp. 82–86; see also Zablocki, 1971). Coser (1974) refers to these and similar groups that try to create *Gemeinschaft* by controlling external and dyadic relations as "greedy institutions," including under that rubric churches, political sects, and the family.[13]

This limited-choice explanation of why individuals participate in corporate groups is not explicit in the community theories; in fact, it has been explicitly denied by, for example, Durkheim.[14] But it is implicitly there. For example, Durkheim saw "moral density" (great numbers of people interacting with one another) as the engine of social change and as the destroyer of corporate groups. As individuals come into contact with more people, they increasingly form extra-group ties and become less committed to family and village (see, for example, Durkheim, 1893: 300). Similarly, Simmel (1908) saw individualism, with both its freedom from corporate group control and its estrangement, as arising at least in part from the numerical expansion of people's relations.[15] Nisbet (1969) is more explicit, explaining the submergence of individual will by "authority." From whence comes this authority? It derives from the power of the group over the individual. With the crumbling of corporate group walls and discovery of functional alternatives outside its confines, the power wanes, so does the authority, and so does the corporate quality of the group.[16] In sum, people participate in corporate groups because of limited choice.

---

[13] For a stimulating essay on the conflict between the need for group cohesion and desire for intimacy between group members, see Slater (1963).

[14] Durkheim at points explicitly rejects this "limited-choice" explanation of collectivism in corporate groups: "If in lower societies so small a place is given to individual personality, that is not because it has been restrained or artificially suppressed. It is simply because, at that moment in history, *it did not exist*" (1893: 194). He would reject our interpretation because it presumes an inherent human egoism (à la Hobbes) and Durkheim contends, as we saw, that there is a dual nature, both egoistic and social. However, elsewhere, Durkheim makes arguments that are at minimum consistent with explaining social consciousness as the result of restrained individualism, and individualism as, in turn, the result of weakened constraints (for example, in his discussion of egoistic suicide).

[15] "The mere fact of multiple group-affiliations enabled the person to achieve for himself an individualized situation in which the groups had to be oriented towards the individual. In the earlier situation the individual was wholly absorbed by, and remained oriented toward, the group" (Simmel, 1922: 151).

[16] According to Nisbet, community is in decline because specialized institutions have usurped these functions from the traditional units of society. For example, the family is no longer the guarantor of education, jobs, or old-age security (see Ogburn, 1954, among others). Nisbet's answer comes down to constraint and interdependence.

Returning to our original question, why would communal relations develop in corporate groups? Based on our exegesis and our effort to cast the community argument into modern terms, the best answer seems to be that *limitations on the choice of social relations promote communal ties.* The more restricted their choice of associates, the more often and longer individuals must interact with, exchange with, and rely upon a small number of people. Thus duration, interaction frequency, and material interdependence lead to communal ties.

People are always greatly limited in the social relations they can form—limited by space, time, energy, material requirements, social norms and values, ignorance, existing social commitments, and so on. These constraints mean that people can know only a tiny proportion of the members of their society and can develop relations with only an infinitesimal proportion. Presumably, the smaller the number of relations, the more often they see those few people and the more they need them, and therefore, the closer they feel. Yet the degree of limitation varies. It varies across individuals within any given society, according to the individuals' locations in the social structure. (This is the variation we shall investigate empirically.) And it varies historically; in particular, the constraints of space and of material requirements have loosened noticeably with modernization. Because primordial corporate groups are formed under conditions of the most limited choice, these traditional groups (for example, family, church, and neighborhood or village) are more promotive of communal ties and are ultimately more promotive of social integration and psychological well-being than are social groups formed out of "mere volition or interest" (Nisbet, 1966: 48).

That limitations promote communal relations appears to be an implicit, but basic, social-psychological proposition in the decline-of-community theory. And it is a proposition we intend to challenge.

THE LOCAL COMMUNITY

The group of people who live together in a locality is, after the family, probably the most significant group in the decline thesis. Physical and social impediments to spatial mobility once restricted almost everyone's activities and personal relations to a single place and thus consigned them to be members of a local corporate group.[17] Urbanization and modern technology have brought instead localities of "limited liability" (Janowitz,

---

[17] This is, of course, a simplified statement, ignoring both nomads and the fact that people have long been more mobile than usually thought (see chapter 10). Yet nomads could not venture far from their "moving-locality" group. And, while individuals in by-gone eras often moved from one village to another, their lives were circumscribed in each place. That is, the daily and weekly ranges of people's lives were quite narrow.

1967): local groups in which individuals are involved only voluntarily, from which they can withdraw easily, and which serve only limited functions.

According to Tönnies, Nisbet, Stein, and others, this change has contributed in large measure to the decline of community. They argue that residential mobility, people's extensive daily travels, the ability to reach outside the locality—through mail, telephone, radio, or in person—to satisfy almost any desire, and similar breaches in the local walls have weakened corporate nature of local social life and ultimately reduced the quality of social relations. The problem posed by this argument is summarized by Minar and Greer (1969: 47):

> Modern life has raised some havoc with men's ability to define themselves with the locality, to create a community in it. . . . It makes urgent the question of whether community can exist for man in meaningful ways without the locality as a nexus of loyalties. *Must community, in other words, be place-oriented?* This is a way of asking if urban life is workable [italics added].

This question, somewhat restated, is our concern through most of Part II. Are local social relations in modern urban settings more likely to be communal than extralocal relations? Does commitment to a place and its residents, because it fosters inwardly focused and interdependent relations, lead to greater intimacy and supportiveness? More generally, what is the role of place in modern social life?

THE HISTORICAL ARGUMENT

The decline-of-community thesis, to conclude our exegesis, presents the following historical argument: Modern society, through changes in its technology, economy, and ideology, has considerably eased the limits on individuals' choices of social relations. People have increasingly taken advantage of this freedom to form far-flung social networks, going beyond the bounds of older corporate groups. The end result, however, is that modern people have frequently sacrificed quality for quantity; they have formed many shallow, instrumental connections and lost the few deep, communal relations that once existed. Thus, the decline of community.

As we said earlier, this book—at least until Chapter 10—does not directly address the historical argument. Instead, several chapters address, within the modern context, the underlying propositions, that the more limited people's choices of social relations, the more communal those relations are, and that local social relations are more communal than extralocal ones.

Limitations on choice are, of course, still present in modern life. Even if the sorts of physical and social constraints that bolstered traditional corporate groups have been significantly loosened, many others persist. Some constraints promote corporate ties; others are simply constraints. People face varying limitations posed by their financial resources, physical health, social activities, family responsibilities, jobs, and other structural circumstances. There is, one might say, a distribution of constraint in this society. It is precisely this distribution that permits us to ask empirical questions related to the decline thesis: How do specific kinds of constraints in modern society affect individuals' social relations? Do they promote communal ties? Are the freer individuals in this society also the more socially estranged?

We base the empirical treatment of these questions on contemporary (1960s) data. Where we draw implications about the decline-of-community thesis from our analysis, we are making a critical assumption: That there continue to be some corporate groups—or, at least, groups with varying "corporateness"—and some communal relations in modern society. If there are no relatively corporate communities at all in modern life (no relatively enclosed families or neighborhoods), and if all social relations are fundamentally estranged, then any comparison among modern social bonds is irrelevant to these historical or sociological questions. All we need to assume is that there is still some variation in modern life from less to more corporateness and less to more communal ties. This assumption is consistent with statements of the classical theorists. Tönnies and Durkheim stated specifically that elements of *Gemeinschaft* persisted even as society became predominantly *Gesellschaft*. Our test of the constraint–communal relations proposition involves examining that variation in modern society.[18]

Procedure

Our study of the structure of social networks and their connections to places rests on two methods: one an effort to review and synthesize the existing literature; the other, a reanalysis of two surveys. The Detroit Area Study of 1965–66 (henceforth referred to as the Detroit survey), conducted at the University of Michigan by Professors Howard Schuman and Edward O. Laumann, interviewed 985 men living in the urbanized sections of the Detroit metropolitan area. The sample was restricted to white males, native- or Canadian-born, between the ages of 21 and 64, and living in primary families. (Details of the sampling procedure and basic findings are reported by Laumann [1973].) The survey obtained information about

[18] Another caveat is in order: We do not intend by this discussion to imply that the only possible or real differences between social relations within and without corporate groups is in degree of communalism. Obviously, there are many differences between relations inside and outside corporate groups.

the men's social networks by asking them to name the three men they felt closest to and saw most often, and then asking about the characteristics of those friends and friendships. We coded and merged 1960 data on the respondents' census tracts with their answers to the survey and were thereby able to explore issues involving the interaction between place and networks that were largely unexamined in previous analyses of this survey (see Chapters 6, 7, and 8). Where our interests overlapped with those of earlier analysts, particularly Laumann (1973) and Verbrugge (1973), we focused on somewhat different variables, used somewhat different methods, and reached somewhat different conclusions (see Chapters 3, 4, and 5).

The second data set we used is a national survey conducted by the National Opinion Research Center (NORC) in 1967. This survey (described fully in Bradburn et al. [1970]) was largely concerned with racial integration in American neighborhoods. For that purpose, NORC selected a sample of neighborhoods which were open to black residents, and then matched these neighborhoods with controls which were white- or black-segregated. Within neighborhoods, households were sampled such that three-fourths of the respondents were women. We merged three distinct sets of data concerning the respondents and their places: (1) responses to the personal interviews collected in the 1967 household survey; (2) census data for the respondents' neighborhoods ($N = 230$), dated 1960; (3) information from knowledgeable informants interviewed by NORC for each neighborhood. The local leaders provided general qualitative assessments of the various locales. We were able, therefore, to create a data file which included not only respondents' answers but also a wide range of independent information about respondents' places. We were particularly interested in this survey's questions concerning neighborhoods and general neighborhood life, rather than those on the topic of integration. Consequently, there is little overlap between our work and that of Bradburn et al. (We will refer to this data as the national survey.)

We sought to make our analysis, some of which was quite complex, accessible to a general audience and at the same time to document it fully for a professional audience. Therefore, we wrote the text for readers with only a minimal knowledge of statistics. The basic issues with which we are concerned are neither statistical nor methodological but theoretical and substantive, and thus should be accessible to all.

We have generally tried to use simple statistics wherever possible, depending heavily on crosstabulation, especially where dealing with questions that have not been explored before (for example, in Chapter 3). The measure we report is usually gamma (γ), which indicates the extent to which individuals ranked on one variable are similarly ranked on another. Where appropriate, we report simple correlation coefficients (r), the degree to which individuals' scores on one variable fluctuate with their scores on another.[19] In more complex analyses, we are often concerned with the association between two variables, holding one or more other variables constant. In the simpler of these cases, we used crosstabulation within levels of control variables, again reporting gammas, or we calculated partial correlation coefficients—what the association would be if the control variables were constant. In a few more complex cases, we wished to control for many variables and to see what the effect of our test variable was with the others simultaneously held constant. In those cases, we used multiple-regression analysis and betas (standardized regression coefficients, β) as our measures of effect. Virtually all the statistical associations we report are statistically significant at the .05 level unless otherwise noted.

A final comment about the logic of our inquiry: In our analysis we usually either test a hypothesis about a specific association between two variables (for example, that nearby friendships are more intimate than distant ones) or explore a specific association for which no theory exists (for example, fluctuations in friendship intimacy across the life-cycle). Unlike many empirical studies, we were not trying to develop or test complete causal models explaining dependent variables (for example, discovering all the statistically significant correlates of friendship intimacy). With rare exception (Chapter 8 being notable), our focus is on the *patterns* of statistical associations rather than on the *size* of statistical associations, on explaining propositions rather than explaining variance.

[19] More precisely, the extent to which the joint scores cluster along the best-fitting linear regression line.

PART I

NETWORKS

INDIVIDUALS' SOCIAL RELATIONS, both personal and intimate ones and impersonal and formal ones, can be thought of as strands in the webs of their "social networks." The networks radiate out from the individual to close associates and then to the society beyond. Conversely, society can be thought of as the complex mesh of all these social networks, an intricate lattice-work. This imagery is a familiar one to sociologists, at least since Simmel's essay on "The Web of Group Affiliations" (1922). The challenge to sociologists is to turn the "network" from image to instrument, to apply the concept in ways that will inform us about the nature of society. Part I is our contribution to this effort.

We explain "social network analysis," describe its contributions to understanding various problems, especially in urban studies, and outline some of its current difficulties. One of those difficulties is deciding what it is *about* social networks that is generally most significant. (What is *specifically* most significant will, of course, vary according to one's specific problem.) We argue and present some evidence that the key attributes of social relations are those that reflect the circumstances individuals face in forming them and maintaining them.

The formation of many social links is quite familiar: We are born into or marry into our kinship ties, our jobs present us with work associates, and so forth. But how these sorts of connections are turned into something greater, into "friendships," is more problematic and therefore more reveal-

17

ing of the processes involved in network formation and maintenance. We examine these processes by focusing on their most common result: similarity among friends. What factors in friendship formation promote similarity in economic position, ethnicity, and age? Our answers are presented in Chapter 4.

Many of these processes are intimately associated with individuals' movements through the different stages of life. Indeed, people's positions in the "life-cycle" are the most pervasive influences on their social networks. That may be obvious with respect to gaining and losing family ties, or meeting and leaving work associates. It is also very true of friendship— as we demonstrate and try to explain in the last chapter of Part I.

2. Network Analysis and Urban Studies

Claude S. Fischer

WHEN ALBERT EINSTEIN completed his university studies in 1900, he could not obtain a job appropriate to his training, in part because he had so antagonized his professors that they would neither hire nor help him. After more than a year of searching and temporary employment, Einstein applied for a post at the Swiss Patent Office and was a few months later called to Zurich for an interview with the office director. In spite of an inadequate performance during the interview, Einstein was hired. As it turns out, the director was an intimate friend of the father of Marcel Grossman, a good friend and former classmate of Einstein. The appointment was no doubt a favor from the director to the Grossmans. Einstein's major scientific insights occurred during his several years at the Patent Office and he later said, in effect, that had he held a faculty position during that period, the pressures for academic advancement would probably have discouraged him from exploring such unorthodox and professionally risky issues as the special theory of relativity (Clark, 1971).

Einstein used his *social network*—the people with whom he was directly and indirectly related—to obtain his first job. (We should note that his problems arose in part *because* of his social network—the professors he had alienated.) Later in his career, he served as an important contact in the social networks of young physicists seeking their first jobs. Social networks are important in all our lives, often for finding jobs, more often for finding a helping hand, companionship, or a shoulder to cry on. Our networks do more than just support us; they also place demands upon us— for assistance, advice, to help a friend of a friend—and they influence our values, attitudes, and decisions.

Network analysis is a style of social science research that focuses on people's social networks as a means toward understanding their behavior.

19

It differs from social science approaches that concentrate on characteristics of the individual (on, for example, Einstein's personality or his academic credentials) and those that concentrate on features of institutions (for example, the Swiss University system or the structure of the Patent Office). The domain of network analysis is the attributes of interpersonal relations.

The concept of social network is new neither to the social sciences nor to the public at large. The common phrase "It's not *what* you know, but *who* you know" testifies to our general experience with using our contacts to achieve our ends. And phrases about "friends in need" reflect the responsibilities we feel to assist those we call our intimates. The concept of social network has long been implicit in sociology. Durkheim's (1897) "egoistic" suicides occur when the individuals are bereft of the social "bonds" (note the metaphor) which could restrain them from performing this supremely individualistic act. (Later, we shall discuss several research traditions in the social sciences that employ more or less consciously the idea of social networks.)

What is new is the development in recent years of explicit efforts to define and study social networks and to use the concept to investigate various topics in the social sciences. Network analysis has made what were latent ideas manifest and specific and has provided a conceptual structure and method of study where there were once only loose applications. Although it has illuminated important processes in many areas of social science research, it has especially helped to advance urban studies. The nature of urban life, opaque and confusing when viewed through the typical sociological perspectives, becomes much clearer and more amenable to investigation when looked at with network analysis. In this presentation of network analysis, we shall (1) review the empirical and theoretical traditions which have converged to produce it; (2) highlight its key theoretical contributions; (3) discuss its particular importance to urban studies; and (4) detail some of its most pressing issues.

Converging Streams

Researchers in a wide variety of fields have found the concept of social network—or one like it—to be a useful tool. The field of network analysis, as a distinctive enterprise, has been built up out of these largely unconnected efforts.

INNOVATION

Social scientists who study the diffusion of innovations have used the concept of networks extensively. In studying the adoption of innovations such as new farming techniques, clothing styles, television, and immunization, they have found that connections among people are crucial. Although some people are more personally disposed to accept innovations than others and some innovations are more useful or advertised than others, the explanation of innovation is not complete without understanding the process of *diffusion,* particularly at the individual level. When an innovation succeeds, it is usually because people who are particularly influential in the community of interest imitate an experimental avant-grade. Others in the community in turn imitate the influentials and persuade their friends and neighbors to follow suit. The hold-outs against the innovation tend to be socially disconnected from the others in the group (see Rogers and Shoemaker, 1971; Burt, 1973; Lionberger and Copus, 1972; Becker, 1970).

For example, Coleman et al. (1966), in a classic study of innovation, found that doctors in four small cities who were friends and professional associates of other physicians were likely to prescribe a new drug earlier than doctors who were somewhat isolated from their colleagues. The channels of diffusion are at least partly personal channels.

POLITICAL AND SOCIAL ATTITUDES AND BEHAVIOR

Similarly, studies of political behavior, such as voting, have found that individuals' attitudes and actions are predicted not only by their own traits —class, race, age, and so on—but also by the traits and political positions of the people with whom they associate (for example, Burstein, 1976; Berelson et al., 1954; Newcomb, 1961); indeed, the effects of individuals' personal characteristics, such as education, may be in part a result of segregating individuals into networks of people holding distinctive views. Political climates of opinion influence individuals only to the extent that they have direct personal relations with people holding those opinions (Putnam, 1966; see also Festinger et al., 1950). And deviates can sustain their positions against general climates of opinion by banding together in cliques (Finifter, 1974).

Even the messages of mass communications are translated by personal relations. Studies of the mass media have identified the "two-step" flow: step 1, a few "opinion leaders" obtain information about products and adopt points of view about issues from the media; step 2, they influence others who have come to respect their judgment (Katz and Lazarsfeld, 1955; but see also Robinson, 1976).

SMALL-GROUP RESEARCH

Studies of small groups have found that personal relations can influence everything from work pace to moral decisions. Many studies have been conducted on "natural" groups such as gangs, school classes, and work groups. Even where the specific topic of interest was not social relations but, for example, the effect of various organizational structures, relations have often turned out to be the explanation of critical processes. In both the Hawthorn Bank Wiring Room made famous by Roethlisberger and Dickson (1939) and Homans (1950) and the federal regulatory agency studied by Blau (1963), productivity depended greatly on the assistance or interference provided by coworkers, and each individual's production was partly a function of his personal relations with the others.

Researchers have conducted many studies on temporary groups formed in laboratories. Again, the influence of personal relations is important: individuals will state that they see things which are patently not so if the group asserts that they are so (Asch, 1956), and individuals will inflict what seems to be great pain on another person if they lack some personal support in their efforts to resist the authority who is demanding this aggressive behavior (Milgram, 1965).

URBAN ANTHROPOLOGY

The greatest spur to network analysis has come from urban anthropologists, particularly from Africanists linked to the University of Manchester (see Mitchell, 1969; Boissevain and Mitchell, 1973).[1] Traditionally, anthropologists have used institutional analyses, focusing on lineages, age-grades, culture areas, and similar categories. Beginning in the 1950s (Barnes, 1954; Bott, 1955) and accelerating through the 1960s, many anthropologists increasingly found it useful to examine the interpersonal ties of individuals, particularly as an aid to understanding urban migration and urban society. For example, they found that networks mitigated the impact of rural to urban migration. Migration from tribal lands usually occurs individually or in a family; in cities, tribal members are often scattered through separate and heterogeneous neighborhoods; tribal institutions—elders, religious totems, allotted lands, extended kin, and so on—are often not present, while instead there are new institutions to confront, such as the industrial labor market, political systems, and bureaucracies. Many observers expected to find that individual migrants suffer psychologically from living outside of the traditional tribal framework and that urban settlements are anomic and chaotic. Neither turned out to be generally true. Instead, individuals more often than not adapt well, are usually integrated into city life, and show relatively few signs of social disorganization (see Nelson, 1969; Gulick, 1973).

Anthropologists were puzzled by their findings until they began to think seriously, not in terms of tribal institutions, but in terms of personal relations among tribal members. This network approach provided a framework

---

[1] Other beginnings to network analysis which did not catch hold as did the Manchester School include Caplow (1955) and Henry (1958).

for understanding the migrants' processes of adjustment: individuals usually travel to cities where they have kin or friends. These associates receive the migrants, assist them in finding lodging and work, and introduce them to more people. The tribal community is maintained by high levels of personal communication among members in the city and with those in the home village. Sometimes formal organizations (for example, churches, clubs) are added to the set of personal relations. Of course, many individuals suffer from inadequate networks but, on the whole, the norms of the group are maintained through ramified and persisting personal bonds (see, for example, Pons, 1969; Roberts, 1973; Perlman, 1975; Gutkind, 1965; and Butterworth, 1962).

OTHER STUDIES

There are many other studies scattered about the social science literature that focus on interpersonal relations. Some of the more recent ones come out of an explicit network-analysis approach; others are in a sense prototypes. Here are some examples:

Bott (1955) found that she could best understand the conjugal relations of married couples by examining their friendships and kin ties: intense and sex-segregated friendships maintained separately by each spouse promoted segregated marital arrangements.

Students of social class structure, ranging from Warner et al. (1963) to Laumann (1966, 1973), have described classes and class boundaries in terms of personal relations: classes are demarcated by the relative absence of relations between sets of people who have many interrelations among themselves.

Networks also influence the direction of migration flows. For example, many Italian immigrants to America followed "chains of migration." The newcomers were drawn to particular cities and jobs by kin and townsmen who preceded them (MacDonald and MacDonald, 1974).

Political economists have studied the informal exercises of economic power by tracing out the business and personal connections of corporate executives and other well-placed people (see, for example, Zeitlan et al., 1974; Levine, 1972).

Sociologists of science have found that research directions and productivity result partly from personal connections among researchers, so that the informal organization of a discipline is often more important than its official associations or journals in determining its progress (see Crane, 1972; Breiger, 1976).[2]

---

[2] This is no less true of network analysis itself. There is a network of "networkers," connected intellectually by the circulation of preprints, personally by frequent conversations, historically by common backgrounds (such as common graduate schools), and locationally by common "home bases," especially the University of Manchester, Harvard University, and the University of Toronto.

Social circles develop, particularly in urban settings, around special shared needs and interests and in turn sustain unique services, activities, and ways of life (Kadushin, 1966).

Researchers on mental-health topics find that individuals' psychological well-being is associated with the support their networks provide (for example, Kleiner and Parker, 1976).

As a final example, Granovetter (1974) found, in a survey of men's job mobility, that the men who received the best job offers were those who tended to have more far-flung networks of acquaintances. These contacts provided them with unexpected opportunities for advancement (see also Katz, 1966; Erickson and Yancy, 1976).

All these studies share a focus on social relations. This is the essence of network analysis. Instead of finding the answers to their questions in the attributes of individuals—personalities, histories, social positions, and so on—or in the attributes of institutions—organizations, norms, functions, and so on—they found answers in the attributes of relations—people known, nature of bonds, extent of interconnections, and so on. The utility of network analysis has become apparent largely through the cumulation of studies such as these.

THEORETICAL TRADITIONS

Two major theoretical traditions have also contributed to the development of network analysis: role theory and exchange theory. These analytical frameworks (they are not really theories) both stress aspects of relations *among* units rather than aspects of the units themselves. Role analysts focus on the positions people hold in the social structure (for example, head of family, or professor). The most important influences on behavior are the normative expectations appropriate to each position's *role relations*. For example, a professor is expected to teach students, follow regulations of deans and chancellors, work with departmental and university colleagues on administrative matters, and engage in intellectual production with other people in his or her specialty (publishing, refereeing, and so on). These behaviors are products of social relations in that they are defined by mutual expectations and obligations held by both sides of a relation. Students expect professors to teach; professors expect students to learn (see Deutsch and Krauss, 1965: Ch. 1; Merton, 1957).

Role analysis assumes that relations are derived from institutions and are not entities in their own right. Positions and role relations are products of an institution; normative expectations for a role relation are part of a greater set of institutional norms; and specific individuals are interchangeable in any given position. The interaction of Professor A and Student B is, according to role analysis, determined by the institutional characteristics of higher education, not by A and B. Thus, role analysis does not stress the interpersonal relation *per se* to the degree that network analysis does. Nevertheless, role analysis has provided an important entrée to network analysis. Many anthropologists, for example, have developed network perspectives out of an appreciation of kinship systems, which are highly institutionalized role structures, as prototypical networks. (There is another difficulty with role analysis: in the "real world," it seems that people often play their roles as much in free-form and *ad lib* fashion as they do by the norms.)

Exchange analysis focuses more strictly on personal relations and is more congruent with the assumptions of network analysis than is role analysis. Individuals are seen as rational maximizers. Interpersonal relations are considered, basically, as interdependencies, where the rewards and costs to one person are at least partly contingent on the actions of another or others. Social relations develop from this rudimentary level as individuals act jointly to "solve" this interdependency, in essence exchanging rewarding behavior with one another (see Thibaut and Kelley, 1959; Kelley, 1968; Homans, 1974; Blau, 1964). For example, a professor's salary (and intellectual satisfaction) is contingent on having students; a student's career is contingent on being taught. Teaching, in its most jointly satisfying way, involves an efficient "exchange" in which both sides "profit."

Exchange analysis has often been attacked as reductionist because it seems to argue that individual acts create social structure. If this critique is valid, then exchange analysis would serve poorly as a basis for network analysis. But exchange analysis need not suffer from such an error. Quite to the contrary, most interdependencies result from social-structural circumstances which confront specific individuals, as in the illustration of the professor and student. And the options available for exchange are usually constrained by institutional norms that exist before and independently of the individuals. (For example, the student could bribe the professor; that is an exchange "solution" to their interdependency. But that solution poses risks in terms of punishment and of guilt—which is not to say that it, or a similar solution, is unknown.) An exchange analysis seems particularly compatible with network analysis and has been a major influence on some of the theoretical development of network analysis in anthropology (see Whitten and Wolfe, 1974; conversely, a network approach helps exchange theory become a social theory—see Emerson, 1976). It also provides a set of social-psychological assumptions which underlie our own work (see Chapter 1).[3]

---

[3] Two other conceptual approaches have contributed to the formation of network analysis: communications and systems "theories." The communications approach presents a metaphor of society and its parts as a communications "net" (see, for example, Deutsch, 1967; Meier, 1962). The singular trait of cities, for example, is that they are central "nodes" or "switchboards," where channels cross and information is exchanged at a rapid pace. Systems approaches stress that the organization of a system's parts is the key to its functioning (see Buckley, 1967; Easton, 1965; Parsons, 1951). Systems theorists argue that, to the degree that otherwise disparate

The Contributions of Network Analysis

Our brief definition of network analysis as a style of research that focuses on relations highlighted three points: it is an approach or orientation, not a theory as such; it concentrates on the personal connections among individuals; and it is thus distinct from approaches that focus on characteristics of individuals or aggregate units. For clarity, let us use a concrete example of a network and of network processes: graduate students finding an initial faculty job (an illustration with which Einstein might have empathized). The question is: Why and how do certain job candidates wind up in certain jobs or, more generally, what is the process of placement?

There are generally three ways of approaching this question. First, we could focus on individual candidates: their graduate careers, intelligence writing, personalities, and so on.[4] Second, we could focus on the hiring departments: their search procedures, preferences, locations, salaries, and, most important, whether they have jobs and what kinds of jobs they have available in any given year.[5] We could even combine the two by analyzing the match between individuals and jobs. Third, we could focus on the set of professional and personal connections that tie the particular candidates to the key decision-makers in the hiring departments: who knows whom through whom? Consider Figure 2.1 as a schematic illustration of this last, network, approach. Circles represent people; lines represent personal relations. The dashed lines demarcate distinguishable groups, both formal and informal.

A network analyst would think it significant that candidates A and B are each linked to Chairperson X in two-step paths (although quite different paths), while candidate C is three steps away and candidate D is not linked to Chairperson X at all. The analyst might predict that A and B would have an advantage in a competition for a job in X's department because they could present their cases more directly to the chair and have more personally involved champions campaigning for them. (On the basis of our own participant observations of faculty hiring, we would confirm these predictions.) A further question that might be pursued is: How is it that the individuals came to have more or less helpful networks? The

---

systems—organisms, machines, societies, and so on—share common organizational principles, their processes and states can be explained by common propositions. This stress on the *organization* of elements, instead of the separate *elements* themselves, articulates well with the network emphasis on *relations* among actors.

4 Schools of social science that exemplify this approach are the fields of personality (e.g., Freudianism), socialization, and the study of attitudes and opinions.

5 Schools of thought exemplifying this approach include structural-functionalism, Marxism, and organizational analyses.

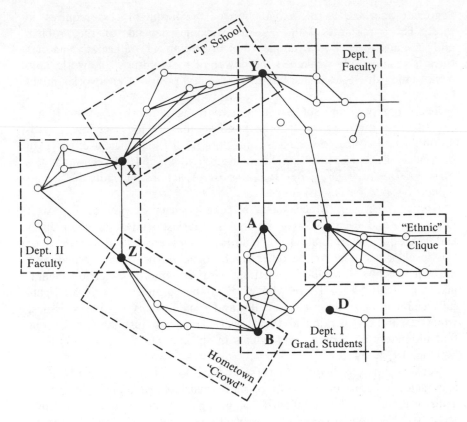

Figure 2.1 A Schematic Illustration of the Networks Involved in Obtaining a Faculty Position

answer might be found in their structural positions (age, ethnicity, sex, class, and so on) and personal qualities.

We can see from this illustration, first, that network analysis is an approach or orientation (as are the other two possible foci); it is not a *theory*. A theory requires specific propositions (for example, "two-step links are more useful than three-step links," or "more publications lead to better jobs"). Instead, an approach indicates the materials from which theories are constructed. Second, the materials which network analysis uses are interpersonal relations, their structure and contents (we will discuss this further in the last section).[6] Third, network analysis is thus quite distinct from, although also complementary to, both individual and

---

[6] Our repeated discussion of *personal* relations should not make us overlook the fact that network analysis has been applied to *intergroup* and *interorganization* relations, as well.

aggregate analyses. A full explanation of the hiring process requires all three. The importance of the network variables depends on the problem and circumstance. For example, the institution of "affirmative-action" rules has supposedly weakened the power of the "old-boy" network; and, were standardized tests instituted for faculty positions, networks might become far less significant than they are today.

There are two kinds of advantages to using network analysis. It has explanatory power, as we demonstrated in the previous section. In addition, network analysis makes contributions to sociological theory. In particular, it bridges the gap between individual and aggregate models of social life, it incorporates the purposeful actions of individuals into models of social-structural processes.

Bridging the gap: Much social science is macroscopic, dealing with large units and even societies as wholes. Marxist studies of colonialism and functional interpretations of cultural values are two illustrations of this level of analysis. At the other level, social science is concerned with individual actors in small-scale settings (for example, research on mental health and attitudes). Those who work at the "grander" level can rightfully claim to be dealing with socially and sociologically significant issues, while researchers working at the "lower" level can justifiably point out that ultimately it is specific individuals in specific situations who act (see Merton, 1974: 34).

Network analysis helps join these two approaches. It describes large aggregates in terms of networks of individuals related to one another in a distinct manner. The boundaries of groups are indicated by a relative scarcity of relations between clumps of interconnected relations. In Figure 2.1, three informal groups are identified by their personal networks: the "hometown" group, the "ethnic" students, and the "J-theory school" of thought. In each case, there is a distinguishable network which is only weakly connected to the others. (There are also formal groups—the faculties and student bodies; these, too, are interpretable as networks, here as networks of formal relations rather than of personal bonds.) The groups themselves are connected in a hierarchical fashion via higher-order networks to form institutions. For example, networks of faculties form institutions of higher education, and networks of schools form disciplines.[7]

A network analyst would argue that the "top-down" effects of institutional factors (for example, political propaganda) on individuals are mediated by this lattice of relations, and that there are also "bottom-up" effects: institutions are shaped by the joint responses of individuals (for example, voting).

An example of the top-down process is the polarization that occurs

---

[7] There have been many advances recently in describing mathematically the social structure formed by social networks. See, for example, White et al. (1976).

during social conflict (see Kriesberg, 1973; Scherer et al., 1975: Ch. 8; Coleman, 1957). In Figure 2.1, competition between A and B for a job in Department II would probably separate their two sets of friends. What is likely to happen is that the two links between A's and B's intimate networks will be severed. In this perspective, polarization is the loss of connections between conflicting clusters of actors.

An illustration of the bottom-up process is the formation of ethnic enclaves. In Figure 2.1, again, a possible history of the ethnic clique of graduate students is that newer members were recruited by the advanced students on the basis of personal ties, thereby forming a distinct entity in the student body. A large-scale example is the formation in this manner of ethnic enclaves, organizations and interest groups by chain migration to cities (see, for example, MacDonald and MacDonald, 1974; Breton, 1964; Wirth, 1928).

These examples illustrate the claim that "network analysis provides the investigator with pathways into the heart of social systems" (Whitten and Wolfe, 1974: 719).[8]

A second theoretical contribution of network analysis is that it permits sociologists to integrate a structural analysis of society with a viable model of the individual, one in which he or she is a participant in the construction of the social world. As we argued in Chapter 1, much of contemporary social science assumes that the individual is an object moved by external forces: norms, structures, institutions, and so on. A network approach is more consistent with a model of individuals as actors who perceive, assess, select, and behave (within limits posed by their circumstances). Networks, unlike categorical groups such as lineages and classes, are visibly constructed and manipulated. We see this daily in our own lives: making friends, avoiding certain acquaintances, deciding which relative to favor with a holiday visit. Boissevain (1973: viii) stresses this point: "Network analysis is . . . first of all an attempt to reintroduce the concept of man as an interacting social being capable of manipulating others as well as being manipulated by them." Social structure impinges on individuals through chains of relations, and it is partly constructed by individuals forming and using chains of relations.

In Figure 2.1 we can observe individuals who are the objects of group pressure and individuals who are creating it. Chairperson X is, because of his or her formal position and network location, under the cross-pressures imposed by Z on behalf of candidate B and the J-school on be-

---

[8] Ron Breiger has pointed out (personal communication) that most network analyses do not fully appreciate the individual-group duality. That is, aggregates are thought of as sets of relations among individuals; but individuals are rarely considered as composed of relations among aggregates (see Simmel, 1922; Brieger, 1974). Although it might seem bizarre, a network approach could be developed along these lines. Its theoretical predecessor is role theory: individuals are the summation of the roles they play.

half of candidate A. Candidate C benefits from a group's moral support, in contrast to D who is virtually isolated. All these individuals are the targets of network pressures. At the same time, we can look at the purposeful actors in the situation: Z (who is under pressure from B) trying to rally members of Department II to influence X; Y asking allies in the J-school to phone X on behalf of A. Networks influence individuals and networks are influenced by individuals. (Of course, some individuals are more often the pressured and some more often the pressurers.)

The recent New York City fiscal crisis provided an illustration of how individuals use and are are used by networks. *Newsweek* reported on the measures Governor Hugh Carey used to pressure United Federation of Teachers President Albert Shanker into signing over pension funds:

> The strategy was to get people Shanker trusted to warn that he would be seen as the villain of the piece. First, Richard Ravitsch, a wealthy builder and friend of both Carey and Shanker, tried to soften up the union boss on Thursday night. On Friday morning, Harry Van Arsdale, Jr., head of New York's Central Labor Council, urged Shanker to relent; so did former Mayor Robert Wagner. Finally, Carey himself took over in Ravitsch's Park Avenue apartment. "The gist of it was that Carey told him, 'The city is in your hands, for better or worse,'" said a top aide to the governor. "They [Carey and three state officials] asked if he wanted to go into the history books as the man who triggered default of New York City."
> The UFT boss didn't (*Newsweek*, October 27, 1975: 18).

Anthropologist Raymond Firth sums up how networks incorporate individual action and social structure: "Social organization [is] the systematic ordering of social relations by acts of choice and decision. . . . A person chooses, consciously or unconsciously [within a range of structurally circumscribed alternatives], which course he will follow. And, his decision will affect the future structural alignment" (quoted by Whitten and Wolfe, 1974: 718).

Networks and Urban Sociology

Urban sociology is fundamentally concerned with the interaction between the ecological characteristics of human settlements and social life (see Fischer, 1975). The causal connections between ecology and social relations have been explored primarily in studies of urban life-styles and personalities (Wirth, 1938; Fischer, 1976). Other studies have focused on them more peripherally. Students of land-use patterns, for example, have sought to understand how the make-up of individuals' families influence their choices of residential locations.

Urban sociology has been hindered by a key conceptual difficulty: understanding the processes by which macroscopic ecological variables (such as size, density, dispersal, and structural differentiation) affect microscopic social variables (such as personality, friendships, and behavioral styles). There have been, to be sure, important speculations in classic essays by Simmel (1905), Park (1916), and Wirth (1938). But these formulations tend to be incomplete. They allude to some sort of reflection in individuals' lives and minds of the urban differentiation around them, or to direct psychic impacts of cities, without detailing the actual chain of events.[9] Partly because of this ambiguity, others have argued that the causal connections do not exist, that the microscopic realms of social life are essentially autonomous of macroscopic variables like city size (Reiss, 1955; Gans, 1962a; Lewis, 1965).

Network analysis makes such theories testable. As Tilly (1972) states, "A network conception permits fairly rapid movement from aggregate characteristics of the community to features of interpersonal relations on a small scale and back again." Individuals are affected through their social networks, and the social structure of a settlement can be expressed and measured in terms of networks (see Tilly, 1972; Craven and Wellman, 1973).

Using network ideas, one can explicate more clearly and persuasively the Park-Wirth hypothesis that population size produces isolated individuals. According to this theory (which is drawn largely from the "decline-of-community" theory), in more populous settlements, individuals quite rationally develop functionally specific relations with many people rather than multi-purpose ties to a few people. They work with one set of people, live with another, play with a third, and so on. Single-purpose relations are not as durable or intimate ("communal") as are multi-purpose relations. Consequently, individuals have many superficial ties, but few if any ties involving intense mutual obligations. In a crisis individuals will be left without important emotional support (see Craven and Wellman, 1973; Southall, 1973). Whether empirically valid or not, this hypothesis and others like it are clearer and more testable when expressed in network concepts.

A second example of how network analysis clarifies problems concerns alternative ways of perceiving urban social structure. Urban life viewed through an institutional perspective must appear disorganized and atomistic, because corporate groups seem weak or non-existent in cities. Local groups (that is, neighborhoods) are amorphous, not distinctly bounded, and their members do not usually act as a coherent group. Kin ties are geographically dispersed, kin interaction is irregular, and relatives often have limited involvement in individuals' lives. Although the work setting often provides a distinct set of contacts, those ties are usually segregated

---

[9] Simmel (1905), for example, assumes that the urban setting directly causes nervous overstimulation in the minds of individuals, leading to personality alterations as means of coping. See Fischer (1972) for an attempt to detail these theories.

from others, there is a good deal of job turnover, and there is rarely an identifiable corporate unit associated with the workplace (a union being the closest approximation).

A different reality appears from a network perspective. Social structure is composed of sets of interpersonal networks, variously based on kinship, common residence, work, recreational activities, or friendship. In small, and particularly premodern, settlements, these kinds of ties are superimposed, almost always joining the same set of persons. And those persons reside close to one another. The individuals will thus appear to form a distinct, bounded, holistic group. However, this appearance may not reflect the significant features of the actual structure. Since networks and not institutional units are considered the bases of social structure in both small and large settlements, the relative absence of visible corporate groups in urban areas need not signify social disorganization. Society is organized in terms of these networks, whether they overlap or not.

A third example deals with the factors that promote neighborhood cohesion. A network perspective suggests that such cohesion will exist when people find social relations in their localities more rewarding than those outside the localities. Three conditions, in particular, produce this effect (see Fischer, 1976: Ch. 5; Keller, 1968): (1) the existence of other, overlapping ties, as in ethnic enclaves (see, for example, W. F. Whyte, 1955) and factory neighborhoods (for example, Kornblum, 1974); (2) logistical difficulty in developing or maintaining extralocal relations, as in isolated hamlets (for example, Freeman, 1970) and among carless suburban housewives (Michelson, 1973a); and (3) an external threat that increases the functional importance of neighborhood ties, as in the case of urban redevelopment and busing (see Suttles, 1968, 1972).

Urban politics provides our final illustration. According to institutional perspectives, city politics can only be a travesty of town-hall democracy (see Dahl, 1967). The masses are herded and stampeded by symbol-waving and slogan-shouting demagogues, while decisions are made in backrooms by a small elite. But network analysis suggests an alternative perspective. Urban politics is seen as an "ecology of games" (N. Long, 1958) in which representatives of different interests—usually large networks of people linked by economic or ethnic commonalities—negotiate coalitions with one another on specific issues. An important ingredient in this process is the formation of direct connections among the leaders of the various networks. The existence of a power elite, for example, might be measured in terms of the relative closeness of these leaders to one another as compared with their separate ties to their constituents. The complexity of the urban setting assures that new and distinct issues constantly arise and that coalitions are thus always in flux.

These examples indicate the contribution of network analysis to the study of urban phenomena: it provides sociologists with a more precise way of thinking about the connections between ecological characteristics of settlements and characteristics of personal life. Instead of seeing urban social structure as formed of weakened and fragmented corporate groups, it is seen in terms of complex networks of relations formed by purposeful actors.

Problems in Network Analysis

Although network analysis is useful as a point of view or an orientation, it is not yet very well developed as a rigorous analytical procedure. There is still little agreement on precise definitions, the important features of networks, how they change, and other similar issues. Each investigator must immediately resolve some of these problems in order to proceed with any specific research. And the field as a whole must eventually reach agreement on these topics in order to develop a general method of study.

Definitions

There is some agreement that social network refers to the relations among social actors. However, there is much less agreement on any more specific definition. Here are three worthy examples of definitions:

> A social network [is] a specific set of linkages among a defined set of persons, with the additional property that the characteristics of these linkages as a whole may be used to interpret the social behavior of the persons involved (J. C. Mitchell, 1969: 2).

> The social relations in which every individual is embedded. . . . In an egocentric sense . . . the chains of persons with whom a given person is in actual contact and their interconnection (Boissevain, 1974: 24).

> A relevant series of linkages existing between individuals which may form a basis for the mobilization of people for specific purposes under specific conditions (Whitten and Wolfe, 1974: 720).

Of these and similar attempts, a paraphrase of Mitchell probably serves best as a generally acceptable and useful definition: *a social network is a specified set of links among social actors.* Social actors can be defined as individuals, roles (for example, presidents of large corporations), or groups (for example, terrorist gangs), depending on the research question. Since groups consist of networks, links among groups form a higher level of network. A *link* is the total set of *relations* between any two actors— that is, the ways in which they are interdependent (more on relations later). Since everyone is ultimately related, directly or indirectly, to everyone else, we must "specify" which links we are interested in for any given network analysis.

Investigators generally define the links which will make up a network on the basis of research interest. Links can be defined as, for example:

—exchanging advice on professional matters
—casual neighboring
—being "close friends"
—conspiring on political decisions

So, for example, a researcher interested in how people come to make a political decision might look at each person's set of political discussion links and define the group of interest as the set of persons joined by the network of these links (see Laumann et al., 1974). However, it is important to see whether some general principles of specification, or "partialling,"[10] can be established.

Network theorists have identified a number of dimensions along which networks can be specified (see Whitten and Wolfe, 1974: 725 ff.). One significant distinction is between *categorically* defined and *ego*-defined networks. In the former, a set of persons is distinguished by a shared characteristic or type of relation. Examples of categorically defined networks are the set of workers in a shop, an extended family, an ethnic group, or city leaders. The basic research problem is to reveal the structure of links among that set—for instance, the political alliances among workers (for example, Lipset et al., 1962; Finifter, 1974), or the personal friendships among members of a political elite (Laumann et al., 1974; Mills, 1956). An egocentric network is defined with respect to a particular actor and includes only those people who are actually linked to the actor in specified ways—for example, the political allies of a politician, or the recreational companions of a given individual.

However, this distinction is only preliminary; it is also necessary to specify networks on the basis of their *relational content*. J. C. Mitchell (1973) has suggested three types of criteria for distinguishing among network contents: norms, communication, and exchange. Normative criteria refer to the expectations associated wtih a relation between social *roles* (re: role theory) and yield distinctions most similar to those in common usage (such as "friend," "kin," "coworker," and "partner"). These distinctions are useful because they employ "folk" categories which carry significant cultural meaning. They also tap latent aspects of relations (for example, the *right* to ask a favor of a sibling; or the *obligation* to assist a friend). However, these normative criteria are unreliable because their cultural meanings are often vague and they often fail to predict behavior. There is great diversity in people's definitions and expectations of "friends," "parents," "neighbors," and similar normative categories. Even

---

[10] "By 'partial network' I mean any extract of the total network based on some criterion applicable throughout the whole network" (Barnes, 1969: 57; see also Wolfe, 1970).

when there are shared expectations for a relation, people may not behave according to those expectations. Finally, the same kinds of interactions may be found in different role relations (for example, people may borrow money from both kin and non-kin friends; one can go bowling with both coworkers and in-laws).

Mitchell's second criterion, communication, can be subsumed within his third, exchange, along with economic trade, collaboration on the job, mutual emotional support, and other kinds of exchanges. A typology of relations based on the exchanges they involve would have two advantages. It would have a conceptual foundation in exchange theory, and it would deal with actual behavior. However, such a typology would also have two difficulties: how to incorporate latent exchanges (rights and obligations) into a description of a relation, and how to categorize heterogeneous exchanges (for example, esteem traded for information). We suggest a yet more general scheme of relational content: to categorize relations by the joint activities of the two actors, for example, placing relations involving the discussion of political topics, attendance at a given church, and cohabitation into separate categories.[11]

Regardless of the set of categories, networks must be delimited and categorized in some fashion in order to pursue network analysis. While *ad hoc* techniques may suffice for particular investigations, network analysts must try to develop general schemes that distinguish networks by their contents. So far there are suggestions along these lines, but no conclusions.

DIMENSIONS

Once a researcher on a specific topic or the discipline in general has satisfactorily delimited the "total, infinite, unbounded, everlasting network" (Whitten and Wolfe, 1974: 725), the remaining problems are, first, to specify and define the critical attributes, or *dimensions* of those social networks, then to measure them, and finally to explore their causal antecendents and consequences.

The critical dimensions of networks can be defined in two ways: by the relational *content* (for example, the extent of financial obligation in a relation, or the physical loci of interaction of a network); or by the network's *structure* (for example, the number of people it connects, or the degree of interconnection). The network literature contains many suggestions for critical dimensions (see collections edited by J. C. Mitchell,

---

[11] This approach seems advantageous for research in that it allows designation of specific behaviors of interest. Its drawbacks as an approach to developing a general scheme include the problem of determining latent activities and more important, the difficulty of formulating a useful typology of all interactional activities. Efforts have been made along such lines by researchers working in the time-budget tradition (for example, Szalai, 1972).

1969; Aronson, 1970; Boissevain and Mitchell, 1973). Some dimensions describe dyadic *links*. These include, for instance:

Multiplexity—the number of relations in a given link
Symmetry—the balance of power or profit
Intensity—degree of commitment in a link

Other dimensions describe the *network* as a whole, or the *set* of links. Examples include:

Range—number of actors connected in a network
Density—the extent of interlinkage among the actors, usually expressed as the ratio of the number of existing links to the number of possible links
Reachability—the average number of links needed to connect any two actors by the shortest route
Clustering—the extent to which the total network is divided into distinguishable cliques

Many of these attributes have been conceived with respect to particular theoretical problems (for example, Bott's [1955] focus on density and clustering). However, the field of network analysis must proceed to develop a short list of key dimensions that are general properties of networks and have substantive implications. (We try to contribute to this development in Chapter 3.)

DETERMINANTS AND CONSEQUENCES

Finally, we must consider the causes and effects of network attributes. We want to understand both the conditions that cause specific networks to fall at various places along those dimensions (for example, why some networks are more dense or clustered than others) and the consequences of that variation (for example, the nature of the relations and personalities in networks of more and less multiplexity, intensity, or reachability).

The antecedent variables most often mentioned in the network literature include urbanism, social class, and residential mobility. Urbanism (as noted earlier) is thought to increase the specialization—reduce the "multiplexity"—of links, and decrease the density of individuals' networks (for explicit propositions, see Henry, 1958; Frankenburg, 1965; Craven and Wellman, 1973). Higher social class is often assumed to have similar consequences. In addition, high status is supposed to produce a shift from kin-based to occupation-based networks (see Chapter 4). Residential mobility is thought to disperse social networks, reducing their density and the intimacy and depth of links (see Chapter 9). Although some systematic studies of hypotheses such as these have been made (see especially Laumann, 1973; Wellman et al., 1973; Verbrugge, 1973; Shulman, 1972), the hypotheses remain plausible but unconfirmed.

There are also some noteworthy hypotheses about the effects of social network attributes. An entire line of research has evolved around Bott's (1955) theory that the extent of overlap between a husband's and a wife's networks influences their marital relationship. One frequently encounters the speculation that individuals who maintain differentiated, single-content networks are less psychologically integrated than others (for example, Merton, 1957; for challenges to this thesis, see Gergen, 1972; Sieber, 1974). Granovetter (1973) has argued that involvement in widely dispersed and instrumental networks provides greater access to resources than does involvement in highly dense and intimate ones. Several sources have suggested that network density promotes consensus and conformity among the connected persons (see Caplow, 1955; Laumann, 1973). These hypotheses also remain largely unexplored but potentially fertile ground for study.

Conclusion

Hypotheses about network dimensions, causes, and consequences chart some of the major work to be done in the study of social networks in their own right. Meanwhile, there is great value in adopting a network approach, even in its more diffuse and general form, as simply a focus on the relations among social actors. At such a rudimentary level, it still illuminates many phenomena, from the spread of a new fad to the nature of political power.

In the rest of this book, we will use network analysis to study the issues of "community," choice, and space. We will ask under what conditions social networks have the attributes described by the concept of community, what the roles of individual choices and constraints are in creating communal networks, and how place and space affect individuals' formation and maintenance of their social networks. These issues have long been of interest to social scientists. Network analysis permits us to frame the questions and organize the investigations more precisely.

3. The Dimensions of Social Networks[*]

Robert Max Jackson
Claude S. Fischer
Lynne McCallister Jones

T. H. MARSHALL ONCE described a sociologist as someone who cries, "Give me a job, and I'll spend the rest of my life polishing the tools." The proliferation of concepts and hypotheses in social network analysis unfortunately conforms to this stereotype. As we noted in Chapter 2, network theorists have offered long lists of "attributes" and "dimensions" but have presented few empirical assessments of the utility of those concepts. In this chapter, we apply some of those conceptual tools and weigh their relative value for future research and theory.[1]

Our specific analysis derives from the general perspective we have been developing in the last two chapters. We assume that people actively choose among alternative social relations, and that the social environment de-

---

[*] An earlier version of this chapter was presented at the meetings of the Eastern Sociological Society in Boston, March 1976.

[1] Although others have conducted similar analyses, their efforts were not as systematic as this one and their conclusions differed from our own. Notable work in this line includes Laumann (1973) and Verbrugge (1973), using the same Detroit data, and Wellman (1976; 1973) and Shulman (1972), on a survey conducted in Toronto. In general terms, our methods differ from those of Laumann in that we examined a number of characteristics which he ignored, particularly those dealing with the content of friendships; we measured heterogeneity, to which Laumann devoted an entire chapter, in terms of *a priori* categories instead of "distances" derived from small-space analysis (an essentially circular procedure); and we analyzed complex associations among variables through multiple contingency table analysis rather than by using less revealing regression techniques, as Laumann did. Our differences with Verbrugge include measuring attributes of friendships rather than attributes of individuals on each end of the friendships. In short, our analysis used some different variables, relied on a different methodology, and stemmed from a different theoretical orientation. Not surprisingly, we reached somewhat different conclusions.

termines the relative costs and values of these alternatives. This "choice-constraint" perspective guides our application and evaluation of network concepts and hypotheses, and the data analyses that follow. These lead us to conclude that, for a large set of questions, the substantive content of personal relations is more important than the formal structure of social networks.

We begin by examining several key propositions in social network analysis, which we then contrast with our own choice-constraint perspective. We derive from our perspective some expectations about the associations among attributes of social networks (for example, multiplexity and intimacy). We then evaluate those expectations by testing them in the Detroit survey.

Attributes of Social Networks

The concepts of multiplexity and density have been especially popular in the networks literature (and, under other labels, in sociology generally). Classical theorists argued that urbanization and modernization created less multiplex and less dense social networks and, as a consequence, people have suffered a loss of social integration and supportive social relations.

Multiplexity has been used in at least two ways. First, it may refer to the number of different *role relations*—such as kin, neighbor, coworker—any two people have with each other. (For example, the link between two people who both work together and belong to the same club has a multiplexity of two).[2] Alternatively, multiplexity refers to the *number of contents* in a relation: the number of distinct activities, exchanges, dependencies, or modes of interaction between two people.[3]

The classical theories of "community" (see Chapter 1) generally suggest that modernization involves a shift from largely multiplex relations, in which individuals interact with one another in a variety of ways, to

---

[2] Boissevain (1974) defines multiplexity as follows: "A social relation that is based on a single role relation [in turn defined as a shared 'activity field'] is described as uniplex or single-stranded, while a relation that covers many roles is termed multiplex or many-stranded" (p. 30).

[3] Mitchell (1969): "Network links which contain only one focus of interaction are called 'uniplex' or, more simply, 'single-stranded' relationships. Those which contain more than one content . . . are called multiplex" (p. 22). In a later article, Mitchell (1973) provides three categories of "content": information, exchange, and "normative" roles (see discussion in previous chapter). The meaning of quantifying "strands," in this definition or the prior one, is unclear because there are no well-defined *a priori* categories which are mutually disjoint or exhaustive. And it is altogether uncertain whether different roles or contents should be weighted equally in an overall index. As long as these problems are unresolved, the construct cannot be applied theoretically or empirically in any precise manner.

singleplex relations, in which individuals know one another in limited, specialized ways. These theories usually assume that multiplex relations are more enduring, supportive, and intimate, largely because they provide more exchanges and involve the individuals' entire personalities (see, for example, Boissevain, 1974; Craven and Wellman, 1973).[4] Consequently, they argue, modernization reduces social intimacy by reducing multiplexity.

Network density is usually defined as "the extent to which links which could possibly exist among persons do in fact exist" (Mitchell, 1969: 18). Density is usually measured by comparing the number of actual relations among a set of people to the number of possible relations. For example, in a set of five people there are ten possible friendships ($[5 \times 4] /2 = 10$). If they report only four actual friendships *in toto,* density is said to be 40 percent (4/10). Under this mathematical firmness, however, is some definitional quicksand. Most analysts ignore variation in the *kinds* of relations people have with one another and define relations dichotomously, as either existing or not. Unfortunately, we are still stuck with this approach in analyzing our data.

According to the classical statements, density, like multiplexity, declines with modernization and urbanization. Required to act in diverse social contexts with diverse kinds of people, the modern individual is connected to people who have no relations with one another. These theories also argue that dense networks can give individuals more concerted social support and bind them more closely to the norms of the group (see Granovetter, 1973; Craven and Wellman, 1973; Bott, 1955; Laumann, 1973). They conclude, again, that modernization reduces individuals' social supports, this time by reducing density.[5]

We will focus on the perspective on social networks that these theories share. They emphasize the *formal* qualities of a social relation, such as its multiplexity, over the *content* of the relation: the actual exchanges or degree of intimacy it involves.

---

[4] Granovetter (1973) has suggested that, although multiplex relations are more emotionally supportive, a network of singleplex relations can yield more material and instrumental assistance.

[5] Talcott Parsons' "pattern variables" represent another and quite different effort to specify the aspects of social relations implied in the classic *Gemeinschaft-Gesellschaft* distinction. In some particulars, there are similarities between the network theorists' variables and the pattern variables: multiplexity is not unlike diffuseness; affectivity and particularism capture elements of intimacy; and ascription-achievement is one way of categorizing the social source of a relation. However, there are major differences between Parsons' approach and the present one which derive from their very different interests. Parsons is trying to describe the institutionalized, normative *orientations of actors* toward situations and relations. Network theorists are trying to describe the empirical uniformities of actual relations. The difference leads the latter to look at variables Parsons does not consider—at the link level, attributes like frequency of contact, symmetry of exchange, and duration—and to consider emergent properties of networks, such as density.

THE CONSTRUCTION OF SOCIAL NETWORKS

In Chapter 1 we distinguished two approaches to analyzing social networks, one which we called "mechanistic," the other "choice-constraint." The first, most common in the networks literature, acknowledges that individuals make choices in forming their social circles but assigns choice a secondary role in the analysis of networks. It largely takes for granted the existence of an individual's network and focuses instead on the consequences to the individual of being "enmeshed" in a given network (Barnes, 1972: 3). This approach concentrates on formal qualities (categorizing networks in ways that will conveniently permit comparisons across egos). Laumann does this quite consciously:

> My theoretical predilections incline me toward the "structuralist" point of view, in which forces typically beyond the control of the individual are regarded as providing the *determinative causal force*, rather than the converse notion, in which the individual essentially creates his primary environment to reflect his preexisting needs and orientations (1973: 118; italics added).

Laumann has created a false dichotomy. Circumstances beyond the control of individuals certainly affect their behavior. But people create networks through a series of choices, and social structure influences their choices by determining the range and relative value of available alternatives.

A choice-constraint approach stresses that networks are the results of individual choices made within social constraints. Although some network theorists acknowledge the choice processes (for example, Boissevain, 1974: 93–96; Mitchell, 1969: 43), they do not systematically explore its implications. To find serious consideration of how networks form and change, one must look elsewhere, to Simmel (1922), to symbolic interactionists (Mead, 1934; Blumer, 1969; Matza, 1969), and especially to social psychologists (Thibaut and Kelley, 1959; Homans, 1974; see also Lazarsfeld and Merton, 1954). Let us be more specific.

As briefly discussed in Chapter 1, the model of behavior we are using includes the heuristic assumption that individuals act as rational decision-makers. People must continually choose among behavior alternatives, each of which promises certain rewards but also involves certain costs (rewards and costs as subjectively assessed by each person). People seek, consciously or not, to maximize their rewards relative to their costs, and they therefore pick the most "profitable" and "rational" alternative. This rationality is "bounded" (Simon, 1957), first, because the choices are made with incomplete knowledge of the consequences and of all the alternatives objectively available, and, second, because of some inaccuracy about the relative utility to the individual of the alternatives. Nevertheless, within limits, people choose what they perceive to be best.

We also assume that social relations are essentially exchanges—both of material goods and services and of less tangible rewards such as advice, comfort, and praise. The costs of relations include the goods and services reciprocated, the bother of maintaining a tie (telephoning and the like), persevering through conflicts and difficulties, and the opportunity cost of alternative relations forgone. Over time, people constantly choose whether to begin, continue, or cease exchanging with other people. And these choices, too, are weighed on the basis of reward and cost, according to "bounded rationality." Of course, people can form relations only with those whom they have met and can interact with at reasonable cost (see also Kerckhoff, 1974). These others will be largely those with whom a social context—work, neighborhood, kinship, social club, and the like—is shared. In sum, people choose to construct and maintain social exchanges with some of the people whom they encounter, and they make that choice on the basis of weighing rewards and costs.[6]

Networks change as a consequence of changes in the factors we have described: rewards, costs, and contexts. What the individual finds rewarding may change as a function of, for example, movement through the life-cycle. Costs may change: others may demand more in exchange; opportunity costs may increase because alternative relations become available; or maintenance costs may increase because of, for instance, greater physical separation. Finally, social contexts may open up or close down. Throughout such changes, we assume that individuals seek to sustain a network structure that provides relatively rewarding relations at relatively low costs.

This perspective yields several specific propositions about the development of networks and the associations among network attributes. (Note: The propositions listed below refer largely to working-age American males —the sample in the Detroit survey—but we believe that many of them are more generally applicable.)

THE CONSEQUENCES OF SELECTION

Our assumption that people maximize their rewards relative to their costs in selecting and sustaining relations implies, first, that when the *costs* of interacting are relatively similar across a set of possible associates, then the *rewards* connected with the different people determine the proba-

---

[6] This is, of course, an abstract *model* of human behavior, not a concrete *description* of it. People have both conscious and unconscious needs and wants (that is, those they are aware of and can verbalize and those they cannot). People often behave in ways that seem "irrational." However, the rational maximizer model assumes, for the sake of analysis, that people act *as if* they were clear-headed calculators. The worth of this assumption depends on how far it takes us in understanding behavior. It is particularly useful to sociologists interested in the effects of the social and physical structures around the actor.

bility of interaction. Conversely, when the rewards for interaction appear roughly constant for all the people, then the costs connected with each determine whom individuals will choose to associate with.

People vary in the opportunities they have for forming and keeping ties (for example, in the kinds of social contexts open to them). And individuals vary in constraints on them (for example, in the time or money they have). We will focus here on two personal circumstances that influence network formation: social class and the contexts from which friendships are formed. (Later chapters deal with other circumstances such as life-cycle and ecological location.) People in higher social classes tend to have more money (with all it can buy, including ease of travel), more social skills, and more control over their time. We would expect that people who can invest more in a relation can thus reap more rewards, and we expect this to be true for higher status men. Similarly, the freedom of movement and range of choice of the well-to-do should permit them to sustain ties from diverse sources. And they may even achieve greater intimacy with their associates.

The contexts in which people participate—work, neighborhood, and so on—delimit pools of possible intimates, each context delimiting a different sort of pool. The costs and rewards of personal relations also depend upon the kind of social context (for example, a coworker can usually be seen with less effort than can an old school chum). Thus, we expect that different kinds of social contexts produce qualitatively different social relations.

When people decide to interact with others, to cultivate a bond or let it lapse, they decide on the basis of the relation's content, not its formal structure. People do not make such choices on the basis of abstract qualities like multiplexity or density, but instead on the basis of the concrete features of the relation (Is she nice to me? Do we have fun going out?). People make choices about their relations on the basis of content (for example, deciding whether a neighbor would also make a good business partner) before the form of the tie is altered (for example, the relation becomes multiplex). This does not mean that formal qualities have *no* effects on relations, but it does mean that the specific contents of relations are casually prior to the forms[7] and, consequently, the content of relations has more effect on social networks than do their formal properties.

This brings us back to the concepts of multiplexity and density, the key formal attributes stressed in classical theories. Our argument implies

---

[7] This does not mean that the content of a relation is *temporally* prior. People born into corporate groups find themselves in a dense network of multiplex relations. However, individuals' choices about which relations to develop and which to let decline are based on the specific content of each. Thus, content is *causally* prior to structure.

that higher multiplexity results when individuals find it worthwhile or necessary to maintain more than one kind of link with one another. For example, a person may discover that a neighbor is a particularly rewarding friend, or relatives become neighbors when they move nearby. Over time, these sorts of conditions can increase or decrease multiplexity. Consequently, the role multiplexity of a relation depends on the context in which it was formed, its duration, and people's reasons for maintaining it. Each of these specific sources of multiplexity influences the quality of a social bond. Therefore, role multiplexity has little effect on the quality of a relation once the source of the multiplexity is taken into account.

We make similar arguments about density. People's friends are more likely to know one another when they live in the same neighborhood or work at the same place, and so on. Furthermore, some contexts promote density more than others do (for example, kinship more than neighborhood). Thus, density is a function of the number of different contexts from which the specific links are drawn; and when the links are drawn from the same context, density depends on the substantive nature of that context. It is, then, probable that density has little effect on the quality of a relation or a network once the substantive sources of the density are taken into account.

We use these propositions to organize our analysis of the Detroit data.

The Dimensions of Friendship Networks

As we noted in Chapter 1, each of the men in the Detroit survey was asked to name "the three men who are your closest friends and whom you see most often. They can be relatives or non-relatives." (Names of brothers and brothers-in-law were subsequently excluded and replacement names solicited.) Later questions asked the respondent to describe the characteristics of his friends and aspects of the friendship.[8]

Guided by theoretical discussions of social networks and by trial and error, we developed a set of critical variables that could be measured in the Detroit survey. Some of these variables are attributes of *links*, the total set of connections between two people. Link variables characterize

[8] These questions were designed to elicit the respondents' intimate (male) networks, but the lists should not be interpreted literally. We have found in our own development of a network questionnaire that the terms "friends," "close," and "frequent" are ambiguous, and the definitions people use are often idiosyncratic. Even in the Detroit data, 5 percent of those "closest" men were later labeled "acquaintances,"and 20 percent of the "most often" seen men were seen, off the job, less than once a month. (Logically, these statistics do not invalidate the questions but suggest that a good deal of "noise" crept into the answers.) We prefer to think of the elicited names as representing some subset of the men's personal social networks, a sample biased toward closeness and frequent contact.

the *relations* between any two men, and not the men themselves. (The Detroit men reported 2,935 friendship links.) [9] Other variables are attributes of *networks*, the set of relations among a man and his friends. Network variables measure emergent properties, characteristic of the network as a whole and not reducible to the link level. (An example of a reducible variable would be the average intimacy of links in a network.) There are 985 networks in the data set.

We use the following variables in our analysis (and elaborate upon their definitions as we proceed):

Attributes of Links

Intimacy: reported "closeness" of the friendship
Frequency: how often the pair "got together outside of work"
Duration: the number of years a man knew his friend
Role Multiplexity: the number of role relations (just friend, relative, co-worker, neighbor, association membership) involved in a link
Attributed Source: the social context from which the friendship emerged

Attributes of Networks

Density: the extent to which the men named by the respondent were, in his estimation, friends of one another
Homogeneity: the age and class similarity among the men in the network
Dispersion: the range of attributed sources from which the friendships in the network were drawn
Dominant Source: the single context (that is, attributed source), if any, that provided most of the respondent's friendships

INTIMACY, FREQUENCY, AND DURATION

Intimacy, frequency of contact, and duration are concepts that appear often in the networks literature. Each presumably indicates the depth, intensity, or *quality* of a relation. The *duration* of a bond reflects the amount of experience shared by two people and how well their tie has endured disruption and competition from alternative relations.[10] We measured it as the number of years the friends were reported to have known one another (collapsed into four roughly logarithmic categories: one to three

---

[9] This means that 2,935 relations served as our units of analysis, and that each respondent is usually repeated in three of the units. And this in turn means that the units of analysis are not quite independent in the simplest sense of statistical analyses. This is analogous to studies sampling people within a number of neighborhoods which analyze the relationship of individual and neighborhood characteristics (see Laumann et al., 1974, for a similar procedure).

[10] We suspect that time is significant in terms of shared experience early in a relation, and in terms of survivability during most of its history.

years; four to seven; eight to 13; and 14 or over). *Intimacy* has many aspects: whether people confide in one another, can depend on one another, and so on. The Detroit survey contained only one intimacy question, whether each friend was considered a "very close friend, or a good friend, or more an acquaintance."[11] *Frequency* was measured as how often the two friends "got together" outside of work.[12]

The associations among these variables form an intriguing pattern: Longer-lasting friendships were more intimate ($\gamma = .35$); intimate friends were seen more often ($\gamma = .14$), *but* friends who were known longer were seen *less* often ($\gamma = -.23$). The first finding is easily explained. The accumulation of shared experiences over time increases intimacy, or men keep their more intimate ties longer, or both. The second finding is also easy to understand. Frequent interaction promotes intimacy, or men seek out intimate friends more frequently, or both.[13] The explanation for the third finding is less obvious. Fifty-six percent of friends known less than eight years were seen at least weekly, but only 34 percent of friends still known after 13 years were seen this often. Why did durable friendships, described as intimate, involve less frequent contact?

Our answer focuses on the substantive meanings of contact frequency and of duration. Basically, the changes that accompany the aging of a close friendship interfere with frequent contact, so that friends can remain intimate but still be prevented by circumstances from getting together frequently. As an intimate relation grows older, it often becomes less convenient for friends to meet, and convenience is the primary influence on interaction frequency (see Verbrugge, 1973; below). Over time, people's life circumstances change and so do their relations. Many of the early supports to a friendship—school, jobs, physical proximity, and so on—fall away. The friendships that are maintained in the absence of such role supports are the intimate ones.[14] However, those role relations provided occasions for frequent contact. Therefore, although people prefer to see their most intimate friends most often, the constraints of day-to-day life cause networks to assume a shape where people spend more time with more recent and less intimate friends but feel closest to old friends whom they cannot see easily. (This argument assumes, first, that frequency is

[11] Wellman et al. (1973) found that a similar question predicted quite well whether an intimate was considered to be available for assistance.

[12] We do not have a measure of the total amount of time the men spent in each other's company. However, the gross differences in interaction frequency considered here are so large that they indicate the relative time spent together as well.

[13] Another possible explanation is that there is a perceptual bias which creates a relationship between closeness and both duration and frequency: "If I've known Joe so long [or seen him so often], he must be close."

[14] One role that facilitates (or obliges) contact, irrespective of duration, is kinship. Kin-source friends are the only ones for whom contact is not negatively associated with duration ($\gamma = .04$, N.S.).

not a cause of intimacy, an assumption for which there is evidence,[15] and, second, that duration is more a result of intimacy than a cause of it.)

We interpret duration, not so much as a formal attribute of a link (that is, number of years), but as the outcome of continuing choice, emphasizing the fact that people periodically decide whether to maintain a relation—even if only by "dropping a line"—or to let it lapse. Focusing on the process of continuing choice allows us to explain the negative association between frequency and intimacy.

REWARDS AND COSTS

Earlier we said we expected, on the basis of our choice-constraint model, that where alternative choices for social interaction have equal costs, their differential rewards should determine which person is chosen. In our data, we can consider frequency of interaction as an indicator of choosing social interaction (selecting which friend to spend time with) and reported intimacy as an indicator of the reward value of those interactions. Two indicators of cost are: (1) the distance from the respondent's residence to his friend's residence, and (2) the source of the friendship (for instance, friends known from work will be relatively easier to see than some other friends). When we removed (by statistical controls) the effects of either distance or source, the association that we reported between rewards (namely, intimacy) and selection (namely, frequency) increased.[16] This evidence is in a sense like an experiment: When a man was "given" a set of best friends to choose from, all of whom were about

---

[15] In this regard, Shulman (1972) found no association between the frequency of contact his respondents reported having with their "intimates" and whether or what they reported exchanging with those people. Wellman (1976) found that people whom his respondents saw most often face-to-face tended to be also reported as more available for help. However, frequency of telephone contact was more critical than in-person contact, and contact altogether was less important in emergency than in "everyday" situations. Kleiner and Parker (1976) found that the frequency with which men discussed things with associates was not related to the men's psychological well-being, although other aspects of their social ties were.

[16] The association between intimacy and frequency is greater among friends living in the neighborhood ($\gamma = .20$) and among friends living outside the neighborhood but in the metropolitan area ($\gamma = .21$) than it is for those living outside the metropolitan area ($\gamma = .01$), or within the total sample combined ($\gamma = .14$). Our interpretation is that when the cost of distance is a constant factor in deciding whom to spend time with, people are free to see whomever they wish in accord with their tastes. All neighbors were within ten minutes; other Detroiters were between ten and about 45 minutes away. Hence, intimacy predicted frequency. However, when distance varied greatly—people outside the area lived from perhaps 20 to 2,000 miles away—distance costs overrode tastes as a determinant and the effect of the intimacy was negligible. Were the opposite of our assumption true— that is, were intimacy mostly an *effect* of frequency—then controlling for distance should have *reduced* the association between intimacy and frequency (because the variation in the "cause," frequency, would have been reduced).

equally as troublesome to see, their differential rewardingness (that is, intimacy) was a more significant predictor of getting together than in conditions when both rewards and costs varied.

The converse proposition is also supported—but only slightly in our own data. When rewards were held constant by looking only at the most intimate friends, the cost of interaction (distance) became a somewhat better predictor of frequency than it was overall.[17] More important, other research confirms the proposition. A few studies have found that propinquity has a strong effect on friendship formation among quite homogeneous populations—for example, married veterans who were engineering students at M.I.T., or police academy cadets (Festinger et al., 1950; Segal, 1974; see also Fellin and Litwak, 1963; W. H. Whyte, 1956). Given a set of very similar people to choose from, the number of steps from one door to another becomes exceedingly important. In more heterogeneous settings, these costs are counterbalanced by variations in rewards.[18]

SOCIAL POSITION

We can conceive abstractly of the exchange processes controlling friendship choice as existing in a series of "markets." As with most markets, the participants are not equal. *Social class* affects the selection and maintenance of a social relation by shaping the opportunities and constraints the individual faces. It influences an individual's access to the social skills and material resources that facilitate finding and keeping rewarding relations. As we expected, men in the higher class levels drew their friends from more diverse sources than did other men ($\gamma = .15$ between occupational status and dispersion of sources). They had relatively fewer friends in their networks who were kin and neighbors (see also Verbrugge, 1973), but more who were fellow association members. They also perceived their friends as being "closer" than did men of lower status ($\gamma = .12$). In general, high status seems to provide more opportunity and fewer constraints in network formation (as it does in other realms of life).

Mirra Komarovsky (1967) reached a similar conclusion in her study of blue-collar families. She argues that for these families

opportunities for enlarging the circle of friends are limited . . . when the husband's job neither requires social entertaining nor serves as a source of

---

[17] The association of frequency and distance is slightly greater among the "very close" friends ($\gamma = .49$) and among friends of longest duration ($\gamma = .50$) than it is overall ($\gamma = .43$).

[18] For example, Gans (1967) found, in his study of the development of community life in Levittown, New Jersey, that the effect of propinquity was overridden by those of class and ethnicity. The minority social class and ethnic group residents searched beyond their immediate neighbors to find friends similar to themselves.

new contacts. . . . Because the choice of friends is made within so small
a group, the chances of finding congenial persons are relatively small (p.
312).

People build their networks by choosing (and rechoosing) friends on the
basis of the differential rewards and costs associated with the alternatives
they face. But those choices are not completely free; they are channeled
by individuals' social positions, which affect the opportunities they face
and their abilities to sustain the costs of social relations.

ROLE MULTIPLEXITY

We were able to construct a crude index of *role multiplexity* for each
link in the Detroit survey by computing the numbers of known role relations between a respondent and each friend. We could count being
friends, kin, coworkers, neighbors, and fellow members in a voluntary
association as separate relations.[19] Twenty-six percent of the links scored
one—that is, the men were "just friends"—43 percent scored two; 26
percent scored three; 6 percent, four; and almost none scored five.[20]

Contrary to the expectations of many network theorists (for example,
Boissevain, 1974: 30; Craven and Wellman, 1973; Mitchell, 1969: 32),
the extent of multiplexity in a friendship was associated with neither its
duration nor its degree of intimacy. Actually, multiplexity was *lower* for
men who knew each other longer ($\gamma = -.17$). Of new pairs of friends
(men knowing each other less than three years), 40 percent shared three
or more roles (including friendship); of old friends (men knowing each
other more than 13 years), only 29 percent shared three or more roles.
One out of eight new friends were "just friends," which one out of three
old friends were. As we argued earlier, old friendships often endure because of their intimacy, even as role supports fall away (see Chapter 5
for further discussion of this topic). Similarly, the greater the multiplexity, the slightly *less* intimate the friendship ($\gamma = -.08$). The more
multiplex a friendship, the more often the men saw one another ($\gamma = .32$),
but this is accounted for largely by friends who shared the role of neigh-

[19] Operationally, kinship was determined by an affirmative answer to whether "any
of the men you have named are relatives of yours" (recall that brothers and
brothers-in-law—4 and 5 percent of the original names, respectively—were subsequently replaced and do not appear in our analysis); coworker status by whether
"you see_____regularly where you work—that is, at least once or twice a week";
neighbor status by whether the friend lives "in this neighborhood—say, within ten
minutes of here"; and associational status by whether the respondent "usually
meet[s] . . . [the friend] . . . in meetings of" various organizations.

[20] In her calculations, Verbrugge (1973) used the names that were first mentioned—
those including brothers and brothers-in-law—and therefore could not count associational ties. Her distribution was 35 percent—52 percent—13 percent—0 percent
(recalculated from her Table 6.4). This leads her to underestimate multiplexity
for fellow association members.

bors. Friends who were neighbors saw one another substantially more often than did other pairs of friends. Sharing other roles besides neighbor, however, increased frequency only slightly.

Thus, role multiplexity did *not* significantly affect the quality of friendships. Even where multiplexity was associated with another dimension of the friendship, frequency of interaction, that association is best understood in terms of the substantive sources of multiplexity (that is, the neighbor role) and not its formal quality (that is, the number of roles). We are led to consider, instead of the *number* of role relations, the *kind* of role relations.

ATTRIBUTED SOURCE

The *source* of a friendship is that social context, or pool of acquaintances, from which the friendship was formed. We were able to attribute a source for 83 percent of the friendships, in the following categories: kinship (7 percent of all friendships), childhood and juvenile friends (20 percent), neighborhood (23 percent), work (26 percent), and voluntary associations (7 percent). Those who had no apparent role relation with the respondent made up the remainder (17 percent). There is a certain degree of error in these assignments (particularly due to change in role relations), but no evident systematic bias.[21]

We argued earlier that the social context in which relations are formed affects their content and quality, because the context delimits the pool of eligibles, the kinds of interactions that occur (for example, task-related interaction with coworkers versus socio-emotional interaction with kin), and the associated rewards and costs. Context should have more effect on content and quality than formal features such as multiplexity, because it is causally prior in the formation of individuals' relations. And that is what we found.

Duration. Kin and childhood friends were known the longest time; work, neighborhood, and association friends the shortest time; and friends lacking role overlaps fell in between (see Table 3.1). The workplace and neighborhood provided 79 percent of the most recent ties (under three years), and only 35 percent of the oldest ties (over 13 years).

---

[21] We categorized each friendship in terms of its history and role relation and selected in a hierarchical manner that context which seemed to be the most probable source of original contact. All friends who were relatives were classified as of "kin" origin; all non-kin friends who were known by the respondent before he, the respondent, was 18 were called "childhood"; all non-kin, non-childhood friends who were seen at work were labeled "work" friends; of the remainder, those residing in the neighborhood were labeled accordingly; and, of those still left, ones seen at meetings of an association were labeled "association." The residual group is "no known roles."

TABLE 3.1   Characteristics of Friendships by Attributed Source

ATTRIBUTED SOURCE	DURATION (% > 13 YRS.)	INTIMACY (% "VERY CLOSE")	FREQUENCY[a] (% > 1 PER WK.)
Childhood (N = *603*)	72	72	54
Kin (*194*)	66	72	40
No Known Roles (*507*)	49	54	20
Association (*199*)	39	51	39
Neighborhood (*678*)	35	43	60
Work (*772*)	30	44	43

a Frequency seen outside of work.

Intimacy.   The men perceived their kin and childhood friends as most intimate, and the friends they found in the work or neighborhood setting as least intimate (see also Wellman, 1976; Fried, 1973: 106). (This difference cannot be explained in terms of duration effects: the same order of intimacy by source displayed in Table 3.1 existed for all friends regardless of duration.)

Frequency.   The key to understanding frequency of leisure-time interaction is ease of access. Living close by generally promoted contact, regardless of the source of the friendship. This was not so, however, for work friends, who were seen equally often regardless of residential distance. This latter finding suggests that work interaction may substitute for leisure interaction in maintaining contact with a friend. After controlling for geographical distance, the differences among sources in frequency of interaction (those shown in Table 3.1) became much smaller, with a slight advantage remaining to kin and association friends.[22] These results suggest that extra-personal supports—proximity, kinship, and clubs—facilitate contact.

In a few respects, work and neighborhood friends can be distinguished as a class from kin and childhood friends. Work and neighborhood friendships were short-term, ethnically dissimilar (see Chapter 4), and not very intimate, but involved frequent contact (neighbors during leisure and co-workers on the job). Kin and childhood friends both tended to be the reverse. They were more enduring, intimate, and ethnically similar, but they were seen infrequently.[23] We might crudely characterize the former

[22] Among friends living in the neighborhood, kin were seen most often (69 percent were seen more than once a week), and association next most often (66 percent). Among friends elsewhere in the S.M.S.A., kin (51 percent) and association (41 percent) were again more frequently seen.

[23] These differences in source types were *not* the result of differences among respondents (for example, that people who picked kin as friends were also the kind who generally had more intimate ties). Source differences in intimacy and duration were as strong among those respondents who nominated friends from three different sources as among those who nominated all from the same source.

as friendships of "convenience," and the latter as friendships of "commitment."

As we suggested earlier, the source context of a friendship has more bearing on its quality than does multiplexity. We can pursue the same general issue of content versus form at the network level by examining density.

DENSITY

The Detroit respondents were asked, "Of your three best friends, how many of them are good friends of one another?" At first glance, dense networks appeared to fit most theorists' descriptions, based on the classic *Gemeinschaft* model, of cohesive, intimate, enduring, and day-to-day primary groups (see, for example, Granovetter, 1973; Tilly, 1972; Bott, 1955; Laumann, 1973). Men whose friends were also friends of one another were more likely to perceive each friend as "very close" ($\gamma = .13$), to have known their friends a long time ($\gamma = .10$), to see them often ($\gamma = .24$), and to get together as a group ($\gamma = .80$) than were men in loose-knit networks.[24]

However, most of these associations between network density and friendship quality were limited to certain kinds of networks. Men in dense networks saw their friends more often than did other men, irrespective of other characteristics. Apparently, having friends who were friends of one another made it easier (or more necessary) to see them frequently. But intimacy and duration were associated with density *only for friends living in the neighborhood*.[25] That is, friends living outside the neighborhood could be long-lasting and intimate *whether or not* the network as a whole was dense; friends living inside the neighborhood were intimate largely *if* the network was dense.[26]

These findings suggest that, at least in the Detroit sample, network density does not generally indicate a primary group with *Gemeinschaft* qualities. Such a group would involve tight connections among local residence, frequent contact, multiplexity, intimacy, and density. This was not a common pattern in our data. Instead, the more intimate friends tended

---

[24] Shulman (1972) did not find an association between density and frequency, but otherwise confirms these findings. He also found that people in dense networks were more likely to report being helped by their intimates, but were no more likely to give help, lend, or borrow than were others. Wellman et al. (1973) found no relationship between density and availability of assistance. Laumann (1973: 123) confirmed our results in his own analysis.

[25] Density X duration: among friends living in the neighborhood, $\gamma = .21$; others, $\gamma = .02$ (N.S.). Density X closeness: friends in the neighborhood, $\gamma = .24$; others, $\gamma = .05$ (N.S.).

[26] That is, in the interaction effect of location and density on each of duration and intimacy, the "deviant" cell was neighborhood/low density. Friendships in that cell were especially short (and only 37 percent were considered "very close").

to live outside the area, regardless of density. (Also, they were seen relatively infrequently, and did not have multiplex ties to the respondent.) The significance of density to intimacy here seemed to be restricted to differentiating among neighborhood friends. Most local friends were not intimate; but those who were intimate were involved in dense networks— networks which typically originated on some basis *other* than locality, such as kinship or childhood. Except with regard to neighborhood friends, then, density affected little more than contact frequency.

To elaborate our analysis of network density, we must explore the origins of density. We can dismiss the possibility that density results from the similarity of friends. We measured *network homogeneity* in terms of the variation in age and occupational status among the respondent and his three friends.[27] Neither type of homogeneity was associated with network density; nor were they substantially associated with characteristics of individual friendships.[28] We had more success in explaining network density and other network dimensions when we returned to the sources of the relations.

NETWORK DISPERSION AND DOMINANT SOURCE

The *dispersion* of a social network refers to the number of social contexts (attributed sources) from which the individual friendships were drawn. If they all came from one context (for example, if the friends were all coworkers), then dispersion is low; if they came from a variety of settings, dispersion is high.[29] (Since the data we are analyzing describe egocentric networks—that is, since they are established on the basis of a respondent's ties—dispersion refers in this case to the number of social contexts which the respondent's friends shared with him rather than with one another.) We measured dispersion as the number of different attributed *sources* represented in the networks for which we had full data (61 percent of the cases).

Early urban sociologists such as Park (1916) and Wirth (1938) referred to something similar to dispersion when they described the diversity of "social worlds" in cities and wrote of individuals whose lives were

[27] Age was measured in years; status in terms of the Duncan SES index; and variation in each as the standard deviation.

[28] See Laumann (1973) for more detailed analysis of occupational homogeneity. Note that he employed a very different measure: a mean "distance" based on the results of placing occupational groups in a two-dimensional space as determined by group patterns in friendship choices. See also our analysis in Chapter 4.

[29] It is common in the network literature (for example, Barnes, 1969) to define "partial" networks by the shared social context—for example, work or neighborhood networks. Here we are referring to a partial network which crosses such bounds. "Friendship" networks are a classic instance; they can include coworker, neighbor, and other links.

divided among a few such worlds. Following the decline-of-community theories, they suggested that, although such dispersed social relations provide access to material resources, they also break up cohesive communities, and produce shallow and impersonal relations (see Fischer, 1976: Ch. 2).

We discovered, first, that the amount of dispersion was lower than chance expectation; that is, the men tended to draw two or all their friends from a single source (26 percent drew all three friends from one source; see also Verbrugge, 1973). Second, as we expected, the more dispersed a respondent's network, the less dense it was likely to be;[30] that is, the greater the number of sources that produced the friendships, the less likely it was that those friends were friends of one another ($\gamma = -.48$). In 57 percent of the networks drawn totally from the same source, all the men were friends of one another; in only 17 percent of networks drawn from three different sources was this so (see also Shulman, 1972: Ch. 6).

Dispersion was modestly associated with the link attributes of duration, intimacy, and frequency—but in a curvilinear manner. Friendships in dispersed networks tended to be average in these respects, while those in single-source networks tended to be either high or low. This was because of the effects of the source: in concentrated networks, friendships varied according to which specific context the network was drawn from; in dispersed networks, the varying sources "averaged out." (For example, in a dispersed network, we might find both a relative who is an intimate friend, and a neighbor who is just an acquaintance.) [31]

In sum, the social-worlds theories' expectations that single-world networks would be intermeshed (dense) were confirmed, but their expectation that single-world networks, regardless of source, would also provide more communal relations was *not* confirmed.

Given that the source of a particular friendship substantially affects the nature of the relation, how does the *dominant source* of the network affect other network attributes? In those cases in which a network was not totally dispersed, we could identify the social context from which most of the relations were drawn. We were able to classify 63 percent of the networks as being "dominated" by kinship, childhood, neighborhood, work, or voluntary association relations.[32] This is more than a random

[30] To some undetermined extent, this finding may be an artifact. Respondents, once having thought of a first friend, may have then recalled others from the same context (rather than their actual next "closest friend").

[31] Dispersion was related positively, though modestly, to role multiplexity ($\gamma = .11$), which means that networks drawn from many sources tended to have slightly more role relations per link than did those drawn from a single source—contrary to the prediction common in the literature.

[32] We were able to classify some networks on dominant source but not on dispersion because there were networks in which we could attribute a source to only two of the friends, but these were friends from the same source.

TABLE 3.2   Characteristics of Networks by Dominant Source

DOMINANT ATTRIBUTED SOURCE	DENSITY (% FULLY DENSE)	AGE HOMOGENEITY (% > MEDIAN)	CLASS HOMOGENEITY (% > MEDIAN)
Kin (N = 23)	44	10	36
Work (211)	39	39	61
Neighborhood (212)	29	48	39
Childhood (167)	34	77	44
Association (41)	34	62	63

model would predict because, as we saw, the men tended to return to the same "well" for their friends.

The associations between dominant source and other network variables are summarized in Table 3.2. Kin, and to a lesser extent, work networks, were relatively heterogeneous in class and age, and were relatively dense.[33] (The relative class homogeneity of work networks was partly an artifact of work settings being class-segregated.) Association and, to a lesser extent, childhood and neighbor networks were homogeneous and not dense. We might see two types of networks in these results: heterogeneous and dense, homogeneous and not dense.

A man will tend to have a dense network when his friends share social contexts with one another, but some contexts (kin and work) promote density more than do others (childhood, associations, and neighborhoods). The difference is probably explained in terms of the degree of choice in interaction. People in the first two settings, kin and work, are more often obligated to interact with one another, and are thus more likely to develop dense ties, than are people in the other settings.[34] (Recall that "neighbor" is defined as someone within ten minutes.) The differences in homogeneity can be explained in a similar way. People tend to choose similar friends (see Chapter 4). To the extent that they have free choice, they will therefore develop socially homogeneous networks. The constraints of kin and work networks partly prevent this from happening, while the relative freedom of choice in club, childhood, and neighbor networks allow the homogeneity to develop. (The modest homogeneity of neighbor networks is probably best understood as following from the fact that simple convenience is important in choosing those kinds of friends.) In what seem to be conditions of widest choice, people choose similarity, while in conditions of limited choice, they end up with density.

---

[33] Laumann (1966: Ch. 5) also finds that kin friends are less similar in social class than are non-kin friends. See also Chapter 4.

[34] Most childhood friendships were probably in dense networks when they were formed, but that density usually breaks up over time.

Conclusion

In this chapter, we used the Detroit survey to assess the significance of various network attributes. Contrary to many theorists' expectations, we found that formal attributes such as multiplexity and density were not very useful in explaining the quality of social relations, and certainly less useful than substantive attributes such as the contexts from which the relations emerged.

In our analysis, we employed a choice-constraint model of the formation of social ties: people construct social relations as a series of exchanges with others; these exchanges arise out of interaction in a shared social context; and the development or dissolution of a relation depends on the rewards and costs it brings to the individuals involved. People confront different opportunities for forming social relations and have varying resources with which to pursue those ties, depending on the individuals' locations in the social structure. Consistent with this model, we saw that:

—the relative rewards and costs associated with friends influenced who was selected for interaction

—men's class positions partly affected the form and quality of their relations by limiting opportunities and resources for social involvement

—the kind of social context in which a friendship was formed made a substantial difference to its quality, while role multiplexity did not

—the dispersion of social contexts from which a network was drawn and the dominant sources of low-dispersion networks largely explained the network's density, while network density itself explained little

—we discovered two "types" of friendships, differentiated by their relative rewards and costs: low-cost and low-reward ties (convenience) versus high-cost and high-reward (commitment)

—we could distinguish two types of network sources, differing in their relative constraint upon freedom of choice and interaction: more constrained contexts (kinship, work) produced high network density and low social similarity, while more voluntary contexts (childhood ties, associations) allowed low network density and high social similarity

Findings such as these encourage us to conclude that the choice-constraint model is a fruitful one.

We should note that our findings concern friendships, one of the least determined and most freely chosen types of social relations. Often people are connected to one another in far less voluntary ways: cognate kinship, ascribed statuses, assignment to a work group, and so on. To what extent are our conclusions applicable to social relations in general? That there is a range of social bonds—from highly limited circumstances in which interaction is virtually forced to situations in which it is almost totally "free"—reinforces our emphasis on *choice-making under constraints*. The task of the analyst is to understand when and how some relations are constrained to happen or from happening. Although our data deal with more affable and willing relations, "friendships," the principle that people choose their ties under varying degrees of constraint holds true more generally. Consider, for example, Rainwater et al.'s (1959) observations about working-class wives:

> Many working class women are family-type people by default. Their best friends are within their family less through choice than by virtue of their social isolation from other kinds of people (p. 116).

Komarovsky (1967) found a similar pattern in the blue-collar families she studied:

> The [economic] interdependence of in-laws makes it difficult for uncongenial persons to go their separate ways. These coercive bonds, therefore, tend to exacerbate the conflict, which might have been muted by infrequent contacts (p. 274).

In this case, structural constraints (economic needs) channel social interaction in directions it would not otherwise take. People make choices within such constraints.

4. Social Structure and Process in Friendship Choice

Robert Max Jackson

WHOM A PERSON CHOOSES as a friend depends on the personalities of the individuals involved and the situations in which they interact. Those situations are themselves the products of the "formal" structures of society —including the economic, ethnic, and age structures. Consequently, the patterns of personal relations—in a sense, the "informal" social structures —are shaped by the formal social structures. In this chapter, we will examine how the choice of friends by men in the Detroit survey was structured by the men's positions in the *economic structure,* as indicated by their *occupational status, economic sector,* and *educational attainment,* their *ethnicity,* and their *age.*

It is well known that men choose friends who are socially similar to themselves. But much else is not known. We know very little about the distinct influences of different dimensions of social structure upon friendship choice, how those effects depend upon the context in which a friendship is formed, how the dimensions of the social structure interact with one another in shaping friendships, or how friendship *networks* affect the formation of individual friendships. We shall address each of these questions, employing a specific model of friendship choice. This model, which is derived from the more general version presented in the preceding chapter, states that the probability that two people will form a friendship depends on the extent to which differences in their social positions promote or limit their opportunities to develop personal relations and on the value such relations would have to them.

A Model of Friendship

The evidence on the social patterns of friendship (reviewed by Riecken and Homans, 1954; Lindzey and Byrne, 1968; Laumann, 1973) demonstrates that friends tend to be relatively similar to one another along whatever dimension is measured: physical location, socioeconomic status, ethnicity, religion, sex, IQ, personality, values, and so on (although people often tend to claim friends of higher status than themselves). There is little evidence that friends have complementary attributes; *similarity* pervades friendship selection. However, the existing research has largely failed to specify the *degree* to which friends are similar, the *conditions* under which they are similar, and, most important, the social *processes* that create this pattern.

There are models of friendship selection available, to be sure. Two in particular deserve mention. The *individualistic* model is the commonsense interpretation elaborated by social psychologists (for example, Winch, 1958; Rubin, 1973). Interpersonal attraction—both friendship and love—are the products of psychological affinity or complementarity. Affect (emotional attachment) is the key element. However, this analysis does not sufficiently explain the similarity of friends. First, although there are very many people who are sufficiently congenial to become friends, only a tiny fraction actually do so. Second, friends do not *find* one another; rather, people construct friendships out of minimal interactions. The individualistic approach may explain which of two structurally comparable persons is chosen as a friend, but it cannot generally explain the effect of social structures on patterns of friendship (see Goode, 1959, on love).

The *values* analysis tries to specify the link between social structure and friendship. It assumes that people generally find it painful to interact with those whose values they do not share and, therefore, will usually select friends from groups whose values are congruent with their own (see Lazarsfeld and Merton, 1954; Maisonneuve, 1966). Presumably, people's formal social positions place them in normative environments which shape their values. They then find friends who share these beliefs and attitudes among people in similar social positions.[1] This analysis also has serious deficiencies. First, values probably affect friendships only to the degree that they are salient and discussed. Therefore, many people with differing values can still be friends (for example, men in an all-white neighborhood who hold differing racial attitudes). Second, sharing values is not enough to create friendship. A rich proprietor and a poor laborer may hold identical values, but would probably not become friends. Third, it appears unlikely that values and social positions are connected strongly and consistently enough to account for the patterns of friendship similarity.

Both values and emotional attraction affect friendship choice, but they are insufficient as explanations for the great similarity of friends' social

[1] None of the writers of the values persuasion has explicitly stated the argument in this manner, but it is a logical extension of their analyses. There is an alternative interpretation as well: that, over time, interaction between friends will lead to similarity in values. Although this reverses the causality of the "values" argument, it is not otherwise germane to the argument we present.

positions. Although both views implicitly treat friendships as *exchanges,* they do not explore the implications of exchange.

OPPORTUNITIES, REWARDS, AND COSTS: EXPANDING THE MODEL

We begin by restating the key points in the theoretical discussion of Chapter 3: two people begin and maintain a friendship because it has value to each of them. The value, or *reward,* of a friendship to an individual depends on the capacity of the other to provide certain "services," such as emotional support, economic assistance, information, allies, and connections to resources outside one's immediate network. The friendship also has *costs*: direct costs, such as the time spent helping a friend; indirect costs, such as the money spent to visit a friend; and opportunity costs, the value of the services a person could obtain in an alternative friendship. Obviously, people do not always make optimal "cost-benefit" decisions; nonetheless, they are capable of comparing their crude net returns from different relations, and they can shift their commitments toward those that they find substantially more "profitable" (see Mauss, 1925; Thibaut and Kelley, 1959; Homans, 1974).

This analysis implies that people must have equal resources in order to develop stable friendships. The resources need not be of the same kind, but unbalanced exchanges—qualitatively or quantitatively—promote power differentials, patron-client relations, and exploitation (see Mauss, 1925). (There are of course many unbalanced relations, but they are not what is usually meant by friendship.) Equality of resources largely depends on equality of social position.

Friendships vary in the extent to which equivalence is necessary. Wolf (1966), for example, distinguishes between *instrumental* friendships, based on frequent, tangible exchanges, and *expressive* friendships based on enduring intimacy, mutual commitment, and symbolic exchanges. (The distinction is similar to the one we made in the last chapter between relations of "convenience" and "commitment.") Social equivalence would be less important for the second than for the first type of friendship.

People try to construct positive relations in each of their social contexts —kinship, work, neighborhood, and so on. Entry to each of these contexts is limited (more or less strictly) to certain kinds of people, often largely on the basis of social position. For example, men of different occupations enter different work settings. Consequently, people's opportunities for forming social relations are to some degree limited to others in similar social positions. Presumably, contexts vary with respect to which social dimension is screened. For example, ethnicity is more important to kin than it (usually) is to an employer, but the opposite is true of occupation. Within any setting, particularly valuable relations expand into "best friend" exchanges. And to the extent that they shift from "instrumental" to "expressive" relations, these friendships become less dependent on the original context and more likely to endure the dissolution of that role relation.

People's choices of friends are also affected by their existing social networks. People constantly construct and maintain not only individual relations but also entire social networks. They therefore consider (although perhaps not consciously) how their current friends will or do react to a potential friend. People may also evaluate how a potential friend complements their existing network, in terms of satisfying unmet desires for interaction and fellowship. And existing friendships can shape the way a network expands by providing introductions to new people.

In sum, friendship is the product of a series of exchanges. It requires that people meet and that they participate in mutually rewarding interactions in which each receives a substantial "return" for his or her "investment." This in turn requires that their resources be roughly equivalent (which resources are relevant depends on the social context). Any single friendship choice also depends on the individual's existing network of friendships.

PROCESSES LINKING FORMAL AND INFORMAL STRUCTURE

Our own and others' analyses of friendship formation suggest several ways by which the formal structures of society shape its informal structures —individuals' personal relations. We list these processes briefly here and will return to them in our discussions of specific structures.

The position of individuals in the formal social structures—economic, ethnic, and age—will influence:

—what they value, expect, or need from exchanges
—their capacities for meeting the direct and indirect costs of exchanges
—their participation in and access to the various contexts in which friendships are formed
—the kind and degree of social pressure brought upon their selections of friends

Social Structure and Friendship: Simple Effects

In this section we estimate the extent to which the structural positions of the Detroit respondents influenced their choice of friends and, in particular, their selection of friends in social positions similar to their own.[2]

[2] Laumann (1973) treated a somewhat similar issue in his analysis of the Detroit survey. However, his work differs from our approach and procedure in significant

We categorized each respondent and each of his friends in terms of economic position, ethnicity, and age, and then tested the association between the respondents' and the friends' statuses. (We note again that this is a sample of American white, working-age men, which does restrict the scope of our analysis.)

THE ECONOMIC STRUCTURE

Men's positions in the economic structure will influence their friendship choices. People in different lines of work are physically segregated on the job; people in different classes are physically segregated by residence and socially segregated in leisure-time activities. There are class differences in the resources available for exchange, in the kinds of exchange that are valued, and in implicit understandings about exchange. Consequently, the more two men's economic positions differ, the less probable it is that they will become "close friends."

Occupation. We placed each respondent and each friend into one of four broad occupational categories and crosstabulated the two distributions (see Table 4.1). The results show the following: (1) Men preferred friends from the same occupational level, choosing 41 to 48 percent of their friends from that category. A summary measure of this preference is the *self-selection ratio*: the ratio of the percentage of same-group friends to the expected percentage had the choices been random. In this case, it ranged from 1.6 to 2.1, averaging 1.9. That is, the men chose friends from their own occupational level about twice as often as would be expected by chance. (2) This self-selection ratio is highest for upper white-collar and lowest for blue-collar men. Men of higher status tended more often to confine friendships to people of their own status level. (3) The farther apart they are in occupational levels, the less probable it is that two men will be friends.[3]

Economic Sector. As a result of sharing and interacting in a common

---

ways, some of which are indicated in subsequent notes. The most fundamental and consequential difference is in intent. His was to describe an underlying friendship structure in terms of occupation and ethnicity; ours is to demonstrate the causal processes by which formal structures influence friendship choice.

[3] Upper white-collar includes proprietors of firms with ten or more employees, managers and officials, and upper and middle-status professionals; lower white-collar includes proprietors of small firms, other professionals, technical and kindred occupations, sales, and clerical; upper blue-collar includes foremen, all crafts, and protection workers; lower blue-collar includes mechanics, repairmen, all operatives, and all laborers. We performed the same analysis using 18 occupational categories. The self-selection ratio averaged 4.3. There was a slight but inconsistent tendency for men to overchoose (or overreport) friends from "higher" occupations. And, again, the farther apart the two occupations, the less likely a friendship.

TABLE 4.1   Friend's Occupational Level by Respondent's Occupational Level

| FRIENDS | RESPONDENTS | | | | |
	Upper White-Collar	Lower White-Collar	Upper Blue-Collar	Lower Blue-Collar	DISTRIBUTION OF FRIENDS
Upper White-Collar	48%	25%	13%	10%	23%
Lower White-Collar	33	44	19	19	28
Upper Blue-Collar	12	16	41	25	23
Lower Blue-Collar	8	15	27	48	26
N *of Cases*	(693)	(646)	(646)	(888)	(2,873)
Distribution of Respondents	24%	23%	23%	31%	

work setting, men find many of their friends in their own economic sector. Residential patterns (such as living near a factory), shared economic interests, and contacts through voluntary associations (like unions and business groups) reinforce these tendencies. We divided the industries into which the respondents and their friends worked into four categories: production, commerce, construction, and state.[4] The men chose from 36 to 63 percent of their friends from their own sectors, with self-selection ratios of 1.3 to 3.8. State employees had high ratios and production employees low ratios. There was no particular pattern to the choices men made of friends *outside* their own sector.[5]

[4] The urban sample precludes an agricultural sector. Production includes all manufacturing, plus transport and communication; it is dominated by motor vehicle–related production. Commerce includes wholesale and retail trade, finance, insurance, real estate, and services. State includes government jobs and social welfare services. The categorization was based upon *a priori* theoretical grounds but checked against the friendship patterns before adoption.

[5] **Friend's Economic Sector by Respondent's Economic Sector**

| FRIENDS | RESPONDENTS | | | | |
	Production	Commerce	Construction	State	DISTRIBUTION OF FRIENDS
Production	63%	30%	33%	24%	47%
Commerce	19	52	18	15	26
Construction	7	7	36	8	10
State	11	11	13	52	17
N *of Cases*	(1,288)	(565)	(196)	(360)	(2,409)
Distribution of Respondents	54%	24%	8%	15%	

Education. Aside from its role in locating people in the occupational structure, education influences friendship choice by affecting people's institutional histories and opportunities for contact, the kinds of exchange they value, and their social skills. Consequently, the more two people differ in education, the less likely it is that they can make or keep a friendship.

On the average, the Detroit men chose twice as many friends at their own educational level as would be expected by chance, with college graduates manifesting the most self-selection. There was also a slight tendency for the men to pick (or, at least, report) friends more educated than themselves. In sum, the greater the difference in education, the less probability of friendship.[6]

All three aspects of the economic structure—occupational level, economic sector, and education—shape friendship choice. The Detroit men selected friends sharing their economic positions. And in the case of ranked positions (education and occupation), the probability of a man's selecting a friend from a given level declined with increases in its social distance from his own.[7]

THE ETHNO-RELIGIOUS STRUCTURE

Ethnicity, defined in terms of religion and nationality, affects individuals' choices of friends through several of the processes described earlier. To the degree that different ethnic groups hold varying positions in the economy, that structure will influence what exchanges people value, how much

---

[6] The four categories of education were less than high school, high school, some college, and college graduate. These calculations are subject to more error than the prior ones. Respondents were not as well informed about their friends' education. They tended to attribute high school education to many who lacked it (Laumann, 1973: Ch. 2).

[7] Laumann's (1973) analysis of the occupational structure of Detroit was based on a "small space" analysis of the Detroit data. After accepting, on statistical grounds, a two-dimensional solution to the "social distances" among the occupational groups —measured as the similarity in the pattern of friendship choices between each pair of groups—Laumann interpreted one dimension as representing status (the education, prestige, and income associated with an occupation) and the other as entrepreneurial-bureaucratic differences in work sites. This follows Duncan (Blau and Duncan, 1967: 67–75). Our analysis clarifies these results, since it shows that both occupational level and economic sector affected friendship choice. Laumann and Duncan melded the two in creating their occupational categories, and so their statistical procedures separated them again. As well as engaging in *post-hoc* analysis, Laumann does not measure the size of these effects, or indicate how they depend on other social characteristics, or integrate these findings into a causal model.

they can exchange, where they meet, and so on. Ethnic membership influences the form of symbolic exchanges as well—for example, styles of interaction. It affects the opportunities for contact and the costs of interaction through residential propinquity and shared activities such as church. A common ethnicity creates some shared cultural values and personal experiences. Finally, the degree of ethnic solidarity affects the extent to which an existing network controls the selection of new friends. Therefore, we expect men to "prefer" their own ethnicity in selecting friends.

We used both nationality and religion to define the categories shown in Table 4.2. These six categories show all the significant and consistent effects that are evident when the analysis is done with 15 categories.[8] Looking at religion alone, both Protestants and Catholics chose their coreligionists twice as often as they chose from the other group (69 percent to 31 percent for both), and Jews chose Jews 80 percent of the time. Looking at our six-category table, men chose friends from their own groups two to four times as often as chance alone would dictate. No group was disproportionately popular as a source of friends.

There is a further pattern to the ethnicity results. As the groups are ordered in Table 4.2, the probability of friendship declines the further apart they are.[9] This suggests that the ethnic groups were more or less similar to one another in the factors—residential location, values, and so on—that influence the selection processes.[10]

---

[8] Respondents were asked to describe the "original nationality" (besides American) and "religious preference" of each friend and of themselves. We joined these two dimensions into one measure of ethnicity, where possible merging small groups, and eliminating others from the analysis. Jews were one of the groups eliminated because of small numbers (30). However, they did show an extreme tendency to choose other Jews as friends. Our decisions on merging were based on theoretical grounds (see note 10 below).

[9] The order was based on a canonical correlation analysis (see below) and maximizes the appearance of an ordered relation.

[10] Laumann's (1973: 42–72) analysis of ethnicity was roughly as follows: Using the pattern of friendship choices made by each of 27 groups, he found a small space solution that described three dimensions. He interpreted these as (1) religion (Protestant, Catholic, Jew), (2) economic status, and (3) possibly religious involvement. We used much fewer groups (initially 15, then 6), merging on *a priori* grounds— cultural origin, immigration history, and class—the many small groups Laumann used (as few as 7 respondents). This allows us to highlight the significant effects of ethnicity implicit in Laumann's statistics, but largely obscured by his analysis: the ordering of South European, North European, and East European Catholics (Laumann, 1973: 63, Figure 3.3a), which he does not discuss, and the Conservative, Anglo, German distinctions among Protestants (1973: 65, Figure 3.3b), which he arbitrarily interprets as based on church attendance frequency. (We attribute them to the different historical experiences of these groups.) Further differences between his and our analysis: (1) we concentrate on causal patterns, not on revealing underlying structures; (2) therefore, our categories are based on *a priori* theoretical grounds; (3) our contingency-table and regression (see below) techniques permit an assessment of the size of the effects; and (4) we simultaneously employ ethnicity and other structures to evaluate relative effects (see below).

TABLE 4.2 Friend's Ethnicity by Respondent's Ethnicity

| | | | | RESPONDENTS | | | | DISTRIBUTION |
FRIENDS	NECP	AP	GP	SEC	NEC	EEC	OF FRIENDS
Northern European Conservative Protestant[a]	42%	8%	6%	5%	5%	2%	10%
Anglo-Protestant	20	47	31	20	20	14	27
German Protestant	8	14	30	8	9	9	13
South European Catholic	8	5	4	28	8	7	8
North European Catholic	12	20	19	23	39	22	24
East European Catholic	10	6	11	15	18	48	18
N of Cases	(249)	(542)	(303)	(143)	(568)	(392)	(2,197)
Distribution of Respondents	11%	25%	14%	7%	28%	18%	

[a] "Northern European Conservative Protestant" includes Baptists and some fundamentalist groups.

67

TABLE 4.3   Friend's Age by Respondent's Age

FRIENDS	RESPONDENTS			DISTRIBUTION OF FRIENDS
	21–34	*35–49*	*50–64*[a]	
21–34	72%	13%	6%	30%
35–49	21	69	33	45
50–64	6	15	52	21
65+	1	3	9	4
N *of Cases*	(911)	(1,278)	(724)	(2,913)
Distribution of Respondents	31%	44%	25%	

[a] No respondents over 64.

THE AGE STRUCTURE

In Chapter 5, we will consider in detail how the life-cycle affects friendship choice and the extent to which people select age-similar friends. Here we shall briefly anticipate some of that analysis. Age differences separate people's activities (residence, work, pastimes), interests, and historical experiences. For these and similar reasons, we can expect many same-age friendships.

We find this in Table 4.3. In more detailed analysis, using age categories of five years' width, we found that men chose same-age friends two to four times as often as expected by chance. We also found what might be called a "boundary effect": men close to the ages of 21 and 65 chose far more of their friends from within the 21–65 range than outside of it. These ages, roughly marking entry into and exit from the labor force, create extensive "faults" in the age structure, making friendship across them particularly unlikely.

Consistent with our expectations, then, the men's positions in the social structure strongly affected their choice of friends. The Detroit respondents were especially likely to pick as friends men sharing similar positions, and especially unlikely to pick as friends men in positions very different from their own. As summary indicators, the self-selection ratios for each structural dimension are: occupational level (16 categories), 4.3; economic sector (11 categories), 3.9; educational attainment (6 categories), 2.2; age (9 categories), 3.3; and ethnicity (15 categories), 3.0. To this point, we have documented more completely and exactly what many other studies claim: friends are similar. Our next step is to demonstrate the causal processes by examining the "simple" effects in more complex ways.

Variations in Selection Patterns

The model we introduced states that social structure influences friendship choice through several specific processes, including the delimitation of opportunities for interaction, the distribution of resources available for exchange, and social pressure from existing networks. It thus implies that social conditions which alter these processes will thereby alter patterns of friendship. In this section, we consider a specific social condition of that kind: the *source* of each friendship. We were able to assign most of the friendships to a probable origin—a social context in which the friends met (see Chapter 3). Our model, in contrast to an interpersonal attraction or values approach, anticipates systematic variations in friendship patterns according to source because these social contexts screen members, partly determine the nature of the exchange, and create varying degrees of personal involvement. The results of our analysis appear in Table 4.4.

Friends who are *kin* will tend to share an ethnicity both through the bloodline and because of social pressures to marry within the group. These friendships are also more likely to be based on intimacy and diffuse commitments, than on frequent material exchanges (see distinction by Wolf [1966], presented earlier). Consequently, we expect kin friends to be relatively similar on ethnicity and dissimilar in economic realms. The data confirm our expectation: 58 percent of kin friends shared an ethnic identity (versus 34 percent for all friends), and kin friends were less

TABLE 4.4   Social Similarity of Friends by Source of Friendship: Percent in Same Structural Category, and Association (Gamma) Between Respondent's and Friend's Statuses[a]

SOURCE	STRUCTURAL DIMENSION [b]				
	Occupational Level	*Economic Sector*	*Educational Attainment*	*Ethnicity*	*Age*
Kin	38%	43%	40%	58%	35%
	(.29)	(.07)	(.40)	(.81)	(.13)
Childhood	40	50	49	45	85
	(.51)	(.42)	(.63)	(.55)	(.94)
Work	60	81	51	23	49
	(.73)	(.85)	(.63)	(.24)	(.70)
Neighborhood	39	42	43	32	53
	(.43)	(.16)	(.51)	(.35)	(.78)
Association	54	60	53	42	56
	(.66)	(.59)	(.77)	(.58)	(.80)
No Known Roles	36	49	46	31	60
	(.37)	(.28)	(.58)	(.44)	·(.86)
TOTAL	45%	56%	48%	34%	58%
	(.52)	(.47)	(.58)	(.42)	(.76)

[a] Gammas are in parentheses.
[b] Categories are: Occupational level, 4; Economic Sector, 4; Educational attainment, 4; Ethnicity, 6; and Age, 9 (five-year widths).

similar to one another in economic position (and age) than were friends from any other source.

Work brings together people employed by the same firm or involved in economic exchanges. Consequently, 81 percent of work friends shared an economic sector (versus 41 percent for all other sources). Within a work context, there is often organizational and spatial segregation by job (see, for example, Kornblum, 1974). Consequently, 60 percent of work friends also shared an occupational status (versus 40 percent for all others). Age and education affect a person's ultimate position in the productive process but are indirectly connected to his specific location. Hence, work friends were moderately similar to one another on these dimensions. Ethnicity has little direct impact on work; work friends were least likely to be ethnically similar (23 percent versus 38 percent for all other sources together). In short, work friends were economically similar and ethnically dissimilar.

Neighborhood friendships are usually casual, not very intimate, and based largely on the low cost of interacting with those nearby (see Chapter 3; Shulman, 1972). Having minimal requirements for the exchanges they involve, neighborhood friendships should show the least selection for similarity. Indeed, neighborhood friends were, after kin friends, the least similar economically and, after work friends, the least similar ethnically.[11] Neighborhood friends were moderately similar in age, perhaps because leisure pursuits and residential locations vary by the life-cycle stage.

Voluntary associations are quite a different context. Participation in them requires some degree of intentional commitment, is based on shared interests, and produces (or requires) personal identification with the group. Since there are many different kinds of association, focused on interests related to different structural dimensions, we would expect friends drawn from them (when considered as a whole) to be similar in all the aspects we measured. Association friends were more similar than the average pair of friends in all regards except age.[12]

Childhood friends usually arise out of social contexts that lose relevance with adulthood—the child's or adolescent's neighborhood and school.

---

[11] We refer here to friends whose only role relation with the respondent was the neighborhood (and perhaps the association). Neighborhood friends also seen at work showed the work-friend pattern described earlier. Note that, although the economic and ethnic similarities of neighborhood friends were relatively low, these were still significantly greater than chance.

[12] If we could separate association friends by type of association, we would no doubt find that members of ethnic associations were especially similar ethnically, members of occupational associations occupationally, and so on. Here we pooled all association friends (because of small sample size). The main types of association were, in order: labor unions, fraternal organizations, church-related groups, sports teams, PTAs, professional groups, neighborhood improvement associations, veterans organizations, and business or civic groups (each had at least 10 percent of the respondents). To fall into our association-friends analysis, respondents had to be sufficiently active in the organizations to see at least one of their closest friends regularly at meetings.

These contexts do freeze one kind of similarity: age. Childhood friends were the most age-similar (85 percent versus 58 percent for all sources combined; see Chapter 5). Maintaining a friendship created in childhood often requires major investment of effort, especially when paths diverge. Thus, most childhood friendships were probably formed out of convenience, like neighborhood friendships, but retained out of commitment, like association friendships. The end product was a moderate degree of economic similarity and a somewhat high degree of ethnic similarity.

We know relatively little about friends who share "no known roles." We might speculate, however, that these friendships are neither constrained to be similar (as work friends are) nor socially supported in the face of dissimilarity (as kin friends are). It is consistent, then, that they were moderately similar on all dimensions.

In summary, kin friends were very similar ethnically but were otherwise relatively undistinguished in terms of structural similarity. Work friends were most similar economically but not especially similar in ethnicity or age. The remaining sources can be ranked on overall degree of similarity: association, childhood, "no known roles," and neighborhood. These variations in the extent to which socially similar friends were chosen cannot, it seems, be easily understood in terms of attraction or values. They are, however, very consistent with a model stressing structured constraints on people's opportunities for exchange and the worth of particular contents of those exchanges.

Our interpretation is further supported by a closer examination of the conditions under which ethnically similar and occupationally similar friendships were most probable. Respondents were especially likely to have friends of the same ethnicity when they lived in Detroit rather than its suburbs, had lived a long time in their neighborhoods, attended church frequently,[13] and had dense networks. These are all conditions that reinforce the processes we have described as producing ethnically similar friends, particularly social pressure and the opportunities for contact. Occupational similarity decreased when family income was statistically controlled; ethnic similarity did not. This supports our argument that the economic structure affects friendships selection at least partly by requiring equality in material exchanges, while ethnic selection is based on more diffuse commitments.

The Interdependency of Structural Dimensions

The next step in our analysis is to consider how the processes by which different social structures influence friendship choice interact with one an-

---

[13] High church attendance was related to similar nationality friendships even when religion was controlled.

other. That is, how do an individual's positions in one structural system—for example, their occupations—affect the development of friendships based on another structure—for example, the age structure? The answers to this question will provide further data against which to examine our model. We have divided the analysis into three more specific questions: (1) How is similarity along one structural dimension related to similarity along another (for example, are age-similar friends also ethnically similar)? (2) How are men's *positions* along one structural dimension related to their degree of friendship similarity along others (for example, do young men have more ethnically similar friendships than old men)? (3) How do men's positions on *all dimensions simultaneously* predict their friends' positions?

SIMILARITY ON DIFFERENT DIMENSIONS

If two friends have one social position in common, are they more likely to have another in common as well? The answer is yes—to the degree that the processes by which the first social position affects friendship choice are compatible with and reinforce the processes of the second. To the degree that the processes are incompatible, similarity on one count is associated with *dis*similarity on another.

The economic positions—occupational level, economic sector, and education—all channel people into workplace settings and influence the resources they have for exchange. Thus, there was some association among these dimensions in friendship similarity. The probability that friends were at the same occupational level was substantially higher when they were also in the same sector (the probability was .23 higher). Occupational similarity was also related to educational similarity (similarity in one brought out greater similarity in the other). The processes by which education and economic sector affect friendship are least similar; the former channels entry into occupational levels, the latter provides contexts for interaction. Friendship similarity on these dimensions was only slightly related (a .06 difference in probability of similarity).

We have already noted the different processes by which economic structure and ethnic structure affect friendship choice: the first through job settings, economic resources, and the like; the second through shared origins, common culture, and so on. As a result, ethnic similarity was slightly *negatively* related to all three aspects of economic similarity. Although the effect was not strong, it was consistent.

Age crosscuts economic and ethnic structure, and the processes by which it influences friendship choice are also distinct. We found little association between being similar in age and being similar in other respects (except slightly with education, a .08 difference).

THE EFFECT OF POSITIONS ON SIMILARITY

Do individuals' positions in one social structure condition the way their positions in other structures shape their friendships? (For example, do upper-class men have more ethnically similar friends than lower-class men do?) There are two general ways by which such a "conditioning" effect could occur. First, it may occur because of a connection between individuals' locations in two structures (for example, upper-class men tend to be "WASP"). People's positions in one structure are related to their positions in other structures. (Anglo Protestants, for example, were least often blue-collar workers, and Conservative Protestants most often were —44 versus 75 percent.) Second, the effect may occur because individuals' positions in one structure "intrude" into the processes by which other structures affect friendship choice. This depends on the degree to which the two social structures have consistent, inconsistent, or independent influences upon the processes of our model. (For example, men in certain ethnic groups may be channeled by their family contacts into particular kinds of work settings that promote occupational similarity.) The set of possible effects to consider is immense (we are summarizing 456 two-way tables), so our report will only highlight major findings.

The Effect of Occupation. Men in higher social class have more resources and mobility to seek and keep friends similar to themselves (and perhaps experience more social pressure to do so). Thus, we found that men in white-collar occupations were most likely to have friends similar on other dimensions (except perhaps industry), while blue-collar workers had the least similar friends. This was especially so when both the respondent and the friend were at the same occupational status.[14]

Economic Sector. When both the respondent and his friend were in the same industry, a consistent order appeared: Men in the state sector were most similar in other respects, followed by men in production, commerce, and, lastly, construction.[15] The differences are partly a result of the types of men and jobs found in each sector (for example, men in the

---

[14] For friends of the same occupational level, the gammas between their educations were: upper white-collar, .68; lower white-collar, .45; upper blue-collar, .52; and lower blue-collar, .38; the percentages with the same ethnicity were 40, 34, 31, 27, and with ages within five years of one another percentages were 69, 62, 58, 51.

[15] For pairs of friends from the *same* economic sector, the associations (γ) between each of their positions in other structures were:

SHARED ECONOMIC SECTOR	STRUCTURES			
	Occupation	*Education*	*Ethnicity*	*Age*
State	.86	.91	.53	.89
Production	.60	.60	.47	.74
Commerce	.46	.45	.28	.75
Construction	.25	.10	.32	.67

state sector tended to have high occupational status, which we saw predictive of similarity) and partly a result of the ways in which the formal organizations of the industries affect friendship choice. State-sector employees work in large, specialized units, with many-layered bureaucracies and rigid lines of authority. This structure limits both opportunities and incentives for diverse friendships. Construction firms are quite the opposite, providing less value or less constraint (on the job) for socially similar friendships (see Stinchcombe, 1959).

Education.   Education is more a historical, personal attribute than a lasting social position. Therefore, educational attainment did not substantially or consistently alter the effects of other dimensions on friendship (except indirectly through its role as an entry requirement for higher occupational levels). Where both friends had the same education, those pairs with college degrees were more similar to one another, ethnically and occupationally, than were other pairs. But, overall, there was little difference.

Age.   Since it crosscuts all levels of other structures, by and large, age had little impact on other dimensions of similarity. Younger men, however, tended to be slightly more similar to their friends than were older men, in various ways. It is not obvious why this was so. Perhaps older men come to value less apparent aspects of a friendship than social similarity; or perhaps older men are less able or willing to change friendships.

The interdependence among the five structural dimensions—that is, how position on one affects friendship similarity on another—can in part be explained by the association among statuses themselves (the first conditioning effect). For example, better-educated men hold higher-status jobs. However, a substantial portion of the interaction between the structures in their effects on friendship patterns cannot be explained by this direct overlap. In particular, the greater similarity of higher-status friends and the economic-sector differences are partly the results of the opportunities and constraints on interaction posed by each of those social structures (the second conditioning effect).

SIMULTANEOUS EFFECTS OF STRUCTURAL POSITIONS

To summarize the effects of the respondents' structural positions on their selection of friends, we examined the association of each social characteristic of a *friend* simultaneously with all five characteristics of the *respondent* who had named him (and all ten two-way interaction terms).[16]

[16] Because ethnicity and economic sector had no *a priori* ordering, they were each used as a set of dummy variables in a canonical correlation analysis. The full set of independent variables (indicating the respondent's social positions, including interactions) was one set of variables, while the dummies for friends' economic sector (ethnicity), omitting one category to avoid colinearity, was the other. In

TABLE 4.5 Regression of Friend's Social Position on Respondent's Social Position (*Entries Are Standardized Regression Coefficients*)

	FRIEND				
RESPONDENT	Occupa-tional Level	Eco-nomic Sector	Educa-tional Attainment	Ethnicity	Age
Occupational Level	.33**	.02	.16**	—.05	.01
Economic Sector	—.03	.34**	.01	—.03	.04
Educational Attainment	.27**	.11**	.40**	—.06	.01
Ethnicity	—.05	—.01	—.04	.42**	.01
Age	.11**	.01	—.01	—.06*	.65**
Occupation × Sector[a]	.06*	.01	.04	—.02	—.02
Occupation × Education	.01	.01	.09**	.02	.02
Sector × Age	—.03	—.02	.00	.07*	—.01
Education × Ethnicity	—.06	—.02	—.09**	—.04	.03
Education × Age	—.09**	—.04	—.11**	.01	.07*
R^2	.30	.16	.29	.20	.42

[a] Regression equation included all ten two-way interactions; only interaction effects effects with at least one statistically significant result are reported here.
* $p < .001$
** $p < .01$

This analysis allows us to estimate the effect of each respondent characteristic while holding the others constant.

The results (see Table 4.5) indicate: (1) A respondent ended up with friends of high occupational status to the degree that he himself was of high status (partial $\beta = .33$), educated (.27), and old (.11). (2) The economic sector of the friend was associated almost exclusively with the

each case the coefficients for the dummies on the two sides of the equation were very similar (that is, for friends and for respondents). A single-scaled variate for sector and ethnicity was formed from those coefficients (after converting them to unstandardized form). These were then used in the regression analysis for simplicity in the presentation of results. The unstandardized coefficients for economic sector and ethnicity are:

		North European Conservative	
Production	0	Protestant	0
Commerce	.26	Anglo Protestant	.18
Construction	.88	German Protestant	.34
State	2.27	South European Catholic	.69
		North European Catholic	.71
		East European Catholic	1.06

Duncan SES scores were used for a rating of occupational level. Age was coded in years. Education was 0 for less than 8 years, 2 for some high school, 3 for completing high school, 4 for some college, 5 for a B.A., and 6 for post-graduate training.

economic sector of the respondent (partial $\beta = .34$), and marginally with the education of the respondent (.11). (3) Friends' education was best predicted by respondents' education (partial $\beta = .40$) and occupational status (.16). (4) A friend's ethnicity was predominantly associated with the respondent's ethnicity (partial $\beta = .42$). (5) Similarly, a friend's age was almost solely correlated with the respondent's age (partial $\beta = .65$).[17]

These findings confirm some of our earlier results—the similarity of friends, the interconnection of the three economic dimensions, the separate processes producing age and ethnic friendship segregation—but do so more fully. They demonstrate that each effect persists when the others are controlled, and the results allow an estimate of relative strength.

The Expansion of Social Networks

In our introductory discussion, we suggested that an individual's social network limits whom he can choose as a new friend. Current friends sometimes introduce new people to one another. Because of time and space restrictions, it is often difficult to keep new friendships separate from old ones. And the current members of a person's social network are likely to resist the entry of "undesirable" new members. This social pressure is greater when the network is denser (when a man's friends are friends of one another). For all these reasons, the network has some effect on friendship choice.

One way to analyze this process is to ask: To what degree does the social similarity of an individual and his most recently met friend depend on the social characteristics of his prior friendships? The most recently met friend should resemble the individual in question more if that individual's previous friends also do. (The earlier friends join to enforce similarity.)

This question is answered for the Detroit data in Table 4.6. The table shows the conditional probabilities that the most recent friend (the third friend) was similar to the respondent on each of the five dimensions, given that (1) neither earlier friend was similar to the respondent, (2) one was, or (3) both were. For each structural dimension, the probability that the third friend was similar to the respondent was at least twice as high when both earlier friends were similar to the respondent than when neither was.

This result could be due to another process. Some respondents may be differentially placed in circumstances that led them *independently* to select

[17] There are also several interactions, the most interesting being between age and education. Both contribute to higher status, but historical changes cause younger men to be better-educated.

TABLE 4.6   Network Effects on Social Similarity of Friends: Conditional Probabilities That Newest Friend Was Similar to Respondent, by Structural Dimension

DIMENSION	NUMBER OF EARLIER FRIENDS SIMILAR TO RESPONDENT		
	0	1	2
Occupational Level	.33	.46	.66
Educational Attainment	.36	.53	.76
Economic Sector	.28	.49	.67
Ethnicity	.17	.30	.52
Age	.32	.47	.71

their friends repeatedly from the same context. But if our hypothesis about social pressure is correct, then the effect we have just observed should be greater to the extent that the respondent's network was dense. If his network was dense, his friends could coordinate their pressure in favor of yet another similar friend.

We therefore repeated this analysis within each of three levels of density: when none of the respondent's friends were friends of one another, when two of the three were, and when all three were. For each of the five structural dimensions, the "similar-friends-beget-similar-friends" effect was greater the more dense the network.[18] This reinforces our hypothesis that social pressure influences friendship choice.

Conclusion

Many studies have demonstrated that people disproportionately select friends who are similar in social position to themselves. Explanations for this observation have focused on individual taste and value similarity. Although they are important to friendship choice, taste and values do not explain the pervasiveness, or the patterns, of social similarity. We elaborated our "choice-constraint" model of network development to explain the common observation. Positions in social structures affect what people value in exchanges, their capacities to sustain the costs of maintaining reciprocity in exchanges, and their opportunities to meet and interact with people in different social positions. Existing networks place pressure on friendship selection that reinforces these processes.

We documented some of these arguments with the Detroit data, establishing the preponderance of friendship similarity on five dimensions: oc-

[18] More specifically, we calculated the *ratio* between the conditional probability (that the most recent friend was similar to the respondent) when both prior friends were similar and the conditional probability when neither were. That ratio was, for increasing levels of density: occupational status, 1.4, 2.2, 3.0; sector, 1.2, 2.0, 5.4; education, 2.0, 2.6, 2.6; ethnicity, 2.5, 2.5, 5.5; and age, 1.9, 2.5, 2.5.

cupation, economic sector, education, ethnicity, and age. More important, we demonstrated that the degree of similarity varies systematically. For most dimensions, the tendency for similarity varied by the source context of the friendship, the degree to which men were similar to their friends in other ways, and the specific social positions men occupied. Economic and ethnic similarity seemed to be traded off against one another, with the workplace being the main source of economic similarity and kinship the strongest source of ethnic similarity. Men in higher-status occupations and men in the state or production sectors were most likely to have friends similar to themselves. Finally, the probability that a man's new friends resemble him socially depends in part on their similarity to his earlier friends. Each of these variations could be explained in terms of the processes we described earlier.

The findings cannot be easily or well explained in terms of individual traits or personal values. Indeed, such factors, when they are not tied closely to social positions, could be applied more usefully to explain some of the *departures* from general patterns of social similarity[19]—general patterns best understood in terms of friendship choices made within a set of structural opportunities and constraints.

Social similarity in friendship is significant not only in its intrinsic relevance for understanding social networks but also for understanding the general stratification of society. Segregation in social networks is the manifestation in informal social structure of a society's formal structure.

---

[19] Some dissimilarity is of course a result of countervailing structural circumstances. But affect—feelings and preferences—does influence choice. Although affect will often disrupt the general social patterns it can reinforce them as well. To the degree that structural positions "socialize" their occupants to different emotional responses and expectations, affect can buttress the structural processes. Such differences have been claimed for gender (Hochschild, 1975) and occupation (Kohn, 1963). Neil Smelser suggested this point.

5. Personal Relations Across the Life-Cycle

C. Ann Stueve
Kathleen Gerson

THE INEVITABLE CHANGES that accompany aging are among the most basic and far-reaching in human experience. As people age, they not only change physically, but also experience a series of transitions through social roles and social groups. At each stage in the life course—school years, early marriage, parenthood, and so on—individuals assume new tasks and responsibilities, privileges and obligations, accumulating experience in the process.

Although social scientists long have studied the ways in which social positions are attached to age (Parsons, 1942; Riley et al., 1972; Neugarten and Moore, 1968; Eisenstadt, 1956), few (with the notable recent exceptions of Hess, 1972; Lowenthal et al., 1975; and Shulman, 1975) have examined how friendship is related to life-cycle stages and the social roles associated with them. This is an unfortunate omission because the nature of personal relations crucially affects both the ease with which people make life-stage transitions and their well-being at each stage in the life course.

The omission of a life-cycle approach is unfortunate for the study of social networks as well. Network analysts (for example, Laumann, 1973) have given largely incidental attention to the influence of marriage, childbearing, and other life-cycle transitions on individuals' networks—even though researchers on the family (such as Komarovsky, 1967) have often reported that significant alternations in personal relations accompany these changes. Our results indicate, in fact, that a major, if not *the* major, influence on individuals' networks is their position in the life-cycle.

In this chapter, we use the Detroit survey on men's best friends to explore how personal relations change over the life course—in particular, changes in the contexts from which friends are drawn, in the characteristics of the friendship, and in the selection of age peers as friends.

The Life-Cycle and Constrained Choice

In Chapter 3, we argued that friendship formation and maintenance can best be understood as a set of choices made within socially structured opportunities and constraints. We contend here that life-cycle stages constitute important opportunities and constraints of this kind. Life-cycle stages structure friendship choice in two ways. First, they partly define the pool of potential friends by influencing the settings in which individuals interact. Second, they affect the rewards and costs to individuals of any given friendship.

In the previous chapter, we examined the processes by which formal structures channel the selection of personal relations. As people age, they move through social positions in many of these formal structures—most important for our purposes is their movement through the cycles of family and work. Over the life-cycle people leave their families of orientation and form families of their own, which in turn eventually dissolve through the departure of children, death, or divorce. Most people (at least most males) also enter and leave school, join and eventually retire from the labor force. These changes in social position are accompanied by changes in people's dependence on, responsibility to, and power over others. Children become parents and novices become "old hands."

In the process of making these life transitions, people's daily settings change, as do their needs and their resources to meet those needs. As people enter new social contexts, they meet new people such as their spouse's kin, other new parents, or fellow workers on a new job. Although interaction with these new people may be restricted to minimal role obligations, individuals can choose to expand these contacts into deeper and more intimate relations. At the same time, people reevaluate old friendships in the context of the demands and opportunities posed by the new roles. For example, after a couple's first child arrives, they may see their friends less often as child care consumes much of their time, energy, and money, and they may choose to see other parents rather than childless friends. Thus people constantly construct and reconstruct their social networks as they move through the life-cycle.

MEASURING THE LIFE-CYCLE

We were able to measure two major components of the life-cycle—age and family status—for the men in the Detroit sample. Age is the basic component of the life-cycle. It is also a key—and easily measured—indicator of other life-cycle factors. First, age is associated with entry into and exit out of life-stage roles. People perceive and generally adhere to a socially prescribed time-table for marriage, birth of the first child, entry into the labor force, retirement, and similar life transitions. As we noted, these stages influence people's pools of acquaintances, their social interests and needs, and their time and resources for social life. Second, age represents the accumulation of experience by an individual, a maturing process that affects social needs and tastes. Third, age locates people historically. People of the same age have experienced the same historical events and cultural epochs. Finally, people use age as a yardstick for measuring how well they and others are keeping pace with expected life changes. Insofar as age indicates people's locations in history, experience, and social positions relative to one another, it guides interaction among them.

We also considered two components of the family cycle: marital status and parenthood. Marriage and the arrival of children each mark the entry of another individual into the most intimate and the most ordinary details of a person's life. New ties with spouse and children may replace other intimate bonds, while the loss of either may trigger a search for new intimates. Spouse and children also connect a person to other networks. A new wife, for example, may inherit many of her husband's friends (Babchuck and Bates, 1963), and she may find little free time to see her old friends as the demands of married life weigh upon her.

In order to explore the effects of aging, marriage, and parenting on friendships, we formed the following sequence of life stages (the numbers in parentheses refer to the sample size at each stage):[1]

1. *Young single* (60):   Age 21–34. Not married. No children at home.
2. *Young husband* (58):   Age 21–34. Married   No children at home.
3. *Young father* (193):   Age 21–34. Married   Children at home.
4. *Mid-aged father* (258): Age 35–49. Married   Children at home.
5. *Old father* (110):   Age 50–64. Married.   Children at home.
6. *Post-parent* (132):   Age 50–64. Married.   No children at home.

By comparing the friendship patterns of men at different stages of life, we can analyze the consequences of being at one stage rather than another. Then using these comparisons, we can draw inferences about how individuals' friendships change over the life course, and especially about how networks change at key transition points (for example, upon the arrival of

---

[1] Marriage and parenting are to some extent correlated with age *within* our age groups. Although this colinearity makes attribution of causality more ambiguous, we believe that the fundamental explanation of our findings is life stage, not biological age. We could not test this further by sub-dividing our cases because of sample size. (And we believe that regression analysis would obfuscate more than it would clarify.)

a first child).[2] We expect to find at these points the most evidence of people altering their personal relations: renegotiating old friendships, dropping those that do not fit their new circumstances, and beginning ones that do. Thus, although our data are cross-sectional (describing a set of men and their ties at one time), we will infer network changes over time and draw conclusions about why these changes occur.

There are other pivotal life transitions that we have not discussed—in particular, those related to the employment career (for example, graduation from school, entry into and mobility within the occupational structure, retirement). Although we could not explore these transitions directly in the Detroit survey, we try to infer their effects from an analysis of the correlates of aging.

The Detroit survey imposes more serious limitations on our analysis of life-cycle and networks. Because of the small frequencies, we can say little about men in "atypical" life stages[3]—for example, unmarried men with children. And we have no information about women, adolescents, or the elderly, since the sample included only men aged 21 to 64. These groups face different contingencies in forming their friendships than do the men we studied (see Lowenthal et al., 1975; Bott, 1955; Komarovsky, 1967; Babchuck and Bates, 1963). They are generally subject to more severe transitions (puberty, childbirth, widowhood, and so on) than are working-age men. Therefore, we can fairly assert that the life-cycle effects found in this sample *under*estimate the full consequences of life-cycle transitions in the general population.

In spite of these limitations, the Detroit data allow us to study the connections between life-cycle and friendship in a large sample, to analyze the consequences of being in one life stage rather than another, and to draw inferences about change over time.

SOCIAL CONTEXTS AND FRIENDSHIP FORMATION

In Chapter 3, we argued that the contexts in which social ties develop seriously influence the nature of those relations. As we suggested earlier in

[2] There are two separable issues: the consequences to networks of *being* in different life stages, and the consequences to networks of going *through* a transition between life stages. We can directly examine only the first issue, but will draw some inferences about the latter.

[3] We excluded 99 respondents who did not fall into our six stages. About half belonged to atypical groups with too few cases for analysis (for example, divorced men with children). It is unfortunate that we cannot study them because their patterns of friendship might illuminate those of the typical groups. The other excluded respondents were married men aged 35–49 without children at home (who number 56). We excluded this group because we could not interpret their life stage based on the information at hand. These men may have had children who had already left home; they may have been awaiting children; or they may never have had children. Given this ambiguity, we could not place these men into our sequential life stages. Nineteen were excluded because life-cycle information was not available.

this chapter, the social contexts in which people participate and from which they draw their friends depend, in turn, on life stage. In addition, life stage influences the value (the balance of rewards to costs) of forming close friends in any given setting. For example, when a young man marries and has children, he may find that involvement in the neighborhood becomes more important to him, while seeing old school friends becomes more difficult.

As these arguments lead us to expect, the sources from which the Detroit men drew their close friends were strongly associated with their stages of life. Not surprisingly, men in the earlier stages were especially likely to report friends formed in childhood (see Figure 5.1 and Table 5.1[A]). The older the men, the less likely they were to report as a best friend someone they had met before the age of 18. This "replacement"—we are inferring change over time—was especially likely to occur at transition points

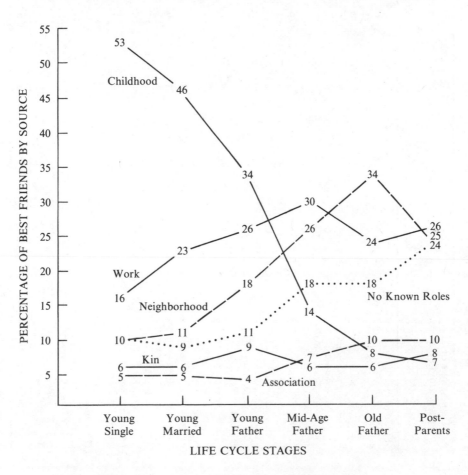

Figure 5.1 Sources of Friendship by Life Cycle Stage

TABLE 5.1 Dimensions of Links by Life-Cycle Stages

Dimensions of Friendship Links	Life-Cycle Stages						Special Case[a]
	1 YOUNG SINGLE	2 YOUNG HUSBAND	3 YOUNG FATHER	4 MID-AGED FATHER	5 OLD FATHER	6 POST-PARENT	MID-AGED HUSBAND
(A) Source:							
% *Kin*	6	6	9	6	6	8	6
Childhood	53	46	34	14	8	7	14
Work	16	23	26	30	24	26	29
Neighborhood	10	11	18	26	34	25	23
Association	5	5	4	7	10	10	7
No Known Roles	10	9	11	18	18	24	21
(B) When Met:							
% *Before 18*	58	50	38	16	10	7	17
18–30	42	49	60	41	24	22	39
After 30	0	1	2	43	66	71	44
(C) Location:							
% *in Neighborhood*	50	33	43	43	48	39	34
(D) Duration:							
% *Less than 4 yrs.*	23	26	23	10	4	6	4
Over 13 yrs.	23	22	27	47	67	68	50
(E) Locus:							
% *Meet in Own Home*	4	14	8	6	6	6	8
in Friend's Home	24	16	9	6	4	7	7
in Both Homes	38	46	55	55	59	53	53
at Work	9	13	14	17	18	14	15
Other	25	10	14	16	13	20	16
(F) Frequency:							
% < *1 per mo.*	8	14	17	24	25	24	19
1 + per wk.	73	59	45	36	40	39	39
(G) Intimacy:							
% *"Very Close"*	58	54	54	53	55	54	47
(Only Friends > 13 yrs.)	(68)	(74)	(72)	(67)	(59)	(59)	(38)
(H) Age Similarity:							
% *"Same"*	71	55	45	34	26	30	32
Maximum N of Friends	175	172	573	1,056	339	368	163

[a] Out of typical life-cycle; see footnote 3.

in early adulthood. Marriage and parenting seemed to pull men away from childhood friendships and toward friendships formed in adulthood. Many of these relations were themselves replaced later in life (Table 5.1[B]).

Close ties formed in the neighborhood and at work became the major substitutes for the childhood friends left behind. With marriage, young men were more likely to draw upon the workplace for intimates—probably because their marriages coincided with entry into their first regular jobs. After marriage, the proportion of best friends who were work friends remained constant until age 65.

For neighborhood friends, the pattern is more complex. We need to distinguish between all the friends who live in the neighborhood, irrespective of source, and those who are drawn *from* the neighborhood during adulthood. While the friends of young single men were largely also neighbors (50 percent), most of these ties were probably inherited from childhood; these young men had formed few local friendships as adults (only 10 percent). Young husbands, on the other hand, reported relatively few friends in the neighborhood (33 percent). Upon marriage, they dropped many childhood friends, probably moved further away from those they retained, and formed few new neighborhood friendships (11 percent). Thus, young husbands had fewer local friends than did young single men. But upon the birth of the first child, the neighborhood again became an important source of friends, as young fathers drew new friends from among their neighbors (18 percent) and generally had more of their friends nearby (43 percent). As fathers aged and settled into their neighborhoods, they continued to convert neighbors into best friends (Table 5.1[C]). Children play a strategic role in linking their parents to the neighborhood; they not only promote contacts with nearby parents but also curtail opportunities to interact socially away from home. The Detroit men whose children had left home appeared to have withdrawn from local friendships: 48 percent of the "old fathers'" friends lived in the neighborhood, but only 39 percent of the "post-parents'" friends were neighbors ($\gamma = .18$). Thus the Detroit men selectively used the neighborhood depending upon the needs and constraints of their particular life-cycle stage.

Many of the Detroit men's adult friends did not have an identifiable source (labeled "no known roles"). Some were probably former work colleagues, neighbors, or association friends whose friendships had withstood the loss of shared roles; others may have been friends of friends. As they aged, the Detroit men increasingly built up friendships based on these past and no longer current connections (see Figure 5.1). Finally, the Detroit men reported about the same proportion of best friends who were kin in all life stages. (As we noted in Chapter 3, kin are underestimated by about half, because closest brothers and brothers-in-law were excluded from the "best friends" list.)

The data reveal, in conclusion, the changes in social networks that occur as people move through the life cycle, constantly forming, altering, or dropping friendships as their circumstances change. In particular, we saw how wives and children provide constraints and incentives that lead men to form new friendships in the workplace and the neighborhood and to sever old ties with their childhood and premarital friends. We suspect that these changes in personal relations are especially likely to occur at transition points, such as the onset of marriage and retirement, when people's positions in major institutions change abruptly. At these life "faults," people must reevaluate and reconstruct their social worlds in light of new needs and new constraints.

The Qualities of Friendship

In this section, we explore the variations in the qualities of friendships over the life-cycle. This analysis follows from a larger concern with the relationship between family life and social ties outside the household. Many theorists have postulated that the modern nuclear family has become increasingly privatized and isolated from the wider community (for example, Slater, 1963; Aries, 1962; Shorter, 1975; Sussman, 1959; Goode, 1963; Parsons and Bales, 1955). Their analysis suggests four historical trends in the relationship between the family and friendship: that (1) ties outside the family have become more fleeting and transitory; (2) social life has increasingly withdrawn from public places into the privacy of the home; (3) frequency of contact with intimates outside the household has declined; and (4) intimacy itself has become increasingly displaced from wider social groups onto the family, and especially onto the spouse in the form of "dyadic withdrawal" (Slater, 1963).[4] (This analysis is related, of course, to the "decline-of-community" thesis.)

We will not consider here the validity of the historical propositions. We will, however, draw from them a set of questions about contemporary family life and social networks. We use a life-cycle perspective to ask: How does the relationship between family status and social ties outside the home—in this case, best friends—change as a person moves through the life course? Specifically, how is stage in the family cycle related to: (1) the survival of friendships (duration); (2) the degree to which sociable interaction takes place in the home (meeting place); the degree to which people are "isolated" from their friends, as measured by (3) how often they see each other (frequency); and (4) how close they feel (intimacy)?

This perspective highlights a fact that many family theorists do not

---

[4] Some argue that, as a result of all these forces, the conjugal unit is itself more fragile. Couples break up under the pressures of having too much responsibility for replacing the emotional support that is no longer available outside the home.

generally consider (Berkner, 1972, is one exception): that people move in and out of family units in the course of a lifetime. For any one individual, there will be extended periods in which he or she is not part of the typical nuclear family (some never are once they leave their parents).[5] And, at any given time, many adults are outside of a nuclear family. Furthermore, over the life-cycle, a person's position within the family changes. If, as family theorists suggest, family life shapes interaction with people outside the household, then people in nuclear families should have qualitatively different informal relationships than those not in them, and people in different family stages should vary in the quality of their extra-household ties.

Do Friendships Endure?

We have argued that life-cycle changes often necessitate adjustments in people's networks. But this does not necessarily mean that friendships are as transitory as some family (and decline-of-community) theorists imply. As we discussed in Chapter 3, friendships of personal "commitment" can withstand life changes, role changes, and physical separation. The great strains on friendship would seem to come early in the adult life-cycle as people begin careers, marry, meet new sets of associates, and so forth. As men pass beyond this early period, they are better able to establish durable relations. Then, later in life, as they settle into families, jobs, and neighborhoods, their chances for forming new friends diminish. Perhaps most important, time allows people to sift through their many acquaintances and friends and to retain those they value most.

Thus, we found that older men were more likely to form and maintain long-lasting friendships. There was much turnover among "best friends" in the early adult years but relatively little in the later stages of life (see also Shulman, 1975). Over half of the close friends of men under 35 had been met within the previous seven years. Less than a quarter of the friends of men 35 and older were so recent; indeed, over half their best friends had been known at least 14 years (see Table 5.1[D]). (Being married or having children was not associated with the duration of friendships.) This finding is not simply an artifact of age—that is, of older men being able to extend their friendships longer. If we exclude the most durable friendships (14 years or more), young men were still more likely to have had quite short friendships. For example, 32 percent of young fathers' 1–13-year friendships were 1–3 years old; only 13 percent of old fathers' 1–13-year friendships were. Young men were *making new best friends* much more commonly

---

[5] In the Detroit data we assume that men living with a wife and children constitute a nuclear household whether or not another relative happens to reside with them.

than were old men; older men were holding onto prior best friends longer.[6] In the long run, it seems, people can settle on and sustain intimate ties outside the family.

PUBLIC AND PRIVATE FRIENDSHIPS

Family theorists direct our attention to the extent to which social life is withdrawn into the home and thus presumably occurs by invitation only. This should depend, however, on whether people have homes suitable for entertaining—itself related to life stage. Life-cycle also affects the extent to which men *can* entertain at home—for example, is there a wife who will act as hostess?—and *must* entertain at home—for example, can the budget support nights out? can a babysitter be found? We suspect that men without families of their own are less likely to be home-centered than are husbands and fathers.

At all family stages, the Detroit men usually get together with their friends (outside of work) in someone's home; at no life stage did the proportion who did so drop below 66 percent.[7] However, there were life-cycle differences in *whose* homes friends usually met. Young singles were least likely to meet friends in their *own* homes, even on a reciprocal basis (Table 5.1[E]). Whereas approximately 62 percent of the friends of husbands and fathers gathered in the respondent's home or in both the respondents' and the friends' homes equally, only 42 percent of the friends of young singles did so. The latter were more likely to gather at the homes of their friends, probably married friends. Young singles were also the most likely to see their friends in public places such as restaurants and bars and at sporting events (25 percent of young singles met their friends in public places while 15 percent of other men did so). Married men and fathers were the least likely to meet friends in public, but men whose children had already left home resumed some outside activities. In short, family life does seem to bring social interaction into the home.

GETTING TOGETHER

In addition to bringing social life into the home, do spouse and children also reduce the amount of time people spend with intimates outside the household? We might suspect that they would, first, because the family, particularly the spouse, can be an alternative source of companionship,

---

[6] Older men could have been making new friends just as rapidly as younger men, but just not included them among the three closest and most frequently seen friends.

[7] The question asked with regard to each friend was: "Where do you most often meet [him]? At one of your homes or somewhere else? [If at home] Is that mainly your home, or mainly his, or about equally both?"

emotional support, advice, and so on. Second, the constraints upon seeing friends becomes tighter when a person takes on commitments to a spouse, children, in-laws, spouse's friends, and other family responsibilities (see detailed analysis by Verbrugge, 1973).

In fact, the frequency with which men saw their best friends did decline steadily from young singles to mid-aged fathers and then leveled off (Table 5.1[F]; see also Shulman, 1975). There was a substantial drop in frequency of contact with marriage (73 percent of young singles' friends were seen at least weekly compared to 59 percent of young marrieds'), another substantial decrease with the arrival of children (to 45 percent), yet another decrease with middle age (to 36 percent), and then frequency stabilized (at 40 percent and 39 percent for the last two stages).[8] This association between life-cycle and frequency of contact with friends ($\gamma = -.25$) among the Detroit men indicates that the family does take time away from friendships. And there are reasons to suspect that this relationship is still stronger among women, because they are more likely to be isolated at home (see Michelson, 1973a).

INTIMACY ACROSS THE LIFE-CYCLE

Does family life reduce the feelings of intimacy people have for their best friends? Apparently not among the Detroit men. Although frequency of contact with friends declined across the life-cycle, reported intimacy did not vary with life stage. In general, men at all stages labeled slightly more than half their best friends as "very close" (Table 5.1[G]). Although spouse and children seemed to inhibit frequency, they apparently did not inhibit intimacy.

However, a different pattern emerged when we controlled for the duration of the friendships. Except for the most recently formed friendships, reported intimacy *declined* slightly with age (Table 5.1[G]). Excluding young singles, the later the life stage, the less likely men were to report their long-term friends as very close. The explanation for this finding may lie in the fact that younger men's friends were likely to be childhood friends while older men's friends were formed later in life. And, as we reported in

---

[8] We explored the possibility that the friends of men in the middle and older stages were seen less often because they lived farther away than did those of young adults. However, the friends of the young adults were actually more likely to live far away (see Table 5.1 [C]). We also tested the hypothesis that older men saw their friends infrequently because these were friends of long duration, friends who did not need to be seen often. Hower, life-cycle differences persisted even with duration controlled. Whether the friendship was initiated recently or many years before, young singles were the most active. Controlling for duration, husbands and fathers still saw their friends substantially less often than did others. Frequency climbed again with older fathers and "empty nest" fathers, although never reaching the intensity of youth.

TABLE 5.2   Percentage of Friends Reported as "Very Close," by Life-Cycle, Controlling for When Friend Was Met

PRESENT LIFE-CYCLE STAGE	AGE OF RESPONDENT WHEN HE MET FRIEND		
	Under 18 (Childhood)	18–30 (Early Adulthood)	Over 30 (Later Adulthood)
Young Single	66%	46%	—a
Young Husband	66	40	—a
Young Father	71	43	—a
Mid-Aged Father	82	52	43%
Old Father	77	55	51
Post-Parent	73	61	49

Duration →

← Time of Formation →   ↓

a Too few cases.

Chapter 3, childhood friends were considered more intimate. This explanation is supported by the results presented in Table 5.2.

Reading across the rows of Table 5.2, we can see that regardless of current life stage, the earlier the respondent had met his best friend, the more intimate he felt that friend to be. Reading down the columns of Table 5.2, we can see that the longer the duration of the friendship, the more intimate it was reported to be. The underlying pattern seems to be this: There are no overall differences in intimacy by life-cycle because of two countervailing effects. Younger men were nearer in time to the kind of friends all men considered most intimate—friends met early in life. These young men consequently had a higher proportion of intimate "types" of friends. However, older men felt more intimate toward any given type of friend (that is, toward friends met in any life stage) than did younger men—probably because older men had had a longer time to sift out the more from the less rewarding friends and to enrich those friendships they retained.

SUMMARY

Does modern family life entail a retreat from communal ties outside the home? We cannot answer the historical question, but we can shed some light on the relationship between individuals' movements through the life-cycle and their close relationships. Our evidence suggests that immersion in marriage and parenthood does affect the quality of friendship ties, but not in any simple "privatizing" or "isolating" manner. Although there is considerable turnover in best friends during the early adult years, men in the middle stages of life are able to build and sustain enduring ties. As their home involvements develop, men increasingly visit with their best friends in the home, rather than in public places. They see these friends less and less frequently as age and its associated social (and physical) constraints inhibit their activities, but there appears to be no net decline in felt intimacy with best friends. A family seems to be a constraint on an active public life, but not necessarily on an intimate private one.

All three components of the life-cycle that we were able to examine—marriage, parenthood, and aging—influenced the men's networks. Of the transitions we looked at, the most pronounced break occurred upon entry into young adulthood, when men married and became fathers for the first time (recall that we do not have retirees in the sample). They left intimate childhood friends behind, formed new relations with people met in adult contexts, and their social life was generally structured by the responsibilities of family life.

Our findings also support two more general arguments of interest to network analysts. First, the life-cycle poses a significant system of opportunities and constraints shaping network formation and maintenance (probably the most significant system—see Chapter 4 for comparisons). Second, network changes occur as a result of *transitions* between stages of the life-cycle. In particular, when people take on adult roles they often sever intimate bonds formed in childhood. In time, they build new relations which mesh more closely with their needs as adults.

Age Peers Through the Life-Cycle

Many observers have noted increasing age segregation and age stratification within modern institutions (such as schools and bureaucracies) and increasing differentiation of life-cycle stages (for example, the emergence of adolescence and youth—see Kenniston, 1971; Aries, 1962). These developments, if real, mean that individuals have a narrowing range of ages from which to draw their friends and are therefore increasingly likely to have friends of their own age. Again, we cannot assess the validity of the historical argument, but we can place this concern within an individual developmental perspective by assessing the effects of life stage on age similarity in friendship and the consequences of age similarity on other properties of friendship.

Many aspects of modern life promote age similarity in social relations, for example, shared historical and cultural experiences, similar positions in the family and work settings, passing through transitions at approximately the same time, relative equality in resources and authority, residential segregation by neighborhood and type of housing, and cultural expectations that make age-similar friendships commonplace and cross-age friendships appear unusual (see Hess, 1972). We suggest that there are two basic processes which make it especially likely that people will form friendships with others of their own age. First, individuals' daily settings are segregated by age, thereby limiting the pools of potential associates to people of the same age. Second, same-age friendships are relatively rewarding, because people of the same age usually share common needs and experiences and have roughly equal resources.

The first factor—age-segregated settings—affects people throughout the life-cycle, but not equally throughout it. Child care centers, "leisure worlds" for the elderly, and young singles' apartment complexes are instances of spatial segregation. Even the suburbs sort families at different life stages into separate neighborhoods. Separation of the generations is apparent within families as well, as the elderly increasingly maintain household units independent of their children (Glick, 1975). Whether this separation is imposed or chosen, it increases the likelihood of intimate ties with people of the same rather than of a different age. Similarly, people of different ages are often unequal in their authority and power, an inequality that probably inhibits personal relations. Although most people are separated by age, the social settings of children and youths are most segregated. Schools are more narrowly stratified by age than are job settings. Consequently, friendships formed in early years should be more age-similar than those formed in adulthood.

The second factor—differential value—also promotes age-similar friendships, because people in the same work and family positions share common life experiences and cultural meanings. Furthermore, people of the same age are likely to make major life transitions at roughly the same time and can therefore sustain their relations.[9] When transitions are not synchronized because of differing ages, friends may lose their shared concerns, as in the case when the older of two coworkers retires.

But, again, this does not affect people equally through the life-cycle. Over a lifetime, *life-cycle stage* becomes increasingly dissociated from *chronological age*. At any age, life stage is probably a more significant criterion for friendship choice than is chronological age. (For example, a married 30-year-old will probably have more in common with a married 40-year-old than with a 30-year-old bachelor.) But as one grows older, each calendar year becomes less significant; the difference in *social* age between a 20- and a 25-year-old is greater than that between a 50- and a 55-year-old. Thus, over the life course, the age range of those who can be rewarding broadens, and we should find that, as they age, people select their friends from an increasingly wide range.[10] In sum, although we expect

[9] For example, Eisenstadt (1956) suggests that adolescent age peers serve as a critical support group in easing the transition between youth and adulthood. They are an alternative source of support to the family of orientation.

[10] This argument implies that the age span of friends continues to widen indefinitely. It does not. As noted in Chapter 4, there is a "fault" at around 65. The retirement and death of men over that age mean that men just under it tend to have fewer friends older than themselves than would otherwise be expected.

age-similar friendships to predominate, they should be less common in the later stages of the life-cycle.

EVIDENCE ON AGE-SIMILAR FRIENDSHIPS

Several studies have found that people tend to choose friends of their own age. Lowenthal and her associates (1975), for example, found that at least 85 percent of men and women in four life stages (high school, newlywed, middle age, and preretirement) reported their closest friend to be near their own age (see also Corgeau, 1975). Similarly, studies of the elderly have found that friendships of the aged are usually with age peers (see Hess, 1972; Riley et al., 1968: Ch. 24). These studies tend to focus upon youth and old age, devoting less of their attention to the young and middle adult years (notable exceptions include Lowenthal et al., 1975; Batten et al. reported in Riley et al., 1968). They also tend to rely upon the respondent's subjective definition of "same age." We can add to this literature an analysis of men in their young and middle years (21 to 64) and a precise measure of age similarity.

In the Detroit survey we were able to calculate the actual age difference between two friends (although we cannot investigate respondents' subjective definitions).[11] We defined "age-similar" as a difference of two years or less between the respondent's age and a friend's. (Since the respondent can be from two years older to two years younger than his friend, our measure of age similarity spans a five-year age range.) The sheer number of age-similar friendships among the Detroit men is striking. Thirty-eight percent of the reported friends differed from the respondent by two years or less; 72 percent were within eight years.[12]

Does this pattern of age-similar friendships vary over the life-cycle, as we expected? Yes, and it does so considerably. As Figure 5.2 indicates, the older the respondent, the more age-*dis*similar his friendships. The major break occurs in the mid-twenties: 68 percent of the friendships of the 21–24-year-olds were with men of the same age, but only 47 percent of 25–29-year-olds' friendships were age-similar. Beyond the age of 29, there was a steady decline in age-similar friendships. Another way of expressing this change is to say that, with age, these men expanded the age breadth of

[11] We are, of course, relying on the respondents' reports of their friends' ages. Laumann (1973: Ch. 2) found in his reliability check that in 86 percent of the cases respondents were accurate within two years of their friends' ages, and that the correlation between the reported and the true ages was .98. In addition, there was no overall bias in reporting their own ages. (That is, Laumann found no significant difference between the average respondent's age and the average friend's age; respondents were not consistently under- or overreporting their own ages.)

[12] These percentages, however, are lower than the 85 percent reported by Lowenthal et al. Perhaps the subjective sense of age similarity tapped by her study exceeds our objective definition of similarity.

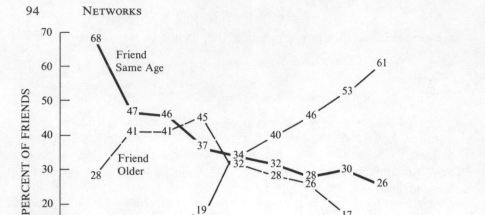

Figure 5.2   Percent of Respondents' Friends Older, Younger, or Same Age* as Themselves, by Age of Respondent

* ± 2 years

their networks. Two-thirds of the 20–25-year-olds' ties were with men no more than two years different from themselves; two-thirds of the 45–49-year-olds' ties covered eight years' difference; and more than two-thirds (actually 76 percent) of the 61–64-year-olds' ties ranged over 16 years. Thus, as these men aged, they chose their friends from a wider age range.

This pattern is consistent with our earlier expectations, but to what extent can it be explained by the processes we described: that the social contexts in which friendships are formed become less segregated by age and that the particular value of age-similar friendships declines with age? Three additional findings support our interpretation. First, we found that friendships formed early in the men's lives were indeed more age-similar than those formed later—irrespective of the respondents' age at the time of the interview. Of the friendships formed before the age of 18, 64 percent were age-similar; of those formed between 18 and 30, 37 percent were age-similar; of those formed after 30, 23 percent were age-similar. In fact, once the age of friendship *formation* is taken into account, the age of the *respondent* has virtually no effect on age similarity. (For example, the friendships old men made when they were between 18 and 30 were about as age-similar as the friendships younger men made between 18 and 30.)

Second, note, in Figure 5.2, that the proportion of older friends *increased* from age 21 to age 39, in spite of a *decrease* in the total number of men who *could* be older than the respondent. Our analysis of social contexts helps to explain this apparent anomaly. The young men were probably moving into new work and neighborhood settings which were populated largely by men older than themselves and from whom new friends were chosen.

Third, the age composition of friendships appears to shift after major life transitions (Table 5.1[H]), especially for men in their mid- and late twenties who were making the break with childhood and assuming the adult status as of spouse, parent, and worker. Of young singles' friendships, 71 percent were age-similar. The proportion of age-similar friendships dropped to 55 percent for young marrieds, to 45 percent for young fathers, and then leveled off. As people leave their childhood friends behind, they leave many age similars behind as well.

In sum, the choice of age similars predominates throughout the life-cycle but decreases in the later stages, probably because the degree of institutional age segregation declines and the degree of commonality diffuses across a wider range of years.

AGE SIMILARITY AND FRIENDSHIP QUALITY

What differences does it make for other aspects of a friendship if two friends are more or less the same age? To answer this question we examined the association between age similarity and three attributes of friendships: role multiplicity, intimacy, and frequency; and we examined the association between age homogeneity of the network and network density.

Role Multiplexity. Same-age friendships were slightly less likely to be multiplex than were others (see Table 5.3). This finding is probably best understood as a result of variations in friendship source. Many age-similar friends were old childhood friends with whom no current role relation existed, while friends with discrepant ages were, as we discovered earlier, more likely to have been met in adult settings, such as work or voluntary

TABLE 5.3   Attributes of Friendship Links by Degree of Age Similarity

AGE DIFFERENCE	PERCENT MULTIPLEX[a]	PERCENT "VERY CLOSE"	PERCENT SEEN 1/WK. +	N OF FRIENDS
Friend Younger 9 + yrs.	36%	44%	49%	(413)
Friend Younger 3–8 yrs.	33	48	41	(462)
Friend Same Age	28	59	38	(1,136)
Friend Older 3–8 yrs.	32	52	41	(523)
Friend Older 9 + yrs.	36	55	54	(429)

[a] Multiplexity greater than 2 (see Chapter 3).

associations. Among older respondents (51–64), the connection between age similarity and multiplexity disappears—probably because by then same-age friends were less likely to be composed of childhood friends.

Intimacy.   We have argued that age-similar friends are especially likely to share common experiences, concerns, and statuses, all of which should promote intimacy. This appears to be the case among the Detroit men. The column in Table 5.3 labeled "% Very Close" indicates that age-similar friendships were slightly more likely to be labeled as "very close" than were age-dissimilar ties. Among the age-dissimilar friendships, the respondent was more likely to report the tie as intimate when he was the younger of the two. Men may feel more involved when in a relation with someone older and perhaps of higher status.

Frequency.   Even though friends of the same age were slightly more likely to feel intimate, they were *less* likely to see one another often. Verbrugge (1973) found the same result: controlling for the effects of respondents' and friends' ages on frequency, contact *increased* with age *dis*similarity. Geographic distance cannot explain this finding: age-similar friends lived no farther apart than did dissimilar friends. Although we have had some difficulty in explaining the relative infrequency with which the men saw their age-similar friends, we suggest two possible explanations: first, two age-similar friends who each have family responsibilities will generally find it more difficult to get together; second, age-similar friendships probably tend to be high on "commitment" but low on "convenience." Although we can confirm neither argument, there is some modest evidence in support of each.[13]

[13] First, most respondents were at stages in the life-cycle when family responsibilities interfere with seeing friends. To the extent that their friends were at similar stages of life (that is, age-similar), the friends' family responsibilities would also reduce contact. That is, getting together requires free time at both ends of the friendship. Consequently, age-similar friends would be seen less often. A few indications in the data support this interpretation. For one, contact was especially frequent when nine or more years separated the two friends (see Table 5.2). More important, the effect—age-similar friends being seen infrequently—was statistically significant only among respondents in the middle years. It was not significant for young singles and older men who were, and whose age-similar friends were, less burdened by home and children. Another piece of evidence that supports this argument is that the similarity–low contact effect did not occur for friends recruited from work, probably because they would be seen in any event. Also, Verbrugge's (1973) analysis generally supports a model in which frequency of contact is a function of time constraints on both ego and friend. Second, assume that there are two general kinds of friends whom respondents nominated to their circle of "three closest": men with whom they had enduring, intimate, and diffuse commitments even in the absence of frequent contact, and men with whom they had frequent and routine exchanges even in the absence of great intimacy (see Chapter 4). Age similarity is related to the first kind of friendship and the second kind tends to be, by comparison, age-dissimilar. (We have seen that age-similar friendships were formed earlier in life, were more often singleplex, and were considered more intimate than others.) These arguments imply the findings in Table 5.2: age-similar friends were considered most intimate but seen least often. They also imply that, if similarity on other social

Density. Finally, the association between the age homogeneity of the network and its density further supports our earlier conclusion that the age span of peer groups widens over the life-cycle. In young adults' networks, the more age-similar a set of friends, the more likely they were to know each other ($\gamma = .18$, $p = .11$). This was not so for the older men ($\gamma = .01$). Apparently, with age, barriers to cross-age friendships are lowered, so that people of different ages can be interlocked despite their age differences.

In sum, men of all ages showed a strong preference for friends of the same age. Yet these kinds of friends became less common through the life-cycle, replaced first by older and then by younger friends. In addition, age similarity was associated—although modestly—with other features of the friendship bond: less role multiplexity, more intimacy, and less frequency of contact. These associations were strongest for the younger men and declined with age. Thus, while age similarity in friendship choice persists throughout the life course, it is more prevalent and of greater consequence in the early life stages.

Conclusion

How does a person's position in the cycles of family and work influence the quality of his informal social relations? By comparing men in different stages of the life-cycle and thus *inferring* changes in their personal relations over time, we have found that movement through the life course leads to significant alterations in men's social networks. For example, as men aged and adopted the responsibilities of marriage and fatherhood:

—their childhood friends were supplanted by friendships formed in adult contexts
—socializing with friends became more home-centered and less frequent, although feelings of closeness apparently did not wane
—the extent of strict age-grading in their friendships declined

We can best understand these and similar changes as the consequences of structural opportunities and constraints posed by different stages of the life-cycle. We suspect that during periods of transition people are most likely to make changes in the composition and quality of their friendship networks. At these times, in particular, new people enter the individual's "life space," old friends become more socially distant, and new needs for companionship arise. As needs and situations change, people reevaluate and reconstruct their social networks.

---

dimensions is also typical of the first kind of friendship (of "commitment"), then, in general, dissimilar friends should be seen more often than generally similar ones. Verbrugge (1973) reports just such a finding. For example, her German sample saw their cross-sex friends more often than they saw their same-sex friends.

Although we have focused in this chapter on regularly patterned movement through the life-cycle, family and work transitions do not necessarily occur at the same age or in the typical sequence for each individual. Furthermore, people make these transitions with varying degrees of ease and success. The role of friendship in these periods is complex. Friends are often needed for support and guidance, but the friendships themselves are likely to be severely tested. We have been unable to fully address these important dynamics of friendship over the life course here. However, we have been able to suggest how the social structuring of the life-cycle (such as the steps from school to job) affects the formation and maintenance of friendships. What are most needed next are studies of personal relations that focus on the periods of transition and on people who take those steps in atypical as well as typical ways.

PART 2

... AND PLACES

IN PART I, we introduced network analysis and examined the composition of social links and networks. We explored the ways in which people, choosing among the alternatives made possible by their positions within different social structures, form and maintain personal relations. We saw how the nature of social ties varies systematically according to the positions people occupy.

In Part II, we direct our analysis toward the variations in social networks that accompany different locations in the *ecological* structure. How do the characteristics of the places people live in affect their social ties? How are people tied socially to the places in which they live?

Chapter 6 tests a proposition that has been quite popular in the last decade, that population density in a neighborhood and crowding in a home inhibit or distort personal relations. Chapter 7 explores the extent to which and the reasons why suburbanites tend to be especially tied to their localities. Chapter 8 deals more generally with the nature of social connection to the neighborhood and surveys various characteristics of people that incline them to be more or less locally involved. Chapter 9 then examines the consequences, especially to people's social networks, of being more or less involved in their neighborhood. The overriding theme in Part II is an effort to understand the relationship between networks and places by understanding that the structure of space and place is also a structure of opportunities for and constraints on the formation of social ties.

6. Residential Density, Household Crowding, and Social Networks*

Mark Baldassare

IN THE PAST DECADE, "crowding" has captured the attention of both the general public and policy-makers. Crowding has been blamed for a host of social ills, ranging from racial disturbances to mental illness. Best-sellers have titillated the popular imagination with gripping descriptions of the bizarre behavior that can emerge under conditions of density (for example, Ardrey, 1966; D. Morris, 1969). The image of densely packed rats attacking and devouring one another has fueled demands for shifting people from large metropolises to smaller communities. Density has become a popular and ubiquitous "scientific" explanation for the urban crises of the 1960s and 1970s.

Population density had previously received some attention from academics. Sociologists such as Durkheim, Simmel, and Wirth speculated about the consequences of density, arguing that it led to social differentiation and the weakening of social bonds. Some researchers studied the social-psychological consequences of slum housing (for example, Plant, 1960; Wilner et al., 1962; see also Biderman et al., 1963). However, the publication in 1962 of an article on crowded rats marked the real beginning of the popularization and widespread study of this ecological variable. John Calhoun (1962) reported in *Scientific American* that, when he allowed a colony of rats confined to a single large pen to breed without limit, the animals went "berserk" (p. 147). For example, they became

* A version of this chapter was presented at the meetings of the American Sociological Association in New York City, August 1976. The two versions differ in emphases and data, although they reach similar conclusions.

either extremely aggressive or withdrawn; they gave up rearing their young (or ate them); and they engaged in homosexual attacks. Calhoun and others were quick to point out a parallel between crowded rats and crowded humans. Some suggested that the "urban crisis" was a consequence of crowding in our cities. Calhoun's paper loosened a floodtide of research, producing a whole academic subdiscipline crossing psychology and sociology and dedicated to studying the effect of density on humans (see Fischer et al., 1975).[1]

Residential Density and Social Networks

Classical sociologists at the turn of the century (for example, Tönnies, 1889; Durkheim, 1893; Spencer, 1895) struggled to understand the great changes accompanying rapid urbanization and tried to predict the shape of the coming society. They saw urbanization as one of the forces, along with the development of a money economy and the influx of heterogenous cultural groups, that were changing the communal, integrated social order (*Gemeinschaft*) into a commercial, anomic one (*Gesellschaft*).

Herbert Spencer (1895) was one of the earliest theorists to argue that the increasing population densities of modern societies fostered the development of highly specialized labor. His rather simplified causal analysis was criticized by Emile Durkheim, who argued, in *The Division of Labor in Society* (1893), that density was a necessary but insufficient cause of complex social organization. Specialization and interdependence were a result of increased interaction (that is, "social density") among members of dense agglomerations. This interaction could, in turn, only occur when there was large-scale agreement upon basic group values (that is, "moral density"). However, Durkheim viewed the kinds of interaction that increase with density as impersonal, functional, and commercial exchanges, accompanied by a qualitative and quantitative decline in personal relations. "Wherever the density of the agglomeration is related to the volume, personal bonds are rare and weak. One more easily loses others from sight; in the same way one loses interest in those close by" (p. 299). George Simmel (1905) suggested, in a well-known essay on the psychological effects of city life, that city-dwellers encounter in their daily rounds sights, sounds, and social contacts which, because of density, exceed the "normal" level of nervous stimulation. To cope with this sensory onslaught, the "metropolitan type of man" must adopt a "reserved" social and psychological style which reduces the number and intensity of the incoming

---

[1] For other recent reviews of the literature, see Freedman (1975), Stokols (1977), and Lawrence (1974).

sensations: avoiding social encounters or keeping them to a superficial level, being blasé in social situations, and maintaining largely instrumental, impersonal social relations.

Stanley Milgram (1970) modernized this thesis by recasting it in information and systems-theory language (see also Meier, 1962). Milgram argued that population density produces high levels of stimulation which threaten "psychic overload." To reduce stress, city-dwellers adopt strategies such as blocking unwanted "inputs" and encounters, "filtering" social stimuli, and allotting less time to each encounter. The result is a way of life in which people have relations that are superficial, specialized, and instrumental, and which ultimately leaves the individual estranged.

Robert Park (1916), a leader of the "Chicago School" of sociology, also argued that the density accompanying urban life replaced intimate relations with impersonal, utilitarian encounters. Drawing on Durkheim as well as on his teacher, Simmel, Park emphasized the changes that population concentration caused in the social structure (for example, specialized labor and land use, mass media). Louis Wirth (1938), Park's associate, summarized these arguments in "Urbanism as a Way of Life" (see Fischer, 1972). Wirth argued that population density was a defining characteristic of urbanism and that intense social contact in dense settings created competition, conflict, and irritability. Density also led to withdrawal and to specialized, transitory, and impersonal social relations; and it created psychological pathologies.

This classical sociological analysis argues, in sum, that *population density inhibits personal relations*. Although the quantity of personal *encounters* increases, the quantity and quality of personal *relations* is said to decrease. More modern analyses come to the same conclusion through other routes. One argument assumes that humans have "territorial instincts" that are thwarted in dense settings. The frustration causes social withdrawal and psychological pathologies. Another argument posits that people carry about them "personal-space bubbles." Intrusion into personal space is thought to cause tension and defensive reactions. Again, density leads to stress. (See Fischer et al., 1975, for an inventory and bibliography of crowding theories.)

We suggest, as an alternative proposition, that population density in neighborhoods need not usually cause stress or tension in residents and, therefore, need not cause a loss of personal relations. Population density may limit individuals' opportunities for certain behaviors (for example, playing a stereo loudly at 3:00 A.M.) but may widen opportunities for others, including meeting people. And if these social opportunities are, as "overload" theorists suggest, too numerous to handle, we assume that most people will pick and choose their interactions precisely in ways that, above all, protect intimate ties. Residents of huge apartment complexes may choose not to know all their neighbors, but they may still have intimates.

What We Know About Population Density

Most of the research on the consequences of density[2] has drawn its analytical model and hypotheses from Calhoun's rat studies and comparable literature in "pop ethology." The research on humans has generally been of two kinds: experimental studies which place groups in confined quarters for one or two hours, and correlational studies which test the association between densities and rates of pathologies across areal units.

The psychological experiments that crowd groups of people, usually undergraduates, into laboratory rooms and the observational studies on groups in natural settings, usually children in playrooms, have in general failed to demonstrate symptoms of pathology or social disintegration.[3] Some subtle effects have emerged in these studies: dense settings were, as one would expect, *perceived* as crowded; males seemed to be made more upset and hostile by dense settings than were females; and density may have reduced the total amount of social interaction in the groups.

However it is unclear what these studies tell us about people in dense neighborhoods or crowded dwellings. There is obviously a substantial gap between the experience of people in temporary and artificial laboratory groups and their experiences in normal settings of daily life. This gap has not prevented experimenters from extrapolating from their laboratories to the metropolis (see Baldassare and Fischer, 1977).

The second approach involves gathering data about rates of "pathology" —delinquency, mental hospital admissions, mortality, and so on—for areal units such as census tracts or health districts and correlating them with population density. The results of these studies have often been contradictory and have not yielded any clear evidence of "density effects" (for example, Schmitt, 1957, 1966; Levy and Herzog, 1974).[4] This research suffers not only from severe methodological problems (for example, multicollinearity, rate validity, ecological fallacy) but also from a difficult analytical snarl. Within a metropolitan area, high rates of pathology tend to occur in dense neighborhoods; poor people tend to live in these dense neighborhoods. Which causes the pathology, the density or the poverty?

[2] Although we have employed the terms "crowding" and "density" synonymously here, in more exact usage, *density* refers to the number of people per area and *crowding* to the subjective perception that there are too many people in a given space. See Stokols (1974).

[3] Examples of the first type are Freedman et al. (1971, 1972), and Griffith and Veitch (1971); of the second type, Loo (1972), and Hutt and Vaizey (1966). See review in Fischer et al. (1975).

[4] One oft-cited study correlated a few indices of density with measures of pathology across 75 "community areas" in Chicago (Galle et al., 1972). The researchers concluded that density did have an independent effect on rates of pathology. However, their findings have been seriously questioned (for example, Ward, 1974; McPherson, 1975), the major objections being with their statistical procedures.

Only a few studies have approached the key proposition, that crowding inhibits personal relations, by testing the association between neighborhood density and individuals' social ties. An American survey found that people in dense neighborhoods were less likely to know their neighbors well than were people living elsewhere (Lansing et al., 1970). But an English survey revealed no difference between people in high-density wards and those in low-density wards in the extent to which they had local friends (Kasarda and Janowitz, 1974). Similarly, a Canadian study also failed to find substantial connections between the density of a family's neighborhood and the nature of the adults' social relations (Booth, 1975a; Michelson and Garland, 1974).[5] And yet interviewers in New York City found that refusals were more common in the denser of two neighborhoods (Davis, 1975; Davis et al., 1974). Perhaps residents in the denser area were screening out "overloading" social encounters (or perhaps they were more frightened of crime).

From this brief review, we draw two conclusions: density has not yet been established to be a cause of pathologies; and very few tests have been conducted on whether density inhibits personal relations.

NEIGHBORHOOD DENSITY AND SOCIAL NETWORKS IN DETROIT

We used the Detroit survey to test directly the association between the population densities of neighborhoods and the characteristics of men's social networks. We measured density as the population of each respondent's census tract, *circa* 1960, divided by the area of the tract. (We measured the total area of each relevant tract on census maps.) We also obtained the total *residential* area of each tract, but for the city of Detroit only.[6] The fact that the population statistics were from 1960, over five years before the survey was taken, introduces some "noise" into our findings, but we have no reason to believe that the error is biased for or against the hypothesis that density inhibits social relations.

We examined the associations between population density and three aspects of social relations: (1) general social involvement—for example, number of friends; (2) involvement in the neighborhood—for example, neighboring; and (3) the dimensions of social networks described in Chap-

---

[5] Michelson and Garland (1974) reported only one variable among the many tested that was related to neighborhood crowding: threat of marital dissolution. The explanation for, and thus, the relevance of, this finding is unclear.

[6] Ann Stueve measured the tract areas. We were forced to use simple areal density (persons per square mile) when we examined the entire Detroit metropolitan area sample. This is only a rough indicator of residential density (persons per inhabited area), a measure that we could only use for the Detroit city sample. (The correlation between the two measures is .51.) This introduces measurement error into our calculations. The mean areal density in our sample was 7,580 people per square mile, the standard deviation was 4,680, and the range was from 20 to 33,700.

ter 3 (multiplexity, duration, intimacy, frequency, distance, density, and dispersion). We calculated the simple correlations between population density and these aspects of social relations. Then we sought to control for the fact that men in denser neighborhoods were poorer than and otherwise different from those in less dense neighborhoods. Thus, we calculated partial correlations, controlling for these confounding factors. All else held constant, did the nature of the men's personal relations differ according to their neighborhood density? [7]

In our first test, of general social involvement, we found that there was *no* correlation between neighborhood density and the *number of friends* a man claimed to have or the *number of days* a week he claimed to see his friends.[8] Controlling for differences in age, education, occupational status, and income did not change this result. Men in dense areas tended to be less involved in *voluntary organizations* than were others, but this was largely a result of their being of lower social status. Thus, neighborhood density seemingly did *not* turn these men into social isolates; it had no association with how many friendships they had or with the amount of time they spent with their friends. There was one notable association: Men in dense neighborhoods reported less talking and *visiting with neighbors* than did other men, and the difference persisted after controls ($r = -.12$; partial $r = -.11$).[9] This finding replicates two North American studies (Lansing et al.'s [1970] American survey and Michelson's [1973a] study of families in Toronto) but contradicts Kasarda and Janowitz's (1974) English study. We can suggest two alternative explanations for an inhibition of neighboring in dense settings. The first follows from a reinterpretation of the psychic-overload hypothesis: the high levels of social stimulation and demands induced in a dense setting lead people to cope by *selective* social withdrawal. They withdraw from less rewarding interactions—chatting with neighbors, for example—in order to protect their time for more rewarding interactions with intimate friends (Baldassare, 1975a: 822). Second, residents of dense neighborhoods may not be overstimulated at all. Instead, they may be in the position, because of all the people concentrated near them, of having the choice of spending their time with people who are more "rewarding" than their neighbors (see Hawley, 1972; Jacobs, 1961). Thus, instead of coping with stress, residents of dense areas may be responding to new opportunities, recog-

[7] We assumed a linear relationship between density and the dependent variables. An alternative hypothesis is that there is a severe curvilinear function or a threshold function such that effects appear only at the high levels of density. We are pursuing this possibility in current research (Baldassare, 1976), although no one has yet reported discovering such functions in previous studies.

[8] Originally reported in Baldassare (1975a).

[9] When we examined *residential* density (persons per acre, excluding industrial and park land) instead of area density, we obtained the same results ($r = -.14$; partial $r = -.13$).

nizing their options, and acting with more discrimination (Fischer, 1973, 1976).

Further examination of our data leads us to consider yet one more explanation for the negative association between density and neighboring. Men in dense neighborhoods are not only themselves of relatively low social status, on the average, they also tend to have *neighbors* of somewhat lower social status than do men in less dense neighborhoods. (The correlation between density and the median income of the tract is $-.51$.) The crowded men may neighbor less because they feel less attracted to their neighbors (see Chapter 8). In fact, controlling for the median income of the tract eliminates the effect of density (partial $r = -.04$). Although it is a less interesting conclusion, it may be that density does not substantially reduce neighboring either.

In our second analysis, we looked more closely at whether neighborhood density altered the nature of the Detroit men's local social relations (Baldassare, 1975b). It apparently did not. (In this analysis, we used a better measure of density—persons per residential acre. But this meant that we could only look at the city of Detroit sample.) With occupational status, age, presence of children in the home, years of residence, and median income of the tract taken into account, there is no association between how dense a man's tract was and the *number of best friends* he had in the neighborhood, the *frequency* with which he saw those friends, how *intimate* he felt toward them, or whether he was a member of a *neighborhood organization*. (The last variable was the only one of these which even showed any zero-order association, $r = -.10$.) [10]

In our third analysis, we examined the effects of neighborhood density on the dimensions of network links identified in Chapter 3: multiplicity, duration, intimacy, frequency of interaction with friends, physical separation, as well as dimensions of social networks—relational density and source dispersion. Instead of considering only local ties, we examined the set of network variables with respect to individuals' entire networks (and employed again gross areal density, which allowed us to use the entire metropolitan sample). If neighborhood density has, as the standard version of overload theory suggests, the effect of making people withdraw from social relations and filter their intensity, we should observe the consequences in the networks of crowded men. Specifically, overload theory implies that the denser a person's neighborhood, the less multiplex, durable, intimate, frequent, and relationally dense the network, and the more dispersed—physically and socially—it is. [11] These expectations were *not* confirmed.

[10] We found, as Davis (1975) did, that respondents in denser neighborhoods tended, as a statistically significant level, to appear more hostile to their interviewers than did those in less dense neighborhoods. Statistical controls reduced this correlation (see Baldassare, 1975b).

[11] If population density produces social withdrawal as a means of coping with the threat of overload, then we would expect: lower multiplexity because simplifying

TABLE 6.1   Correlations Between Areal Density[a] and Dimensions of Social Networks *(Detroit Survey)*

	ZERO-ORDER r	PARTIAL r[b]
Average Role Multiplexity[c]	− .005	− .001
Average Duration	− .011	.021
Average Intimacy	− .011	.038
Average Frequency of Interaction	.065*	.022
Average Physical Distance of Friends	.028	.015
Network Density	.106**	.077+
Network Dispersion	− .082*	− .029

[a] Persons per square mile in respondent's census tract (1960).
[b] Controls: age, occupational status, children at home, years in the neighborhood, and median income of tract.
[c] For definitions, see Chapter 2.
+ $p < .10$
* $p < .05$
** $p < .01$

Men did not differ according to the density of their neighborhoods in the average multiplexity, duration, intimacy, or physical distance of their network links. Contrary to what overload theories imply, men in dense settings saw their friends slightly *more* often ($r = .06$), had slightly *more* relationally dense networks ($r = .11$), and had slightly *less* socially dispersed networks ($r = −.08$) than did low-density men (see Table 6.1). However, when age, education, income, occupational status, children, length of residence, and median tract income are taken into account, even these effects are reduced to insignificance. All that remained of even marginal interest is the association with relational density. The more the population density in a man's tract, the slightly more likely it was that his friends were friends of one another (partial $r = .08$). Although this finding brings to mind "urban villages"—dense neighborhoods populated by cohesive ethnic or class groups (see, for example, Gans, 1962b; Young and Willmott, 1957)—it might be explained by other, uncontrolled factors (such as the age composition of the tracts). In any case, it is the opposite of what the density theories suggest.

In summary, the personal relations of the thousand men interviewed in the Detroit area do not seem to have been inhibited by the degree of neighborhood density. At most, men in more dense locales may have known their neighbors less well than did men in less dense environments,

---

relations to single purposes is a method of withdrawal; less duration because people withdraw from friendships; less intimacy because it means less intensity; less frequency because it protects the individual from too much interaction; more physical separation as a way of reducing demands of one's associates; less network density, so that social life can be compartmentalized into manageable, low-intensity segments; and more dispersion for the same reason.

but their general social lives seem, in net, unaffected. We are aware of the limitations of the Detroit data for testing theories of density. For example, the sample is entirely male, and the density statistics are six years dated. Nevertheless, the survey provides a unique source of information on the key proposition that density inhibits personal relations. Furthermore, our findings are generally consistent with the few other studies that have been conducted thus far.

Why did the density predictions fail, here and elsewhere? The presence of many people near one's home or in one's streets may simply not cause stress or "overload." It there is no problem, there is nothing to solve by means of social withdrawal. Furthermore, even if urbanites do face the threat of overload, they can control potential negative consequences to their intimate relations by minimizing *certain kinds* of social encounters. Instead of responding with some "natural" coping mechanism which automatically produces withdrawal, people *consciously* and *rationally* choose which social interactions will be maintained and to what degree other interactions will be limited. Individuals would presumably leave their intimate friendships intact and reduce their openness to less significant ones. The "rational" urbanites, often pitied by classical sociologists, are capable of making these decisions concerning their social world. They are also rational enough not to destroy their intimate relations when attempting to limit the attention they give to less meaningful interactions.[12]

Household Crowding and Social Networks

The most important residential setting in which personal relations are conducted daily is the household. The smallness of the dwelling unit and the intimacy of the interactions which occur there have led some authors to suggest that the neighborhood may be the wrong context for discovering the effects of crowding. Instead, high dwelling densities are seen as the real cause of our social ills (see, for example, Jacobs, 1961: 208).

The social significance of the family also makes it an important context for studying density. Stokols (1974), for example, has argued that the effects of feeling crowded will be more severe in "primary settings," such as dwellings, than in "secondary settings," such as public spaces, because family activities and relations are so significant to individuals. (Feelings of crowding are inevitably dependent upon experiences of density.) The overload thesis, applied to the household, states that crowding disturbs interaction in the home and, because of the defensive social withdrawal

---

[12] Milgram's (1970) statements approximate this line of reasoning, although he seems to believe that the coping mechanisms adopted for handling incidental encounters come to pervade all of an urbanite's social life.

it produces in individual personalities, it impairs people's personal relations outside the home as well (see also Suttles, 1968: 75–78, 90–92).

WHAT WE KNOW ABOUT HOUSEHOLD CROWDING

The limited evidence on the correlates of household crowding fall into
two general categories: descriptive accounts from various cultures and
survey studies, largely of apartment residents.

Although cultural differences in spatial behavior and standards (Hall,
1966; Baldassare and Feller, 1976) make it difficult to generalize such
findings, several anthropological reports suggest that there are no pathological effects of crowding: !Kung Bushmen "like" crowding and live at
high densities, although they have opportunities to do otherwise, and they
suffer no apparent pathological consequences (Draper, 1973). Many
Chinese families living outside of mainland China choose to share a single
bedroom, renting the other bedrooms to a family apiece, even when there
is no great financial necessity to do so. Efficient scheduling in the use of
common public rooms avoids tension (Anderson, 1972). After surveying
several ethnographic and historical sources, R. E. Mitchell (1975) concluded that social-structural factors mitigate any simple and "pathological"
effects of crowding.

Several studies have examined the effect of household density, particularly in apartment buildings, on relations among family members. In general, crowded adults do not differ much from uncrowded adults in their
family relations. An exception is an Italian study that found more quar-
reling between spouses in crowded homes (Gasparini, 1973). When adults
must share crowded quarters with non-relatives, strain between them does
seem a probable outcome (R. E. Mitchell, 1971). The most consistent
effect of crowding, discovered in a few studies, concerns children. In more
cramped families, there tends to be more tension among children and between mothers and children, and less supervision of children (Chombart
de Lauwe, 1961; Gasparini, 1973; R. E. Mitchell, 1971; and Booth,
1975b). Unfortunately, it is difficult to distinguish in these studies between
the effects of household density—people per space—and those of the
number of children (see Baldassare, 1976).

Only a few studies have looked at the effects of household crowding on
the extra-household relations of family members. A Toronto study found
no signs of social withdrawal (Booth, 1975a); a Hong Kong study found
only that crowded families entertained neighbors relatively infrequently
(R. E. Mitchell, 1971); and a New York study found that parents in
crowded dwellings tended to be less willing to allow their children to
bring friends indoors to play (Davis et al., 1975).

In sum, the existing research does not provide much support for the
thesis that household crowding creates disorders or the inhibition of social

relations among adults; it may have such consequences for children, although it is difficult to separate the effects of spatial constraints from those of family size.

HOUSEHOLD CROWDING IN THE NATIONAL SAMPLE

The NORC national survey (see Chapter 1) provided us with an opportunity to examine the association between household crowding and personal relations. Unlike the previous studies, we have a national and approximately cross-sectional sample within which to test the psychic-overload hypothesis. Our measure of household crowding was the number of residents in the home divided by the number of rooms.[13]

We examined, first, the association of the crowding measure to relations with neighbors.[14] We found that relatively crowded adults were *not* less likely to report having friends in the neighborhood or to report seeing or spending time with neighbors (before or after controls—age, occupational status, family income, presence of children, and years in the neighborhood).[15] Having children promotes neighboring (see Chapter 8), but crowding neither promotes nor retards neighborhood ties.

We also tested the associations between household crowding and other aspects of the respondents' social involvements. Again, we found negative results. Crowded respondents were no less likely to report meeting new people, having high friendship density, or being sociable. We explored the possibility that crowding effects varied by sex (as they do in some experiments) and found only one small difference: crowded women felt slightly less "sociable" than uncrowded women (whites only, partial $r = -.08$), but there was no association among men (partial $r = .02$).

RECONSIDERATION

In all, we found little evidence to support the proposition that household density affects adults' social relations. There are, of course, limitations on our own analysis. The measure of household crowding may be too crude (see Morris and Winter, 1975; Greenfield and Lewis, 1969), and there may be aspects of social relations that we did not measure.

---

[13] Unfortunately, we were unable to obtain areal density measures for the national sample, or household crowding measures for the Detroit sample.

[14] We excluded people living alone from this analysis because their densities are asocial (simply the reciprocal of the number of rooms). Results for the total sample, including the singles, were not different than the ones reported here.

[15] In the white sample, no zero-order r was greater than .06; no partial r was greater than .03. Findings were similar in the black sample, except for one result: among both black men and women, crowding was *positively* associated with chatting with neighbors outdoors (partial $r = .11$ for both).

Nevertheless, our analysis was conducted on a fairly large and comprehensive survey base. The negative results, especially when added to the findings of previous studies, seriously challenge the "density leads to general social withdrawal" hypothesis.

It seems that, over all, household crowding—at least within the range captured by these studies[16]—does not have negative effects on adults' social networks. A few studies indicate, however, that crowding may affect family relations, and that it may especially affect children, who suffer from getting underfoot, being pushed outdoors, and having their activities controlled by parents (R. E. Mitchell, 1971; Davis et al., 1974; Gasparini, 1973; Booth, 1975b; Chombart de Lauwe, 1961). In this section, we will attempt to reconcile these two sets of findings. We suggest moving away from pure crowding-overload models to ones that focus on the instrumental use of space and the power to control it. Instead of people in a small space "overloading" individuals' psyches, what they do is compete for an instrumental resource, the space needed to engage in preferred activities (and perhaps to avoid the possibilty of overload).

Because indoor space, unlike public space, is usually controlled by a clear status and power hierarchy, the family,[17] dominant members of the family can obtain the space they need for their activities (entertaining guests, cooking, and so on) by taking it from subordinate members. (On the use of threat and force in intimate relations, see Goode, 1972, 1973.) It is thus reasonable to assume that adults can maintain their social networks in spite of crowding by appropriating space when it is needed. Children cannot obtain space and can lose rights to what they have when others demand more, and so children suffer.[18] Anthropologist Carol Stack (1974: 7) has described this process in the case of poor black families:

> Social space assumes great importance in a crowded living area. . . . The paucity of personal space leads to efforts by the adults, often extreme, to protect themselves from encroachments, and their space from violations, particularly by children. (This space varies according to a person's mood, but children are often kept as far as four or five feet away from adults.) A child who entered an adult's social space would be punished.

Among the adults, tension can arise when their roles and statuses are unclear, as in unrelated families (R. E. Mitchell, 1971); in the "overseas

---

[16] Among whites in the NORC sample, the mean household crowding rate was .65 persons per room (standard deviation was .3). In the black sample, the mean was .8 (standard deviation, .4).

[17] D. Smith (1971: 65) alludes to this when she discusses the findings by Lewis (1961) that crowded Latin homes are especially dominated by fathers.

[18] Booth (1975b) reports that crowded households had a slight negative impact on children's school work and health (that is, height and weight). He also argues that this may be due to children's limited power (p. 747).

Chinese" case (E. Anderson, 1972), the homeowner had obvious dominion, although equitable rules were established.[19]

Studies have shown that children's play activities are pushed out of the home when space is in short supply. The same sort of inequality in power between husbands and wives may create marital tension when the males demand limited space (Gasparini, 1973); we found a hint of such an effect in that crowding was related to reports of unsociability among women, but not among men.

An argument that focuses on the *power* individuals have to command the space they need and to control the activities of others in cramped quarters seems to account more satisfactorily for the presence or absence of crowding effects in the home. Although the present data are admittedly scarce, this explanation is more in line with the results that we and others have found than are quasi-biological or psychological explanations.

Conclusion

Despite the alarms sounded by ethologists and crowding theorists, there is not much evidence to support their warnings that crowding in residential environments has a direct effect on adults' social networks. (Note that we are speaking here of density within the range of modern residential settings and not of catastrophic circumstances, such as overcrowded refugee camps.)

However, this conclusion does not lead us to dismiss the study of crowding. It suggests, instead, certain directions for future research on crowding that may lead to more useful conclusions. Rather than focus on general social involvement, withdrawal, or pathology, investigators should consider how people in dense neighborhoods *choose* their social interactions. Given their many more neighbors, how do people in dense environments select among them? If certain social interactions are suppressed, which ones are they?

The theoretical distinction between density in a neighborhood and that in a home should be underlined. While the consequences of areal density *might* be understood in terms of a modified "stimulus overload" model,

---

[19] Shibutani (1961: 504) has pointed out that people can maintain smooth interactions when their roles are clearly understood and agreed upon. This observation is relevant to the topic of crowding and power in two respects. First, when an individual's power is considered as legitimate authority, he or she can divide and allocate limited space with a minimum of conflict. Second, when roles are clearly understood by all, it is easier to coordinate physical movements in small areas; people can avoid intruding on or interfering with one another. Problems arise in crowded situations when roles are not understood or agreed upon. (We thank Christiane Taelemans for bringing the symbolic interactionist perspective to our attention.)

household crowding calls for other explanations. Space is a resource, and the consequences of spatial constraints depend on individuals' abilities to command the space they need to do what they want. This, in turn, depends on the power certain individuals have over the activities of other group members. Thus, children may suffer from high dwelling densities while their parents (or, at least, fathers) do not. In general, attention should be given to the effects of density for particular groups, examining the consequences of crowding for people of different ages and classes, for example (see Baldassare, 1976).[20]

There are more general lessons to learn from recent studies of crowding. Much of the ealier (mid-1960s) speculation about crowding, because it emerged from animal studies, assumed an implicit model of people as simple reacting organisms: "placed" in dense settings, they "reacted" by withdrawal or aggression. This is too simplistic and misleading; most people—at least adults—can choose their settings, and people *act* as well as react.

With respect to choosing: It remains true that dense neighborhoods are the sites of more pathology—crime, malnutrition, psychological disorder, and so on—than are less dense locales. But this correlation is mostly, if not totally, a result of *choice* or the *lack of choice*. People with the capacity, skills, and affluence to choose spacious settings do so; they also suffer from fewer pathologies—not because of their space, but because of their advantages. People who are disadvantaged suffer both from pathologies and from lack of choice; often the only places they can live are crowded ones. The oft-observed correlation between density and pathology is therefore largely a result of *self-selection*.

With respect to acting: individuals do not simply react to their environments but act to build and preserve their social relations. Just as people is different stages of the life-cycle construct supportive networks out of the human material available to them (Chapter 5), so do people in different environmental settings. People strive to have and maintain intimate social ties up to a manageable level, and so we should not be surprised that people in different settings achieve it. Problems arise when, as in the case of children or disadvantaged groups, freedom of choice is constrained.

This brings us to understanding the nature of environmental settings for people. According to the theories we have critiqued, dense settings produce stimuli to which people must respond. Although one can demonstrate physiological reactions to intense crowding in the laboratory (Aiello et al., 1975), and although noise in dense neighborhoods disturbs people, the research we have reviewed and the new data we have presented suggest that this conception is basically inadequate. Instead, the spatial di-

---

[20] Another interaction of interest is between household and neighborhood crowding. Does their joint occurrence, for example, yield effects not discovered with each of them separately? (Booth, 1975a; Michelson and Garland, 1974; Baldassare, 1976).

mension of people's living environments presents to them a set of opportunities and constraints which they use to achieve their goals. It is a medium of human behavior, just like time or money; having lots of it opens up new possibilities while closing off others (Hawley, 1972). So, for example, people in apartment buildings are effectively prevented from activities that disturb their neighbors, while people in isolated settings are given a smaller choice of neighbors with whom to engage.

Given a set of relatively important ends, such as maintaining intimate social relations, adults will purposefully use what space they have in ways to achieve those ends. If they have much space, they may send their children to play in another room; if they have less, they will send them outdoors. If there are competing demands for a space (or too many stimuli per given time unit and area), its use will be scheduled—if there is a procedure for making such decisions in the group. And if worst comes to worst, people will even put up with squabbling children in order to engage in personal relations. For people who have some say in the matter, spatial constraints probably affect not *whether* they maintain their social lives but *how* they do so and at what costs. Finally, density is itself amenable to much human choice. For example, people may forego having children when space is limited or add to the space when children arrive (Felson and Solaùn, 1975).

This understanding of density—as a constraint on or opportunity for individuals' achievement of their ends—is, we argue, probably a more rewarding approach. It is also consistent with an emerging perspective on urbanization. Unlike the thesis of classical sociologists that urbanization directly altered people's social relations, replacing intimate ones with transitory ones, urbanization is increasingly seen as presenting people with more choices—the possibility of transitory ties *in addition to* intimate ones (for example, Bruner, 1973; Fischer, 1976). It is then the task of individuals to construct out of these possibilities the most supportive networks they can.

7. Suburbanism and Localism*

Claude S. Fischer
Robert Max Jackson

SCHOLARLY OPINION on the quality of suburban life has undergone a historical cycle. At the turn of the century, many social theorists and reformers thought that living on the border of city and country was invigorating and ennobling. "Out of this joyous union," wrote new-town planner Ebenezer Howard, 'will spring a new hope, a new life, a new civilization" (Donaldson, 1969: 23; see also Tarr, 1973). By the middle of the century, most observers saw the suburbs differently, as the breeding grounds of conformity and neuroticism, and as fitting homes for mass society's "organization men": "We can clearly see the most grievous human loss that life in the suburb entails. Dedication to a status-dominated life style forces individuals into a rigid mold from which they can see only limited aspects of human reality. . . . Emotional growth stops at [a] 'juvenile' phase" (Stein, 1960: 286; see also Riesman, 1959; W. H. Whyte, 1956). Although some writers continue in this tradition of criticism (for example, Alexander, 1967; Coles, 1975), the scholarly cycle has come back to the center. Contemporary writers more often argue that suburbs are essentially neutral and do not cause any particular life-style or personality type. Herbert Gans (1967: 288) best sums up the contemporary opinion: "When one looks at similar populations in city and suburb, their ways of life are remarkably alike. . . . The crucial difference between cities and suburbs then is they are often home for different kinds of people" (see also B. Berger, 1960; Donaldson, 1969).

We accept Gans' statement as a general conclusion about the social-

* This chapter draws substantially from Fischer and Jackson, "Suburbs, Networks, and Attitudes," in B. Schwartz (ed.), *The Changing Face of the Suburbs* (Chicago: University of Chicago Press, 1976), pp. 279–307. A more technical discussion of our research can be found there. The chapter also draws upon Chapter 9 of Fischer (1976).

117

psychological consequences of suburban residence (see Fischer, 1976: Ch. 9). Some life-styles that many have thought to be a product of living in suburbs do not turn out to be characteristic of suburbs after all; other life-styles are suburban only because certain kinds of people (especially child-rearing and affluent people) have brought them to suburbia. Yet one dimension of social life on which suburbanites differ from city residents may be a consequence of suburban residence. That dimension is *localism*: the extent to which people's social networks are centered and their attention is focused on their neighborhoods. In this chapter, we review the evidence on the localism of suburbanites and extend it with some new analyses. We also attempt to explain *why* suburbanism might promote a local orientation. And we attempt to understand how people both anticipate and adapt to the consequences of suburban living.

Before proceeding further, we should define *suburbanism*. According to the census definition, suburbs are political entities: all the municipalities in a metropolitan area except the central city or cities. In the San Francisco Bay area, for example, San Francisco and Oakland are central cities. Every other city—Berkeley, Sausalito, Milpitas, and so on—is a "suburb." Although we must rely on this definition in much of our research, arbitrary political lines are not very satisfactory boundaries from a sociological point of view. More social definitions have been suggested, stressing life-style—for example, middle-class consumerism, or family orientation. These definitions, of course, beg the question of whether suburban residence promotes certain ways of life. Ecological definitions have also been suggested; they define suburbs on the basis of land use, recency of development, low housing density (particularly detached, single-family homes), and the like. These ecological variables can be reduced to (explained by) a single fundamental factor: *distance from the center city*.

This simple spatial variable will serve as our definition of suburbanism and the critical independent variable in our analysis: the farther a metropolitan neighborhood is from the center of the area's population, the more suburban it is. In modern cities, distance is a direct and major determinant of housing patterns. It is a simple geometric fact that the farther from the center one moves, the more land there is (that is, the area of a circle increases in proportion to the square of the radius); an economic fact that the farther out, the cheaper the land; and a historical fact that the farther out, the more recent and less complete the construction. These patterns mean that distant land is more likely to be used for new and spacious housing. And, because of this new and spacious housing, distant land tends to be settled by affluent home-buyers (Evans, 1973; Treadway, 1969) and growing families (T. Anderson and Egeland, 1961; Guest, 1972).[1]

[1] This description of the ecological consequences of suburban location is, we recognize, an oversimplification. The pattern we describe is not valid for many cities outside North America—although these cities are beginning to resemble North Amer-

Although the ecological variable we use in our conceptual discussion of suburbanism is distance, we are in many cases forced to rely on approximate indicators of distance in our data analysis. Many published studies (and the national survey conducted by NORC) provide only the political distinction of center city versus other places in the metropolis.

Models of Suburbanism

Expectations about the relationship between suburbanism and localism (that is, focusing social life in the local area) vary with one's theoretical perspective on suburbs. One such expectation is the null hypothesis: suburbanism neither increases nor decreases localism. A second is that suburban residence *reduces* localism. The argument here is intriguing. Several casual descriptions of suburban life and some more serious speculations about the process of urban dispersal (for example, Webber, 1968) suggest that suburban residence might be associated with a metropolitan-wide lifestyle. They suggest that work commuting, the sprawl of housing, and the distances separating activities and people in suburbia would encourage a less localized life-style than is the case in the center city, where people have services and associates close by. Persuasive as this argument is, we shall see that the prediction is wrong. Suburban life is *more*, not less, local. The third expectation is the one we shall consider most closely: that *suburbanism promotes localism*. There are three noteworthy (and not incompatible) models which explain why suburbanites are more locally oriented than city-dwellers.

1. Herbert Gans (1962a, 1967) and others suggest *self-selection*, that

---

ican cities in these respects (Hoyt, 1969; Hawley, 1971). Even in the United States, other factors besides distance either help to explain the pattern of housing (for example, zoning restrictions) or to disturb it (for example, the spurt of apartment building in the suburbs during the 1960s). Nevertheless, this "model," which explains population distribution as a function of the geographic and economic correlates of distance, remains a powerful one. We can provide some evidence for this model from 1960 Detroit census data.

Ann Stueve coded the census data for 218 tracts in the Detroit metropolitan area—the tracts from which the Detroit survey drew its respondents. We found that distance from the Detroit central business district (CBD: the corner of Michigan and Woodward Avenues) explained 53 percent of the variance in the proportion of housing units which were single dwellings (that is, single-family homes; $r = .73$) and 59 percent of the variance in the proportion which were less than two years old ($r = .77$). Distance explained 42 percent of the variance in the proportion of the population which was under 18 (that is, families; $r = .65$) and also 42 percent of the variance in the median income in the tract. The correlation between distance and children is almost totally accounted for by the mediating effects of single-unit housing and new housing (partial $r = .08$); the correlation with income is largely accounted for in the same way (partial $r = .24$). This pattern of findings largely confirms the argument in the text (see also Fischer and Jackson. 1976: 280, n. 4).

the suburbs attract locally oriented individuals by providing spacious homes and open land at relatively affordable prices. Therefore, people who are raising children and people who are interested in at-home activities such as gardening would be found more often in suburban neighborhoods (see Guest, 1972; Zelan, 1968; Michelson, 1973a). These types of people have localized social lives. Once this self-selection is taken into account, there should be no effect of suburbanism.

2. A *contexual effects* model argues that, irrespective of the individual's characteristics or interests, being surrounded by locally oriented people promotes localism. Suburban housing attracts and concentrates relatively well-off, home-owning families. People in such families tend especially to be involved in their neighborhoods (see Chapter 8). The concentration of these people around any individual further encourages the latter's inclination toward localism because, for example, neighbors drop by, or the local neighborhood association solicits memberships. They have this effect regardless of the individual's original inclination to have a local social life or not.

3. Another model emphasizes the role of *distance and cost* in social relations. The distances separating suburbanites from the mass of the population and its activities increase the costs of extralocal involvement as compared to those costs for a city-dweller. This implies that suburbanites tend to "settle" for "cheaper" local activities and relations. Because this explanation is the most difficult of the three, we discuss it further in the next section.

DISTANCE, ACCESS, COST, AND CHOICE

One of the cost factors that people must weigh in forming and maintaining their social networks is distance (see discussion in Chapter 3). Distance is a cost insofar as it translates into problems of *access*, the ease with which a person can reach people or places. Obviously, the amount of cost varies by individual circumstances. To a laborer, three thousand miles is virtually insurmountable; to a jet-setter, the price of a coast-to-coast jaunt is almost negligible. Nevertheless, in both cases distance is a cost. Consequently, the farther apart two people are, the less likely they are to meet, remeet, interact regularly, and form a binding link. The farther apart two previously linked people become, the less likely they are to maintain their relationship (the likelihood of maintaining a tie also depends, of course, on the reward the link provides).[2] Suburbs raise the cost of inter-

---

[2] The effect of distance also varies with the nature of the link. Professional ties and kinship obligations are probably least likely to be affected; ties of casual sociability will be most affected. For links that are multi-stranded, distance may sever certain strands (for example, neighborly aid) and not others (for example, confiding of intimate problems). We extend the analysis of distance and networks in Chapter 9.

action by reducing access from individuals' homes to the homes and gathering places of people who are their actual and potential associates.[3]

To see how suburbanism influences the costs of social relations, let us assume for purposes of illustration an ideal-type metropolis. It is circular in shape, highly dense at the center, and less dense as one approaches the periphery. In such a metropolis—holding everything else, such as the existence of radial highways and ethnic enclaves, constant for the moment—the farther from the center individuals live, the greater the average distance (thus, the less the average access) to other people in the metropolis and the fewer people there are within any specific distance. The costs of meeting and keeping in touch with people in the area are, in general, greater for the suburbanite than for the city-dweller. (Put geometrically, if one summed up the distance between each individual residence and everyone else's in the metropolis, each individual's total would increase with his or her distance from the center.) Suburban residence also poses indirect costs to social networks by increasing the costs of necessary and competing journeys, such as shopping and commuting, thereby leaving less time, money, and energy for social trips.

If we add to this fact, the greater average costs for suburbanites, two assumptions—that people seek to maximize the rewards from social ties and that they seek to minimize the effort, or cost, of those ties[4]—then we

---

[3] The problem of access is more complex than this simplification implies. The relationships among distance, access, and cost are most probably not linear. Further, individual *perceptions* of access costs, which perceptions will determine travel behavior, are also not linear functions of distance. We recognize these problems. but the model we employ here suffices for present purposes.

[4] These two assumptions are linked. And they are significant because alternative assumptions would predict just the opposite outcome to that discussed in this paragraph. The first assumption, that people seek to maximize their rewards, is one we have held throughout the book. The second assumption, that people seek to minimize costs—in this case, effort—is in a sense reciprocal to the first, but it also has larger implications. There is a school of thought that holds that the "attraction" between two places (for example, in terms of migration patterns) or two people is an inverse function of the intervening distance. This is the "principle of least effort" made famous by Zipf, or alternatively, the "gravity" model (Carrothers, 1956). In an abstract sense, we are saying that individuals act as if they evaluate all of their possible associates, each of whom can be ranked on degree of "rewardingness" and degree of "distance-cost" to the individual, and then select those with the highest ratio of the first to the second, picking from the top of the list down. If, as we are supposing for the sake of argument, these associates are randomly distributed across the metropolis in accord only with the area's density patterns (high in the center, low on the periphery), then the city-dwellers' distance-costs tend to be lower than suburbanites' for associates of equal rewardingness. This difference affects the structure of choices each person faces: the marginal return for distance is greater for the city residents than for the suburban ones. Put another way: Because of geometry and density, each extra radius mile away from suburbanites' homes brings in fewer high-reward associates for the extra cost of travel than does a mile from the city-dwellers' homes. Hence, the suburbanites are less likely to go the extra mile, and more likely to rely on those close by.

What would alternative assumptions predict? We could assume (1) that people

can derive the following prediction: On the average, all else still held constant,[5] *the farther from the city center people live, the more localized their activities and social networks will be* (that is, the more their social networks and activities will be centered within the physically proximate area). The more suburban individuals' residences are, the higher the "schedule of prices" they must pay to interact with people throughout the metropolitan area. Suburbanites can respond to these higher "prices" in one or both of two ways: They can spend the extra time and money required to maintain the same social network they would have if they lived nearer the center. Alternatively, they can ignore or drop distant associates in favor of nearer ones, even if the nearer ones are less rewarding. Suburbanites do both. We shall discuss the first strategy, expending more effort, shortly. The second strategy is of more immediate concern, because it implies that suburbanites' social networks will be more localized than those of city residents. All this, put simply, says that suburbanites are more localistic because they are too far from people other than their neighbors.

In presenting this model, we do not intend to exaggerate the effect of home location on social networks. People develop and maintain significant social relations based on other places (for example, the workplace) and on non-spatial factors (for example, kinship). However, we do contend that suburban residence localizes social networks, particularly, we will argue, for certain groups.

Actually, there is one other possible outcome of suburban distance. Some people neither have the extra resources to keep up their social networks nor can they substitute local relations for extralocal ones, because they are insufficiently compatible with their neighbors. The outcome for these people is isolation. So, there are three possible outcomes of suburbanization: greater expenditures for social ties, more local ties, or greater isolation.

---

seek satisfaction—selecting the first associates whose rewardingness exceeds a specific threshold, and (2) that the "attraction" between people and places is an inverse function of "intervening opportunities" (Stouffer, 1940), as well as distance. This would lead us to predict that *city residents would be more local than suburbanites,* because the density function puts more intervening opportunities that satisfice close to the city-dweller. There is some reason to prefer the gravity model over the intervening opportunities model. For example, Catton and Smirchich (1964) have demonstrated with regard to marriages that the gravity model is more accurate than the intervening opportunities one. (And T. Smith [1976] has shown that the gravity model is a better predictor of criminals' target selections. However, the evidence on inter-city migration tends to support the opportunities model [Ritchey, 1976:374].) In addition, we have generally used "maximizing" rather than "satisficing" assumptions in this book. Of course, both models are extreme abstractions, not yet made concrete by real social structures.

[5] One of the *ceteris paribus* assumptions is that individuals' terms of trade (quality of a relation versus its distance-cost) do not differ between suburbanites and city-dwellers.

ANTICIPATIONS AND ADJUSTMENTS

The localizing effects of suburbanism predicted by these three models, particularly the distance-cost model, can be offset by two human habits that befuddle many social science theories: anticipation and adjustment. Most people are aware of the ecological and social attributes of suburbia, including the kinds of people found there and the potential problems of access. Therefore, in moving to or staying in suburbia, they may anticipate certain consequences, and thus seek those effects, avoid them, or cope with them (see Michelson et al., 1973).

One possibility is that these anticipations create or *increase* city-suburban differences in localism. Some have suggested that it is precisely those persons who desire local social life who move to suburbia (for example, Bell, 1959; Fava, 1959). However, while such moves occur, their number is minimal. Residential movers who are interviewed rarely list such considerations as reasons for leaving a place, and only in a minority of cases as significant reasons for picking another place.[6] Far more important are concerns for space, housing, and neighborhood quality. A mirror process, moving to cities to avoid neighbors, may also occur in a few cases. But, in general, self-selection based on a preference for localism probably contributes very little, if at all, to city-suburban differences.

More significant are anticipations and adjustments that mitigate, if not nullify, the effects of suburbanism. There are three general ways in which this can happen.

1. Self-selection: People often decide whether to move, and how far out to move, partly on the basis of their social networks and their abilities to protect those networks. They try to avoid stretching their real or potential networks beyond tolerable distances. What is tolerable depends on individuals' willingness and ability to do without some existing bonds. Research indicates that those who care most about access to people or places stay in or move to the center city. For those who care more about housing values, "the break of social ties of the past represent[s] a price paid for suburban residence" (Clark, 1966: 140). What is tolerable varies even more by individuals' freedom of movement. We have already seen that suburbanites are especially likely to have high incomes. These kinds of self-sorting tend to neutralize the differences in access between city and suburb.

2. People move to where their "significant others" live and encourage such cherished associates to move near them. On a larger scale, such chain migration produces suburban ethnic or occupational enclaves. This, too, mitigates the effects of location.

[6] Butler et al. (1969), Hawley and Zimmer (1971), Lansing and Hendricks (1967), Michelson et al. (1973), Rossi (1956); neither is there evidence for subconscious sociability seeking in the suburban move (Baldassare and Fischer. 1975).

3. As we have mentioned, many suburbanites pay the extra price necessary to maintain a constant radius of interaction. They take longer trips, buy second cars (Clark, 1969: 119), perhaps spend more time on the telephone, and generally extend themselves more than comparable city-dwellers do to sustain the same kind of social networks. Automobile ownership and use are particularly significant modes of adjustment. Suburbanites are much more likely to have automobiles than are city residents, particularly than residents of dense central cities (Kain, 1968).[7] This difference is not explained away by either income or employment status. Especially among low-income people, suburbanites are more likely to have cars than are city residents (Foley, 1975). Organizations and institutions, as well as individuals, adjust to the strains of distance. Governments build highways and subsidize long-distance rail lines (for example, San Francisco's BART system) to accommdoate suburban commuters. Retailers open shopping malls in the suburbs, and businesses bring jobs and services to suburbia (Zimmer, 1975; Kasarda, 1976). These actions also reduce the effects of distance—at least for the affluent. In fact, one of the side effects of these changes has been to increase the problems of access for city residents through, for example, job relocation and deterioration in public transit (Stegman, 1969; Foley, 1975).

Individuals' and institutions' adaptations are plainly visible. In fact, they *demonstrate* the costs of distance. At the same time, however, they mean that city-suburban differences resulting from distance will be minimized. At least, the differences in social networks predicted by the distance-cost model would be greatly reduced. (The effects of individual traits and contexts might persist.)

Yet we may still expect suburbanism to result in at least some localization of social life because of inefficiencies and lags in the adaptive processes. In addition, four sets of suburbanites should be affected more than others. The first three are those who anticipated alterations in their social networks but welcomed them; those who did not anticipate the problems of distance; and those who through necessity or taste traded off those consequences for other benefits such as a large home. William Michelson's study of movers in Toronto is particularly informative about the latter two groups. He found that movers from the city to the suburbs characteristically ignored

[7] Our own data confirm this pattern. In the Detroit *city* census tracts ($N = 128$), distance from the central business district correlated .87 with the proportion of households which had at least one automobile (the statistic was unavailable for suburban tracts). In the national data, we were able to estimate roughly the minimum number of cars in the household (based on how members went to work). This measure correlated .17 with city versus suburban residence (a dichotomy). Controlling for family income reduced it to .12. (In evaluating this statistic and other correlations with city/suburb in the national data, one must keep in mind not only that the suburban measure is a dichotomy, but also that we are comparing very heterogeneous cities—for example, New York and Eugene—to very heterogeneous suburbs—for example, Skokie and Scarsdale.)

or discounted the problem of access in their decisions and anticipations. Over time, access became an increasingly acute source of dissatisfaction for them (Michelson, 1973a: 41–42). Fourth, an important population which shows the effects of distance is composed of people who lack the means to compensate for distance; they cannot pay the higher price to maintain their networks. Dramatic illustrations of this problem appear when authorities put public housing projects in inaccessible suburban locations (for example, Young and Willmott, 1957; Cooper, 1972; Perlman, 1975).

Cultural minority groups, whether based on ethnicity, age, or life-style, ought also to be affected, although in a complex manner. Members of such groups have a narrower selection of possible associates; it is less likely that they can settle for local relations (unless they live in a suburban enclave). Thus, they are either especially likely to pay the higher price necessary to sustain relations with their fellows, *or*, if they cannot pay the price, they are especially likely to be isolated in suburbia, to have fewer associates, or to see them less often.

Summary of Models

We have examined five predictions about the relationship between suburbanism and localism: (1) that suburbanism is *not* associated with localism; (2) that suburbanism leads to a *less* localized social life; (3) that suburbanism is associated with *more* localism, but only because locally oriented people move to the suburbs; (4) that suburbanism is associated with *more* localism because the concentration of locally oriented people influences *other* individuals to be locally oriented; and (5) that suburbanism promotes localism because, above and beyond the previous factors, distance from the urban center increases the costs of extralocal ties.

Testing the Suburban Models

We turn now to the evidence on suburbanism and localism. We will consider both published research and our own analysis of the national and Detroit surveys.[8] Our purpose is to test the five predictions we discussed in the last section.

[8] A more detailed report of our data analysis is presented in Fischer and Jackson (1976). In this chapter, we will summarize some of the findings from that paper. Where there are differences between the statistics reported there and those reported here, they result from efforts to simplify (for example, collapsing tables), or further reanalysis of the data (for example, in the national survey, adding new control variables, and considering the southern as well as non-southern sample).

CITY-SUBURBAN DIFFERENCES

Many studies show that suburbanites are *more* locally-oriented, in a variety of ways, than are city-dwellers. In leisure activities, for example, suburbanites tend to be involved in home pursuits, such as gardening and entertaining, while people living nearer downtown tend more often to use public facilities, such as theaters and museums (Gruenberg, 1974; von Rosenbladt, 1972; Wallden, 1975). Suburbanites also "neighbor" more than city-dwellers do. That is, they more often talk casually with their neighbors, visit one another's homes, become active in neighborhood organizations, and the like.[9] And suburbanites seem to draw their friends from their neighborhoods more often than central-city residents do.[10]

The national and Detroit surveys provide further evidence on neighboring. In the national sample, suburbanites (defined as metropolitan residents living outside the central city) were more likely than city-dwellers to report chatting with neighbors in their own or the neighbor's home ($\gamma = .28$), having dinner or a party together ($\gamma = .20$), attending meetings of a neighborhood group ($\gamma = .26$), and similar local involvement (Fischer and Jackson, 1976: Table 1). In the Detroit sample, men living outside the city of Detroit were more likely to report often visiting their neighbors at home than were men living in Detroit (15 percent to 7 percent; $\gamma = .40$).[11]

The findings on the localization of friendships were more ambiguous in the national sample, where suburbanites were only very slightly more likely to report that most or some of their best friends lived in the neighborhood than were respondents living in the city (36 percent to 33 percent; $\gamma = .08$; chi square $p < .10$). In the Detroit survey, however, men living in the suburbs were more likely to report that two or all three of their best friends lived in the neighborhood than were respondents living in the city (42 percent to 32 percent; $\gamma = .21$). Friendships with men who were *not* seen at work were most affected by suburban residence.[12] The reader should note

[9] Fava (1959), Fischer (1973: 320), Greer (1976), Greer and Kube (1959), Hawley and Zimmer (1971), Lopata (1972), McGahan (1973), Michelson (1973a), Roberts (1973), J. Smith et al. (1954), Sutliff and Crabbe (1963), Tallman (1969), Tallman and Morgner (1970), Tomeh (1964), and Wallden (1975), among others.

[10] Most of the studies cited in note 9 suggest this difference. See also B. Berger (1960), Clark (1966). Gans (1967), and Michelson (1973a), Lopata (1972) reports a contrary finding: City housewives stated more frequently than did suburban housewives that the couples with whom they were friendly were neighbors. However, Lopata herself questions this finding.

[11] "Detroit" includes two municipalities entirely surrounded by the city of Detroit. Here, as in a few other cases, we found that the Detroit city line had some significance above and beyond its distance from the central business district. There seemed to be a noticeable threshold effect (see Fischer and Jackson, 1976: Table 4).

[12] Nonwork friends of suburban men were more likely to live in the same neighborhood as the respondent than nonwork friends of Detroit city men (50 percent to 40 percent; $\gamma = .20$). The differences were not as great for friends seen at work (34 percent to 29 percent; $\gamma = .12$, N.S.).

that *these statistics underestimate the extent to which suburbanites tend to draw their friends from the neighborhood,* because suburbanites have less dense neighborhoods, so that they start with a much smaller pool of men within a fixed distance from which to draw.[13]

The Detroit data reveal another aspect of suburbanites' localized social networks: they got together less frequently with their best friends than did city-dwellers. Suburbanites and urbanites were about equally likely to get together weekly with friends who lived in the neighborhood ($\gamma = .05$, N.S., Detroiters more often), but the city men were more likely to see weekly their friends who lived *elsewhere* in the metropolitan area than suburbanites were ($\gamma = .11$, $p < .10$). Suburbanism seemingly reduced extralocal social contact disproportionately.

Our data corroborate the typical finding that suburbanites' social activities are more local than are those of city-dwellers. We can therefore dismiss the first two of the five propositions listed earlier: that suburbanism is unrelated and that it is negatively related to localism.

INDIVIDUAL DIFFERENCES

Gans' statement that "when one looks at similar populations in city and suburb, their ways of life are remarkably alike" (1967: 288) suggests that the localism of suburbia is best explained in terms of the characteristics of the individuals who live there: their social class, stage in the life-cycle, home ownership, and so on. Individual differences do account for a great deal of suburban localism (as we shall see below). The interesting point, however, is that individual characteristics do not explain all of it.

The inclination of suburbanites to pursue home-oriented leisure activities cannot be completely accounted for by personal differences between suburban and city residents (von Rosenbladt, 1972; Wallden, 1975; Gruenberg, 1974). People who move from city to suburb often change their leisure pursuits in that direction even when they had not intended to do so (Michelson, 1973a; Gans, 1967; Clark, 1966). And suburbanites tend to neighbor more than city-dwellers do even if they are otherwise similar to the city residents (Fava, 1959; Tomeh, 1964; Tallman and Morgner, 1970; Lopata, 1972: 279).

The published research provides relatively little information about what

---

[13] That is, if all men picked their friends without regard for geography, then a *smaller* proportion of suburbanites' friends than of city-dwellers' friends should live within ten minutes of their homes, because there are fewer adult men who *could be* friends within a suburbanite's neighborhood than within a city-dweller's. Yet we found the opposite to be true.

The Detroit results are also underestimates for another reason: they refer to the respondent's three best friends. As we argued in Chapter 3 (and will again in Chapter 9), intimate friends are least likely to be affected by distance. Had the Detroit survey inquired about more friends, we expect that the effect would have been greater.

we call the localization of social networks, drawing friends and associates from the locality. William Michelson's (1973a) study is the most useful. The reader will recall that he interviewed middle-class couples in Toronto before and repeatedly after they moved. He found that couples who moved from the city to the suburbs, particularly to suburban homes, either increased their involvement with neighbors *or* became somewhat isolated. They also tended to increase their at-home activities. Couples who moved to the city maintained or increased their interactions with friends and relatives rather than with neighbors. Since these were, of course, the same people before and after their moves, something about their new locations promoted differences in life-styles.

We examined the association of suburbanism to localism in the national and Detroit surveys, trying to see whether differences remained once individual traits were taken into account. To do so, we turned from cross-tabulation to multiple-regression analysis in order to control for several variables simultaneously. (In the Detroit data, we used two measures of suburbanism: distance from the central business district and zone. *Zone* is a four-part division of the Detroit area: inner city, outer city, inner suburbs—those sharing a border with Detroit—and outer suburbs.[14] We will summarize the details of these and other results, presented in Table 7.1.

We found that after controlling for personal characteristics such as having children, social class, employment status of the women in the household, and years of residence, the differences in neighborhood involvement between suburbanites and city residents narrowed, but suburbanites still neighbored somewhat more. (In the national data, the correlation between suburban residence and a four-item neighboring scale is .17, but the partial correlation—holding constant life-cycle stage, social class, women's employment, religion, and years in the neighborhood—is .12. In the Detroit data, controls reduced the original association even less.)

In the national data, we were also able to control for characteristics of the dwelling unit: the value of the house and whether it was owned or rented (renting was virtually synonymous with apartment residence, $r = .82$). These characteristics explained a small part of the reason suburbanites were more localistic than city-dwellers. Suburbanites were more likely to own expensive houses, and people in expensive houses were more likely to be locally involved. (Controlling for the two variables reduced the partial correlation with neighboring from .12 to .10, and with neighborhood organizational involvement from .10 to .08). There is a problem of interpertation here, however. Are home characteristics like individual traits, in that the correlation they create between suburbanism and localism is explained by self-selection? That is, the kind of people who want to and can buy

---

[14] Although these two measures were highly correlated ($r = .78$), they behaved somewhat differently and interacted somewhat complexly (see Fischer and Jackson [1976]).

TABLE 7.1 Independent and Indirect Effects of Suburbanism on Localism *(National Survey and Detroit Survey)*

NATIONAL SURVEY (N ≅ 2,300)[a]

DEPENDENT VARIABLES

	NEIGHBORING	ORGANIZATIONAL INVOLVEMENT	FRIENDS IN NEIGHBORHOOD
CONTROLS	*Partial Correlations with City/Suburb*		
None (zero-order r)	.17	.15	.05
Individual Traits	.12	.11	.05
. . . and Dwelling Unit	.10	.08	.05
. . . and Contextual Variables	.05	.08	(.03)
	Direct and Indirect Effects of City/Suburb[b]		
INDIRECT THROUGH:			
Presence of Blacks	.02	.00	.01
Neighborhood Growth	.00	.01	.01
Neighborhood Quality	.00	.00	− .01
Neighborhood Activism	.01	.02	.02
Rent/Own	.01	.01	− .00
(Direct)	.06	.08	.03
Sum of Suburb Effects[c]	.10	.12	.06

DETROIT SURVEY (N ≅ 900)

DEPENDENT VARIABLES

	KNOWING NEIGHBORS	PERCENTAGE OF FRIENDS IN NEIGHBORHOOD	FREQUENCY OF "GET TOGETHER"
CONTROLS	*Partial Correlations with Zone and Distance*		
None (zero-order r)			
Zone	.09	.10	(− .02)
Distance to CBD	.12	(.04)	− .03
Individual Traits			
Zone	.09	.11	(− .02)
Distance to CBD	.12	(.06)	(− .06)
. . . and Contextual Variables			
Zone	(− .00)	(.04)	(− .03)
Distance to CBD	(.00)	(− .04)	− .09
	Direct and Indirect Effects of Distance[d]		
INDIRECT THROUGH:			
Median Income	.10	.06	.01
Percent Youth	.03	.08	.08
Zone	− .01	.13	.06
(Direct)	.00	− .22	− .24
Sum of Distance Effects	.12	.05	− .09

[a] Correlations in parantheses are statistically not significant.

129

TABLE 7.1 (Continued)

b For the full regression equations, see Appendix Table 8.1, page 161. Indirect effects were calculated by assuming that city/suburb was causally prior to the contextual variables, and multiplying the correlation between city/suburb and each of the contextual variables with the standardized partial regression coefficient for the contextual variable.

c Discrepancy between total effect and zero-order r is due to indirect effects through individual trait variables, joint effects, and rounding.

d As noted in the text, zone and distance are alternative and colinear measures of suburbanism. Distance is considered prior to zone and to the contextual variables. Each indirect effect is equal to: $(r_{Dc_i})(\beta_{Yc_i})$ where r_{Dc_i} represents the correlation between distance, D, and a given contextual variable, C_i, and β_{Yc_i} represents the standardized partial regression coefficient for that given contextual variable, C_i, in the full regression equation predicting the dependent variable, Y.

VARIABLE DEFINITIONS

National Survey (see also Chapter 8)

DEPENDENT VARIABLES

Neighboring: Four-item scale based on whether respondent's family had talked on street, chatted in home, dined, or otherwise got together with neighbors.

Organizational Involvement: Two-item scale—attended neighborhood meeting or belonged to neighborhood organization.

Friends in Neighborhood: Respondent reported at least "some" friends in the neighborhood.

INDEPENDENT VARIABLES

INDIVIDUAL TRAITS:

Prechildren: Dummy—under 36, without children

Children: Dummy—have one or more children at home

SES of Household: Scale combining family income and head's education

Woman Works: Dummy—woman of household works at least part-time

Religion: Three dummies—Catholic; Jewish; other or Atheist

Length of Residence: Scale of years (approximate log)

DWELLING UNIT:

Rent vs. Own (correlates .82 with apartment vs. house)

Monthly Cost: estimated for home-owners; rent for others

CONTEXTUAL VARIABLES

Presence of Blacks: Scale combining percent black and distance to nearest black neighborhood (latter logged and inverted)

Percent Catholic: Proportion of neighborhood population estimated to be Catholic

Neighborhood Quality: Scale combining
(a) median house value
(b) percent of sound housing
(c) rated physical appearance
N. B.: This correlates .82 with a scale composed of the income and educational levels of residents.

Growth:
(1) *Age of Housing:* years since last new housing built
(2) *Proportion Newcomers:* percent of population which lived elsewhere five years before

Crime: Scale combining rated safety and percent of informants who cite crime as major problem.

Activism: Scale combining informants' rating of social activity level of residents and number of local organizations.

Suburb: Dummy—suburb vs. city (political definition)

Detroit Survey

DEPENDENT VARIABLES

Knowing Neighbors: How much respondent interacts with neighbors, 4-point scale, low to high.

Percent Friends in Neighborhood: Proportion of "best friends," *other than those seen regularly at work,* who live in neighborhood.

Frequency of Contact: Sum of 6-point response scale, for each "best friend," on frequency with which respondent gets together with him, only for those who report three "best friends."

INDEPENDENT VARIABLES

INDIVIDUAL TRAITS

Age

Number of children at home

Whether wife probably works (constructed from indirect indices)

Occupational prestige

Ethno-religiosity (six dummy variables)

Years in neighborhood

CONTEXTUAL VARIABLES

Median income of tract—c. 1960

Proportion of tract population under 18—c. 1960

ZONE: 4-point scale: inner Detroit, outer Detroit, inner suburbs, outer suburbs (see text)

DISTANCE: of tract from central district (to nearest half-mile)

---

houses pick the suburbs to live in and also pick to be locally involved. Or should we understand this localism to be a real, if indirect, effect of suburbanism? Where such houses can be found is, after all, strongly related to suburban location (see note 1). Thus, suburbs, in a sense, provide the houses, which in turn encourage localism. In any case, even after taking dwelling unit into account, suburbanites were still somewhat more localistic than were city-dwellers.

In sum, the slightly greater localism of suburbanites cannot be completely explained by their personal characteristics, as Gans suggests. Something that these people find in suburbia—such as single-family homes or compatible neighbors—also promotes localism. We turn, therefore, to our fourth prediction, that suburban localism is encouraged by the concentration there of locally oriented people who influence others to be locally oriented.

CONTEXTUAL EFFECTS

Since published studies providing evidence on such contextual effects are extremely rare (for example, Gates et al., 1973), we must rely on our own data analysis.

In the national survey data, we were able to create several measures of neighborhood characteristics from census materials NORC obtained and the interviews it conducted with knowledgeable informants about the neighborhoods (Houston and Sudman, 1975). We examined many indicators of the social and ecological features of the neighborhoods and after exploratory analysis settled on the following as a comprehensive but parsimonious list: (1) the physical quality of the neighborhood, (2) the age of the housing, (3) the proportion of residents who had recently arrived, (4) the perceived amount of crime, (5) the extent of residents' involvement in local groups (as reported by informants), (6) the percent of residents who were Catholic, and (7) the proportion and proximity of blacks. (This last measure is partly confounded with suburbanism because it includes, in addition to percent black, the distance from the nearest black neighborhood, which is likely to be toward downtown.)

After controlling for these seven contextual variables (in addition to the previous 11 individual traits), we found that suburbanites neighbored very slightly more than did otherwise comparable city people (partial $r = .05$), that they were a little more involved in local organizations (.08), but were not any more likely to report their friends to be in the neighborhood (.03, N.S.). A little effect of suburbanism alone remains, but not much.

In the Detroit data, we found that respondents were most localistic when they lived in affluent census tracts (those with a high median income for families and unrelated individuals) and in tracts were many of the residents were under 18 years of age. (Both of these variables were highly related to the respondent's distance from the central business district, $r = .61, .65$.) When these two factors were taken into account, along with individual traits, we found that suburban men were no more likely to neighbor or to report a high proportion of neighborhood friends than were city men. However, the tendency of men living far from the central business district to see their friends infrequently became sharper (partial $r = -.09$; see Table 7.1).

From these two analyses, it would seem that contextual variables are the best explanations of the localism of suburbanites. Once they have been taken into account, only a minute direct effect of suburbanism itself—distance from the metropolitan center—remains. That is, the individual traits and contextual effects models most explain suburban localism; the distance-cost model provides additional, but marginal, explanation.

Earlier in the chapter, we pointed out that many of these contextual variables were themselves largely the result of suburbanism (distance from the center city). In this sense, being located on the urban periphery promotes localism *indirectly* because that is where the contexts—detached houses, middle-class residents, and so on—that support local social life are found. We estimated these "indirect effects" in the national data, looking at several ways that suburbanism might indirectly promote localism.

The idea of this procedure is to derive a numerical estimate of the total extent to which suburbanism influenced people to be more localistic, discounting the differences between suburbanites and city-dwellers that result from individual self-selection. To do this, we added the independent, "direct effect" of suburbanism (the differences in localism between suburban and city residents once everything else was held constant, presumably the result of "distance-cost") to the indirect, contextual effects of suburbanism (the differences that result from suburban neighborhoods being contextually different from city neighborhoods and those differences, in turn, promoting localism).[15] This total was real, although modest, in the national data (.10 for neighboring, .12 for organizational involvement, and .06 for reporting friends in the neighborhood). We conducted a similar analysis with the Detroit data to see how distance was related to localism both directly and indirectly (through the peripheral location of well-to-do people, families with children, and political zones).[16] We obtained "total effects," exclusive of individual traits, roughly equal to those in the national survey (.12 for neighboring; .05 for proportion of friends in the neighborhood; and —.09 for frequency of contact with nonwork friends—see Table 7.1). In sum, the direct plus indirect association of suburbanism with localism is real and consistent, although small. Thus predictions 4 (contextual effects) and 5 (distance-cost) are both partly true.

When we add our findings to those of prior investigators, we draw the conclusion that suburbanism—individual traits held constant—is related, although slightly, to localism in the general population. The small size of the associations, direct or otherwise, must be interpreted in light of our earlier discussion on "anticipations and adjustments": that is, the direct spatial and the indirect contextual effects of suburbanism can be seen both as "inefficiencies" in people's abilities to overcome distance, and as irreducible spatial costs and constraints. In our discussion of anticipations and adjustments, we also suggested that the consequences of distance and cost should be more acute and more visible in certain populations. We turn next to that prediction.

[15] The contextual variables were: whether the respondent rented or owned a home; the level of neighborhood involvement (as rated by informants); neighborhood physical quality; neighborhood growth; and the presence of blacks. The last variable was included largely because one of its components, proximity to nearest black neighborhood, is a close proxy to suburbanism. (It correlates —.34 with city/suburb; the total presence scale correlates —.32 with city/suburb.) Variable definitions can be found in Table 7.1.

[16] "Zone" was created as an alternative measure of suburbanism. As we pointed out earlier, it is highly colinear and interacts complexly with distance. Nevertheless, it can be seen as dependent on distance, since political bounds are based on geographic contiguity. Calculating the indirect effect of distance through zone also helps avoid the confusion in interpreting the significant and oppositely signed regression coefficients of zone and distance when entered together in a regression equation (.16 and —.22 for friends in the neighborhood; .08 and —.24 for frequency; Fischer and Jackson, 1976: Table 5).

SPECIAL GROUPS

The research literature indicates, first, that suburbanism affects the sexes differently. Wives are more likely to be and to feel separated from relatives and friends than are their husbands. Usually, wives can compensate for this loss by becoming socially involved with their neighbors, but when their neighbors are not sufficiently compatible, they must remain isolated.[17] With generally less access to cars and more responsibilities in the home, women more often suffer the stress of distance. Gans concludes: "If there is malaise in Levittown, it is female but not suburban" (1967: 22). We suggest that it is both female *and* suburban.[18]

The problems women face in maintaining satisfying social networks in the suburbs are compounded when the women also fall into another category identified in the published studies: immobile cultural minorities. These are sets of people with special needs and with limitations on their mobility. Adolescents, the elderly, single people, ethnic minorities, and the culturally sophisticated tend to be more isolated in the suburbs than their neighbors are or than are their kind in cities (Gans, 1967; Tomeh, 1964; Abu-Lughod and Foley, 1960). To quote Gans once again: "The smallness and homogeneity of the population made it difficult for the culturally and socially deviant [that is, the different] to find companions. Levittown benefitted the majority but punished a minority with exlusion, what Whyte called the 'misery of the deviate' " (1967: 239).

The elderly provide a case in point. Because of physical and financial problems, they are relatively immobile, and therefore suffer more acutely from problems of access than do younger people (Foley, 1975). A study of the elderly conducted in San Antonio, Texas, found that the farther from the center they lived, the fewer friends they reported, the less socially active and the lonelier they were (Carp, 1975; see also Bourg, 1975; Cantor, 1975).

These patterns of findings are best explained by distance and its depressive effects on access to population. Michelson's (1973a) study revealed this problem sharply, leading him to recommend policies to alleviate sub-

---

[17] Michelson (1973a: 33 ff.), Berger (1960), Clark (1966), Gans (1967), Fava (1975: 20–23), Tallman (1969), Gillespie (1971), Abu-Tughod and Foley (1960: 186).

[18] The national survey allowed us to compare men and women, and it yielded unexpected findings: males showed more city-suburb differences than did women, particularly on the question about the proportion of friends reported to be living in the neighborhood ($\gamma = .24$ for males, .01 for females; non-southern sample). However, these findings are probably not representative of sex differences in the general population because of the sampling procedure used by NORC. They interviewed households, accepting either husbands or wives as spokespersons for the household. Consequently, they interviewed three times as many women as men, and the men they did encounter were an unusual sample, probably disproportionately retirees. (They were, for instance, noticeably older than the women; $\gamma = .13$.)

urban women's "vulnerability," "isolation," "boredom," and lack of extra-residential activities, which are currently only partly relieved by intensified neighboring.

We examined both the national and Detroit surveys for evidence that suburbanism was differentially related to localism for certain populations, particularly groups that are relatively less able to overcome the constraints of distance.[19] First, we looked at class differences. We initially assumed that people of lesser means would most evidence the localization associated with suburban residence. We found just the opposite, that city-suburban differences in localism tended to be greater among those of *higher* status. Further examination of the national survey suggested that this pattern reflected the connection between suburban life and social class: the better-educated suburbanites differed much more sharply from the better-educated city-dwellers in both personal characteristics (having a house, having children, or being a housewife) and neighborhood features (economic and racial homogeneity) than the less-educated suburbanites differed from the less-educated city dwellers. It would seem that the better-educated are more easily able to move between city and suburban areas to match their own needs. When we controlled for personal and neighborhood characteristics, the unexpected class differences were eliminated, leaving a small difference for all educational groups—suburbanites slightly more localistic.

We also looked at constraints on travel in other ways. The elderly are relatively immobile. In the national sample (three-fourths female), living in the suburbs and having a local social life went together most consistently among the elderly. In the Detroit sample (all male) also, the oldest respondents (50–64) exhibited the greatest city-suburban contrast, but this was of a different kind: older men living far from the center were not especially likely to neighbor, but were especially likely to be isolated.[20]

Home-owners are more committed to and spend more time around their homes than do apartment-dwellers (Michelson, 1973b). In the national survey, city-suburban differences in localism among the owners were sharper than among the renters.

Children also impede travel, and so we thought that respondents with young children would be most affected by suburbanism. As in the analysis of class, the opposite of our expectation was true. The explanation for this unanticipated finding appears to be that children are so much a force for involving people in the neighborhood (see Chapter 8) that virtually *all* young families are relatively involved locally, regardless of their residence.

---

[19] The following discussion summarizes pp. 292–93, 300–301—Fischer and Jackson (1976).

[20] Distance slightly reduced neighboring (partial r after all controls $= -.06$, N.S.), the proportion of friends in the neighborhood (partial $r = -.20$), and frequency of contact with friends (partial $r = -.20$).

So, it is instead among the childless that place makes a difference and that one can see the localizing consequences of suburbia.[21]

People are also more vulnerable to the constraints of distance when they lack alternative sources of social relations (pools of potential associates). Kinship and the workplace are two such important sources of ties, and they are, as we argued in Chapter 3, relatively independent of locality. The less the extent of people's involvements in kin- or work-based networks, the more their relations are influenced by suburbanism, because the more they depend on residence-related connections. We found evidence to support this hypothesis. In the national sample, among families that did *not* see their kin often, the suburbanites were more locally involved than were the city-dwellers; there was a smaller city-suburban difference among families that did see their kin often. Similarly, suburban families *without* working wives were slightly more localistic than city families without working wives; there was no city-suburban difference among families in which the woman worked. We noted earlier, with respect to the Detroit survey, that the friends of suburban men were more likely to live in his neighborhood than were the friends of city men—when those friends were *not* seen at work ($\gamma = .20$); for friends seen at work, the city or suburban residence of the respondent was less important ($\gamma = .12$, N.S.)

Although the effects of suburbanism on social life are statistically small, they form a roughly consistent pattern: a general tendency toward localism, accentuated among people who are most spatially constrained or oriented. Together with the findings reported in earlier studies, they support the argument that, in spite of anticipations and adjustments, suburbanism itself —distance from the metropolitan center—promotes or reinforces localism.

Conclusion

We repeatedly found in our data, as other researchers found in theirs, that the differences in localism between suburbanites and city-dwellers, both before and after controls, are real but usually quite small. The differences seem especially small when compared to factors such as having children or length of residence (see Chapter 8). However, the size of the associations belies their substantive significance.

First, we are interested in testing a particular theory, not in accounting for some large proportion of variance. It is hardly surprising that individual differences in behavior are more effectively explained by individual

---

[21] In the national sample, among city-dwellers, having young children discriminated those who neighbored highly from those who did not: partial $\beta = .126$, $p = .015$; among suburban dwellers, having children did not discriminate: partial $\beta = .064$, N.S. (A similar difference appeared in the Detroit survey). That is, suburbanites tended to neighbor, with or without children; city-dwellers neighbored more when they had children.

differences in personal and enduring characteristics, such as sex, race, and number of children, than they are by enviromental variables. Our purpose, however, is not to explain localism but to test a theory linking localism to suburbanism. Given that end, the issue is not size of associations but pattern of associations.[22] In terms of that standard, our findings lend credence to the distance-cost hypothesis.

Second, an ecological variable such as distance affects groups of people rather than isolated individuals. While it may be that each suburban individual becomes more localistic only to a minute degree because of his or her location, the suburban neighborhood as a whole is composed of a set of individuals all influenced the same way. The concentration of such small effects can have greater consequences at the aggregate level.[23] These gathered-together individuals will reinforce each other's localistic tendencies and act collectively in localistic ways: for example, by forming neighborhood associations or resisting low-income housing.

Third, and most important, the consequences of a structural variable such as geographic location cannot be evaluated simply in terms of a single determinative effect on behavior. A structural variable has indirect effects by being part of the "givens" in a situation. Other factors which influence behavior more directly develop in response to the structural givens. In the case of distance from city centers, these other factors include the availability of land, its costs, and the kind of housing that is built on it (see earlier discussion). Furthermore, a structural variable, because it is not a mechanical "force" but part of a matrix of opportunities and constraints, does not necessarily lead to a single behavior; rather, it leads to a set of behavioral options. In this case, the options include, besides localism, spending more time and resources on maintaining social networks and resigning oneself to solitary activities. Such actions as driving and telephoning in order to mitigate or nullify structural constraints are available to many, if not most, people in this society. They have sufficient freedom of choice and resources to anticipate and adjust to ecological constraints. This means that one observes the consequences of structural variables mostly in indirect fashion. The distance-cost of suburbanization is revealed not so much by the loss of customers for center-city business as by the enterprises' moves to the suburbs (for example, suburban shopping malls, sports complexes); not so much by the isolation of housewives as by the purchase of a second car.

Yet, these alternative options are not equally available to all. Even for

---

22 *Size* of statistical associations may be important for inductive explanations of variables (and for some policy issues). The *pattern* of associations is critical for evaluating theories.

23 This phenomon is the other side of the "ecological fallacy" coin. While ecological correlations underestimate individual variability, individual correlations can underestimate aggregate consequences.

those to whom they are available, they are not completely efficient. And so, one finds that suburban residence does indeed lead some individuals to become slightly more locally oriented than they would otherwise be, and it leaves others somewhat isolated—in both cases, a contracting of social ties.

The difference between city-dwellers and suburbanites in localism is partly explained by individual traits. People with certain characteristics— education, affluence, being or having a housewife, having children to rear— move to the suburbs; these are characteristics that encourage local involvement. The reason these people move to the suburbs is largely that the suburbs provide certain ecological and contextual features—spacious housing, open space, and other white, middle-class families as neighbors—that the movers seek; these features of suburbia encourage localism above and beyond the effect of the individual characteristics. Finally, the very nature of the suburb as an outlying part of the metropolis contributes, at least marginally and for at least some groups, to localized social ties and interests.

These effects are, we repeat, small. However, we should not allow small individual differences to mislead us about potentially significant community effects. As American society continues to suburbanize, a larger proportion of its population shifts from a city to suburban location and social context. Slight as the effects might be for each person, the balance moves increasingly, for better or worse, from urban ways of life to suburban ones. That shift in population produces, for example, structural changes which make it easier to become a suburbanite and more difficult to remain in the center: highway construction, dispersal of jobs and businesses, decline of cheap mass transit, and so on, all accelerate the shift.

Scott Greer (1972: 63) has observed that "the culture of the suburb is remarkably similar to that of the country towns in an earlier America." In localism, as well as in other ways, small towns and suburbs are similar. In that sense, the increasing suburbanization of America, may mean, in part, the deurbanization of America.

8. Attachment to Place*

Kathleen Gerson
C. Ann Stueve
Claude S. Fischer

WHAT DOES IT MEAN to be "attached" to one's place of residence? What kinds of people are most likely to be attached and what kinds of places are most conducive to attachment? These questions are of interest to sociologists and policy-makers alike, largely because of worry about the consequences of *not* being socially and psychologically committed to a place. The lack of attachment is thought to represent a "loss of community," to threaten individuals with alienation and neighborhoods with disorganization. In the next chapter we will directly consider the *consequences* of being locally involved or not. In this chapter, we are concerned with the questions that must be asked first about the nature and causes of attachment.

While the specific definition of "attachment" or "local involvement" varies from one investigator to another, we will proceed with the general understanding that attachment to place refers to *individuals' commitments to their neighborhoods and neighbors.* This commitment takes two general forms: *social involvement* and *subjective feeling.* In this chapter, we argue, on the basis of both published research and our own analysis, that (1) attachment to place is not a unitary dimension but, instead, social involvement in and subjective feelings toward a place can take several forms; and (2) people choose to become attached to places in different ways, depending on their personal needs, opportunities, and resources, and on the characteristics of the homes and places in which they live.

* This chapter is a revision of Stueve, Gerson, and Fischer, "The structure and determinants of attachment to place," presented to the American Sociological Association, in San Francisco, August 1975; available as Working Paper No. 225, Institute of Urban and Regional Development, Berkeley.

We will make these abstract propositions more concrete when we turn to the evidence on attachment. Before doing that, however, we must place these arguments within their appropriate context, a theoretical controversy concerning the nature and sources of attachment to place. This debate is over how social networks (and their psychic concomitants) come to be "rooted" in a location—"localism," in the language of the previous chapter—and what happens if they are not.

Perspectives on Attachment to Place

Opinions about the relationship between people and their places fall along a continuum from theories that posit internal, psychic sources of attachment to those that find the source of attachment in social structure. At one extreme, *psychological approaches* posit inherent needs for local ties. There are a few variations among these approaches; for example, ethological analyses hold that attachment to place is rooted in a "territorial instinct" (Ardrey, 1967; van den Berghe, 1974; for critiques, see Martin, 1972; Montagu, 1973). Cognitive approaches state that a sense of place is necessary to maintain psychological stability (for example, Nisbet, 1969). They argue that place is a reference point from which to view the world and a basic source of identity. Consequently, individual well-being depends upon a sense of being rooted to a place. Finally, learning or associational models focus upon the processes by which people come to cherish places. People come to value a physical location as a result of the experiences they associate with it (for example, Tuan, 1974).

Sociological analyses argue that attachment to place is founded on the type of social relations individuals have in a particular neighborhood or town. Classical community theorists, for example, focused upon the material interdependence of individuals in a local area (see discussion in next chapter and in Hunter, 1975). They saw communal bonds as arising out of local relations such as employment, recreation, and consumption, as well as casual interaction. In turn, these bonds provide the foundation for psychological identification. Contemporary analysts (Suttles, 1972; also Heberle, 1960; Leeds, 1973) see the locality, not as a "crescive" (emergent) and "primordial" social unit that arises naturally out of social intercourse, but as a creation, almost an imposition, of the larger society. Geographic areas provide convenient units of organization for classifying people, collecting and dispensing resources, and pursuing collective goals. According to this view, attachment to place fundamentally involves an instrumental membership in a local unit. There is nothing necessarily communal or psychologically important about place. Presumably, as non-spatial dimensions of social organization (for example, occupation or political persuasion) become efficient organizing principles, place decreases in importance relative to "non-place communities" (Webber, 1970)—without any necessary loss of services or communal bonds and without any necessary psychic costs to the individual.

According to an *economic perspective,* attachment to place is understood in terms of factors like housing costs (for example, W. Clark, 1976). Usually, it is seen as the product of an implicit calculation of costs and benefits. In these calculations, people compare the features of their residences to those of alternative residences (see Wolpert, 1965), contrasting, for example, space and convenience, but also the social and psychic rewards associated with a place (such as the glow of fond memories). People decide accordingly to move or to stay, and if to stay, how much to invest themselves in their neighborhoods.

These perspectives differ in the kinds of factors—psychological, social, or economic—that they emphasize. Explanations of attachment to place also vary in terms of their logical structure. A few theories are essentially *functional* explanations. They argue, for example, that because local attachment satisfies certain social or psychic needs, people suffer without it. Second, there are *mechanistic causal* models. These might argue, for example, that the more time people spend in a place, the more familiar with and attached to it they become. Third, *decision-making* models interpret attachment as an outcome of choice. In these models, people select their places and choose whether and how to be attached to them on the basis of relative costs and rewards. (This fits well, of course, with an economic perspective.) This last approach is consistent with our view that social networks should be understood as the results of individual choices made under constraints.

Our own model of attachment to place is based on the economic-decision-making approach but emphasizes more strongly the consequences of *structural alternatives.* People do not choose among endless possibilities; social and economic constraints define and limit the alternatives that are available to them. Poverty, for example, obviously restricts the range of neighborhoods and the quality of housing from which families can choose. Furthermore, because of their social positions, not everyone needs the same kind or degree of involvement; what is a rewarding tie for one may be a costly tie for another. And certainly not everyone has the resources to obtain the ties he desires. The immobile elderly and young mothers, for example, are more often constrained to the local area and therefore more likely to need and want local ties. For young singles, on the other hand, too much involvement may be a cost, not a benefit, precluding their chances to take advantage of extralocal opportunities. In this chapter, we consider a few choices: whether to stay in a neighborhood or leave, and, if to stay, how deeply to plant one's roots. The constraints are posed by resources (or their lack), family needs, and other structural circumstances.

People's socioeconomic positions, the stages of life they are in, and the types of neighborhood they live in all structure their decisions. First, socioeconomic positions and stage in the family cycle affect how dependent people are on the local area and their opportunities for local or extralocal involvement. Second, both these characteristics sort families into different locations by influencing where they want to live and where they are able to live. After people move to a location, features of the local environment come into play. Some neighborhoods foster more involvement than others. Thus, as we pointed out in the preceding chapter, the connection between specific places and extent of attachment to them is in part the result of contextual factors (such as characteristics of neighbors) and in part a result of their ecological features (such as distance from the center).

All these factors influence satisfaction with the neighborhood and the desire to stay or leave, in part by influencing local ties. These subjective feelings about a place, or "affective attachment," are a consequence of behavioral attachment, the pleasurable or distasteful characteristics of the environment, and people's abilities to select the kinds of places where they want to live.

Forms of Attachment to Place

The first issue these perspectives lead us to consider is the constitution of attachment to place. In particular, to what extent is there a single global dimension on which people can be ordered according to their degree of local involvement? Or, is there instead a multiplicity of independent ways people can be attached? Another way of posing the same question is: To what extent are people who are attached to their locations in one specific way likely to be connected in other ways as well? Certain approaches, particularly psychological ones which view attachment as a fundamental human relation or need, imply that attachment is holistic. Others, particularly economic and decision-making perspectives, imply that there are many forms of attachment, as people pick and choose the relations and activities they want and can afford. Professional people who own their own homes, for example, may join a neighborhood organization but not spare any time to kibitz over the back fence; young mothers who are home all day may see their neighbors often but not belong to any local organizations.

Although many studies have been conducted on neighborhood involvement, few have explored, even tangentially, the extent to which there are multiple forms of attachment.[1] One notable exception is a survey conducted in Chicago by Albert Hunter (1974), who found that people who

[1] Most adopt a single measure of attachment; some combine various indicators into a single scale; only a few use multiple indicators or distinguish local social ties from feelings about localities (see, especially, Kasarda and Janowitz, 1974).

reported "feeling attached" to their neighborhoods often did not particularly like their neighborhoods, and vice-versa. The longer people had lived in an area, the more likely they were to report feeling attached, even though they were no more likely to evaluate the area positively. We used the national survey to pursue this issue in a more comprehensive way.

Drawing upon the many questions NORC used to probe respondents' involvements in their neighborhoods, we constructed seven measures of neighborhood attachment (the details are presented in the Appendix). These are:

1. *Institutional Ties*—the extent to which the respondent's family was formally involved in the neighborhood through church, school, or work
2. *Sociable Neighboring*—a scale measuring the degree to which members of the respondent's family talked, dined, and spent leisure time with neighbors
3. *Organizational Involvement*—membership and activity in a neighborhood organization
4. *Kin in Neighborhood*—whether various relatives lived in the neighborhood
5. *Friends in Neighborhood*—the presence of at least some of the respondent's friends in the neighborhood
6. *Happy with Neighborhood*—how happy the respondent was with the neighborhood
7. *Unhappy to Leave*—how unhappy the respondent would be if he or she had to move

We crosstabulated these measures, each against the others, to see whether people who were attached in one way were likely to be attached in other ways as well. They were, but not to a great extent. Table 8.1 shows generally low associations among the attachment measures; that is, one kind of tie did not necessarily imply another. In sum, *attachment to place was not unitary but multidimensional.*

In spite of the generally low associations among the measures, there is some clustering. People who reported being happy with their neighborhoods were largely the same ones who said they would be unhappy to leave ($\gamma = .67$). There was also a strong tendency for respondents who neighbored a good deal to be active in local organizations ($\gamma = .50$), and for those attached in either of these ways to report some friends in the neighborhood ($\gamma = .39$ for both). The cluster—local friends, neighboring, and organizational involvement—suggests that people who maintained voluntary commitments of one type tended to have other such involvements as well. Although respondents who had kin nearby tended to also have friends nearby ($\gamma = .23$), there were notable differences between those with local kin and those with local friends. People with relatives in the neighborhood were hardly different in other kinds of attachment from

TABLE 8.1 Associations Among Attachment Measures (*Gammas*)[a]

	INSTITU-TIONAL	SOCIA-BLE	ORGANI-ZATIONAL	KIN	FRIENDS	HAPPY	UNHAPPY
Institutional Ties	1.	.17	.33	.09	.12	.09	.04
Sociable							
Neighboring		1.	.50	.01	.39	.22	.12
Organizational							
Involvement			1.	.07	.39	.24	.15
Kin in							
Neighborhood				1.	.23	.05	.07
Friends in							
Neighborhood					1.	.30	.29
Happy with							
Neighborhood						1.	.67
Unhappy to Leave							1.

[a] Measures explained in Appendix.

those without local kin, while those with friends were more attached in other ways than were those without local friends. Having kin nearby seemed to do little to root people in other ways; friends, however, were an important link to general neighborhood attachment, either promoting other local ties, or resulting from them, or both.

By examining these results, as well as considering the manifest content of each measure, we can identify four forms of attachment, one involving feelings and the others, social ties:

1. *Institutional Ties*—as described above
2. *Social Activity*—neighboring and organizational involvement
3. *Local Intimates*—having kin and/or friends in the neighborhood [2]
4. *Affective Attachment*—feelings about the place

In sum, attachment to a place appears to be multidimensional. We cannot conclude that one local attachment necessarily implies another. There are multiple ways in which families use neighborhoods, ranging from purely utilitarian concerns to sources of emotional support, and these forms are relatively independent. In particular, feelings about a place are not necessarily contingent upon behavioral involvement. The multiplicity of ties and lack of overwhelming "clustering" recalls Janowitz's description of the modern neighborhood as a "community of limited liability"— people are involved in specific and limited ways.[3]

[2] Having friends in the neighborhood was placed in this category even though it correlated more highly with the social activity items, because of its *conceptual* similarity to having local kin. Later results (see Appendix Table 8.1) show that the types of people who had local friends were more similar to those with neighborhood kin than they were to people who neighbored.

[3] We reproduced Table 8.1 within five levels of family life-cycle stage, four levels of family income, and four levels of location (city apartment, city house, suburban

Who Is Socially Attached?

Having identified separable forms of attachment to place, we next ask: What kinds of people are most likely to be attached in these various ways and what kinds of places are most likely to foster such attachments? In this section, we focus on social involvements: institutional ties, local social activity, and the presence of local intimates. In the next section, we examine affective attachment.

Many previous studies have dealt with this question, but almost all have been seriously limited. Most did not employ multiple measures of attachment (with the notable exception of Kasarda and Janowitz, 1974), have been limited in scope, have examined few if any attributes of the places themselves, and have not systematically examined the concurrent effects of family characteristics.[4] Although our discussion draws upon these studies, we rely primarily on our own analysis of the national survey. We have tried to fill in the gaps in the existing research by using several measures of attachment and by assessing the independent effects of a wide

apartment, and suburban house). Our major finding (results not shown here) is that the associations among neighboring, organizational involvement, and local friendships—the major "cluster" described earlier—are consistent across all levels of family stage, class, and location. We think this is so because social ties are equally important to everyone and this common need minimizes differences in the structure of attachment across families that may vary in other respects. There were, however, some differences worth noting. Older families had less strongly clustered attachments; for them, each measure was more autonomous of the others than was true for younger families. In addition, higher-income families were more consistently high or low (that is, more correlated) in their neighboring, organizational involvement, local friendships, and institutional ties. It is not clear whether these variations by age and income resulted from variations in opportunities for involvement, in constraints, or preferences. For example, were poorer families less consistent in their involvement because they preferred mixed patterns, or because they had to make trade-offs such that they could be involved only one way or another, or because their neighborhoods provided fewer opportunities for multiple involvements? Having kin in the neighborhood was more likely to be associated with other kinds of ties among low-income families. For them, local kin was highly associated with having friends in the locality ($\gamma = .39$), perhaps because the kin and friends were the same people. This was less likely to be the case among high-income families ($\gamma = .10$). Many ethnographic studies (Bott, 1971; Young and Wilmott, 1957; Gans 1962b) have similarly found more kin-centeredness in the lower classes. Finally, among families living in suburban homes, institutional ties and local kin were relatively unrelated to other attachment dimensions, suggesting that suburban residence promoted informal participation even in the absence of local kin and formal ties (see Chapter 7).

[4] More specifically: (1) few individual-level variables have been employed as predictors, especially in multivariate analyses; (2) rarely have more than one or two attributes of a place, if any at all, been used as predictors; (3) the simultaneous analysis of both individual and place variables is extremely unusual (Kasarda and Janowitz, 1974; Gates et al., 1973, being exceptions); (4) it is rare for more than one dimension of attachment to appear as a dependent variable (Kasarda and Janowitz, 1974, being a notable exception here); and (5) studies have usually been restricted to single neighborhoods or cities. Our analysis avoids all these shortcomings.

variety of individual and place characteristics. For each characteristic of a person—life stage, class, and so on—and each neighborhood feature— quality of the housing and the like—we estimated how people or places who differed on *that trait alone* but were otherwise comparable differed in attachment. (We used multiple-regression analysis; the basic results are summarized in Appendix Table 8.1.) [5]

Before discussing how different people are socially attached to their neighborhoods, we note that the overall results confirm our earlier finding that attachment to place is multidimensional. The kinds of people (and places) that were highly attached in one way were not likely to be attached in other ways. In particular, families of higher social status, all else held constant, tended to engage in a variety of social activities with their neighbors (partial $\beta = .17$), but not to report having local friends $(- .10)$ or kin $(-.06)$. Families with children also neighbored $(.13)$, yet they would not have been especially sad to leave the neighborhood $(-.16)$. Thus, different types of families and families living in different types of places were attached in different ways. [6]

TYPES OF PEOPLE AND TYPES OF TIES

How do each of the following characteristics of people's families affect the ways and the extent to which they are socially involved in their neighborhoods: life-cycle stage, whether the woman of the household works, social class, and length of residence?

[5] Drawing on the research literature and our own "structured choices" perspective, we sought to formulate a comprehensive list of possible correlates for the forms of local involvement identified earlier. In developing measures of places, we selected a wide variety of indices from both the census and neighborhood informant files, factor-analyzed them within previously specified domains (for example, class composition, physical attributes), and then reduced the data by creating scales and eliminating colinear items. We ran preliminary regression analyses in order to eliminate variables that were insignificant or redundant. In assessing the correlates of affective attachment, we included behavioral forms of involvement as well as individual variables. Appendix Table 8.1 summarizes the results of our final regressions. The equations reported there tend to have relatively low explained variances $R^2s \cong .13$). We attribute this largely to the categorical and skewed nature of some of the dependent variables, and in a couple of cases to low reliability. We do not think, however, that these defects distorted the general *pattern* of the results, but only reduced their size.

[6] Similarly, we note that the relative importace of personal and place variables differs by type of attachment. Family variables predominate in predicting local ties, accounting for about 75 percent of the explained variance (data not shown). However, house and neighborhood variables are slightly more important than individual traits in predicting affective attachment. Local involvements, while significant predictors of affect, are not very substantial ones (adding about one-third of the explained variance). One interpretation of these findings is that individual attributes and local involvement are less intrinsic to affective attachment than are attributes of the house and place. Perhaps people within a neighborhood involve themselves socially to varying degrees in accord with their personal traits, but their satisfaction with the neighborhood and their preferences for staying or leaving are determined more by the physical place itself than by their social relations in it.

Life-Cycle Stage. We saw in Chapter 5 that people's life-cycle positions shape their social networks. Life-cycle position also shapes social connections to the neighborhood. Being married, and especially having children, influences both people's needs for local involvement and their opportunities to achieve that involvement. Children, for example, connect their parents to the neighborhood in a variety of ways: they demand supervision (which means being with them in the local area), promote informal contact with residents through the children's friends, generate parental interest in the neighborhood and membership in community organizations (Janowitz, 1967; Kasarda and Janowitz, 1974; Gates et al., 1973; L. Long, 1972). And at the same time, family commitments tend to impede the maintenance of extralocal relations. Family characteristics also influence the kinds of places in which people will live, by affecting their needs for space and the local facilities they require. Birth of the first child, for example, often prompts people to move from rented apartments to mortgaged homes (Rossi, 1956; Simmons, 1968).

Analysis of the national survey supports the findings of previous studies on the importance of life-cycle positions to local attachment. Families with children were most strongly connected to the neighborhood—to local institutions (partial $\beta = .35$), local kin (.18), and in every other way. Among respondents without children, young people were more likely to have kin and friends nearby (.13 and .08). Older people whose children had left home or who never had children tended to be relatively unconnected to their neighborhoods (holding constant length of residence and other family and neighborhood characteristics). Children do open new avenues of involvement in the locality and effectively close off other opportunities outside it.

Women's Employment. Wives who are not employed outside the home link themselves and their families to the neighborhood more closely than do working women. They have more time to develop local ties, and they lack the workplace as an alternative setting in which to interact casually and build intimate relations (Michelson, 1973a; Gates et al., 1973; Fellin and Litwak, 1963). Working and nonworking women differ also in their housing needs and preferences. The former, for example, are more willing to sacrifice spacious suburban houses for the relatively cramped but convenient quarters near the city center which allow them to pursue a cosmopolitan life-style (see, for example, Michelson, 1973a, 1973b).

In the national survey, we found that families in which the women worked tended to be a little less locally involved than were others. (Institutional ties were an exception, because women who worked in the neighborhood had a local tie, by definition.) As noted in Chapter 3, workplaces constitute alternative contexts for social involvement, both providing opportunities for extralocal ties and reducing opportunities for local encounters.

Social Class. The socioeconomic position of a family appears to affect local involvement in complex ways. Suzanne Keller (1968) has argued that the life-styles of the middle and upper classes seem to foster local voluntary activities such as *casual* neighboring and participation in local organizations. At the same time, higher-status people may have less *intense* relations with their neighbors, instead drawing their intimate ties from outside the locality. Lower-status groups are less likely to enjoy easy access to areas outside the immediate neighborhood and, as a result, may be more dependent on the locality for a few intimate ties. Yet lower-status people may be less involved casually with most of their (largely low-income) neighbors because of mutual suspicion and distrust arising from the insecurities of lower-class life (see, for example, Suttles, 1968; Zehner and Chapin, 1974).

Our findings are consistent with Keller's analysis. Families of higher social class, compared to those of lower status, tended to participate in local organizations (partial $\beta = .16$) and to neighbor (.17), but they were less likely to have kin or friends in the neighborhood ($-.06$, $-.10$). People of higher status seem able to segregate their social lives, living apart from intimates while being active in a casual way with neighbors.

Length of Residence. Prior research has clearly shown that the longer someone lives in a neighborhood, the more involved he or she is (see especially, Kasarda and Janowitz, 1974; also, Gates et al., 1973; Smith et al., 1954).[7] Yet, we cannot simply conclude that residing in a neighborhood a long time causes involvement there. No doubt, time in a place provides greater chances to meet people, develop friendships, and join organizations. However, length of residence can be a *result* of local involvement: the more involved people are, the more reluctant they are and the more difficult it is for them to leave. Since virtually all existing research (ours included) is cross-sectional these two processes cannot be disentangled.[8]

We found that, even after holding constant many other characteristics of people and neighborhoods, the longer respondents had lived in a place, the more involved they were (from a partial $\beta = .07$ for neighboring to a .18 for friends in the neighborhood). All else held equal, time increases the rewards for staying and the costs of leaving.[9]

---

[7] Hunter (1975) reports a noteworthy exception. He found, in a neighborhood that was being "upgraded" by incoming young professionals, that length of residence was (non-significantly) negatively related to local involvement.

[8] Cross-sectional analysis has a bias that increases the apparent influence of length of residence. Pople who are unattached to a neighborhood are likely to leave it and, instead of appearing an unattached, *long-term* residents in the old neighborhood, they will appear as unattached, *recent* arrivals in another neighborhood.

[9] There is little in the way of religious or ethnic differences reported in previous survey studies of local attachment, and we found few in our analysis. (Our sample in this analysis is all white.) Catholics and Jews tended to be slightly more involved than Protestants or those who reported no religion. Catholics were particularly prone (all else equal) to have kin nearby (partial $\beta = .14$). This may reflect either the desire to live in an ethnic neighborhood or the inability to leave it.

Summary.   Stage in the life-cycle, social class, length of residence in the neighborhood and women's employment each independently influences the extent to which people are socially involved in their locales. These findings may be best understood in terms of people's incentives for involvement (for example, having children in the schools), their opportunities for involvement (for example, lengthy residence), and constraints on their alternatives (for example, limited resources for going beyond the local area).

TYPES OF PLACES AND TYPES OF TIES

Personal and family characteristics also affect people's local involvements by directing their selection of homes and neighborhoods. Where people live is a result of their needs, tastes, and budgets.[10] Growing families seek large dwelling units, usually detached houses; young singles or marrieds without children move toward the "bright lights"; and, of course, people can live only where they can afford to. These simple facts have serious implications for the study of local attachment, and particularly for understanding how features of *places* affect local ties. Places differ in the degree to which their residents are involved, in part because of *self-selection*—that is, because of the types of people who choose to live in them. In addition, some differences between places are are results of *social context*—that is, due to the influences of the kinds of people immediately around each resident. And finally, differences in attachment may be the result of *ecological* features of places, such as housing stock, or access to other areas. (These distinctions are related to the suburban localism models presented in Chapter 7.) By statistically controlling for characteristics of the household, we can rule out most of the differences in attachment that result from self-selection. This allows us to concentrate on the contextual and ecological aspects of places which affect attachment. The question then becomes: Once people have sorted themselves into different neighborhoods, how do features of the neighborhood influence local involvement?

The Home.   For a number of reasons, people who live in houses are more likely to be locally attached than those who live in apartments. First, people who want a home- and neighborhood-oriented life-style tend to select houses. Second, home ownership (which is virtually synonymous with house residence in America) implies greater investment in the locality (Michelson, 1973b; Bradburn et al., 1970; Tomeh, 1967). And, third, home ownership decreases the likelihood of moving away (Nathanson, 1974; Wilkinson and Sigsworth, 1972), thus providing time for building local ties.

---

[10] It is also a result of their information about places to live; unfortunately, we cannot investigate that here.

Respondents to the national survey who owned homes tended to be more locally involved than those who did not (from $r = .07$ for local friends to $r = .16$ for organizations; having local kin was not related). However, this difference was not a result of home ownership *itself*. When individual characteristics—particularly home value, length of residence, and the presence of children—and characteristics of their neighborhoods are held constant, owners were no more likely than renters to be locally involved (except for a tendency to join neighborhood organizations).[11]

Features of the Neighborhood. Existing theories and prior research have little to say about which particular aspects of neighborhoods influence local involvement. Therefore, we examined many neighborhood features, including in our analysis measures of social context—both the composition of the population and the social behavior of the population—and of ecological factors. The final set of variables, after considerable experimentation and winnowing, was composed of: a scale indicating the presence and promimity of blacks, the proportion of Catholics, the proportion of residents in 1960 who had arrived since 1955, the estimated crime problem, the estimated neighborhood activity level of the residents, the quality of the housing (strongly associated with the class level of the residents), the age of the housing, and whether the neighborhood was in a suburb or center city. (See notes to Appendix Table 8.1 for definitions.) Our discussion will stress only the more noteworthy results.

Some published research suggests that the higher the *social class level* of a neighborhood, the more the residents neighbor (Smith et al., 1954; Gates et al., 1973), although the evidence is not unanimous (Bell and Boat, 1957). In an analysis of the Detroit survey reported elsewhere (Fischer and Jackson, 1976), we found that the median income of the tract was the single best predictor of reported neighboring. Respondents to the national survey were also somewhat more likely to neighbor and to belong to local organizations if they lived in tracts with higher-quality housing ($r = .14, .16$). However, when other factors were taken into account, particularly the class level of the respondents and the values of their homes (both of which were strongly associated with neighborhood quality, $r = .42, .50$), then the quality of the place had no effect of its own on these two local ties.[12] It did have an independent effect, though, on local intimates. All else equal, the higher the physical quality of their

---

[11] Having an expensive dwelling was independently associated with more organizational involvement (partial $\beta = .08$) and, since home-owners tend to have more expensive quarters, they were in that way more likely than renters to be organizationally involved.

[12] The differences between these findings and those from the Detroit survey might be explained by gender. The Detroit survey was all male; the national survey was mostly female. Gates et al. (1973) found that the class level of a neighborhood promoted neighboring among men, but not among women.

neighborhoods, the less likely people were to have kin or friends nearby (partial $\beta = -.08, -.06$).

This last finding warrants an effort at explanation. Obviously, the high-quality neighborhoods do not drive people's kin and friends elsewhere; instead, it reflects structural circumstances that people must face. Perhaps these families traded off neighborhood quality against proximity to intimates, since it may be generally difficult to have both (the friends and relatives must also be able to afford the location).

In addition, several other neighborhood features also influence local involvement, but only slightly. First, *racial and ethnic homogeneity* seems to promote attachment. In our all-white sample, the closer people lived to blacks, the less likely they were to neighbor (partial $\beta = -.09$; see also Keller, 1968; Gans, 1967). Second, *suburbanites* were slightly more likely to neighbor (partial $\beta = .06$) and to belong to neighborhood groups (.08) than were otherwise identical city-dwellers (see also Chapter 7). Third, the more organized *local activity* there was in their neighborhoods, the more likely people were to be involved and to have friends nearby (partial $\beta = .07$ for both). Finally, the more *crime,* the less people neighbored (partial $\beta = -.06$), but the more likely they were to have kin nearby (.07) and to belong to local organizations (.06).[13]

Perhaps the most notable result of our analysis of neighborhood features is that the characteristics of the place were much less important than the characteristics of families in affecting the extent of local involvement.[14] Yet people were still influenced by the places in which they had chosen to live (or lived in with little choice). In particular, the kinds of people around them helped shape their social ties.

TYPES OF PEOPLE AND AFFECT

Life-Cycle. People in different stages of the life-cycle varied not only in the extent of their local involvement, but also in the extent of their emotional involvement—although in a quite different manner. People with children tended to be *less* happy with their neighborhoods and *less* reluctant to move than were those without children who were otherwise similar (partial βs $= -.13, -.16$). Perhaps the presence of children raises a family's needs, especially for space, to levels which many cannot meet.[15]

---

[13] We also found that the older the housing stock in an area, the less likely it was that residents had kin or friends nearby (partial βs $= -.07, -.06$), but were unable to explain it.

[14] When house and neighborhood variables are added to the regression equations, they further increase the explained variance over that accounted for by personal traits by 29 percent (institutional), 31 percent (neighboring), 30 percent (organizations), 50 percent (kin), and 60 percent (friends).

[15] Indeed, the zero-order correlation between having children and being unhappy to leave the neighborhood ($r = -.09$) is eliminated by controlling for household density (persons per room, partial $r = -.01$).

Or, perhaps many people live in certain neighborhoods "for the children" and would personally prefer to live elsewhere.

Women's Employment. Respondents from families in which the women worked liked their neighborhoods as much as other respondents did, even though, as we saw earlier, they were less attached to their places socially.[16]

Social Class. Socioeconomic position limits a family's ability to satisfy the needs generated by its stage in the life-cycle by placing constraints upon where people can choose to live. It is not surprising, then, that in most, but not all, studies people in higher social classes tend to be more content with ther locations (Lansing and Ladd, 1964; Kasarda and Janowitz, 1974; Hunter, 1974, 1975; Wilkinson and Sigsworth, 1974—but not Marans and Rodgers, 1975; and Fried, 1973: 96). While this appeared to be the case in the national survey as well ($r = .09$ with "happy"), once factors such as the quality of the respondents' housing and neighborhoods were taken into account, people in higher social classes tended to be *no* happier with their neighborhoods and were *less* sad at the thought of moving than were others (partial $\beta = -.08$). Perhaps affluent people are more confident of finding new, suitable neighborhoods than are the less well-to-do. Higher social class may simultaneously provide individuals with a greater choice *of* neighborhoods and a greater freedom *from* neighborhoods.

Length of Residence. Several studies have indicated that the longer a person resides in a neighborhood, the more likely he or she is to be satisfied with it (for example, Kasarda and Janowitz, 1974; Nathanson, 1964; for an exception, see Morgan and Murray, 1974). The longer respondents to the national survey had lived in their neighborhoods, the more likely they were to feel happy with their places ($r = .08$) and reluctant to leave them ($r = .17$). However, this was largely explained by their social connections to the neighborhood. When social ties were held constant, long-time residents were no happier with their places and only slightly sadder to leave them (partial $\beta = .07$).[17] If it were not for these social connections then, time would have little impact. This finding challenges— although it certainly does not dismiss—those perspectives on attachment to place that understand it to be a direct consequence of residence (for example, that "familiarity breeds content," or that "sense of place" serves cognitive functions).[18]

[16] Even when social involvements in the neighborhood are not controlled, respondents in families with working women were no different (all else constant) from others in happiness with, or reluctance to leave, the neighborhood.

[17] The introduction of the "ties to the neighborhood" variables reduces the partial coefficient of length of residence from .08 ($p < .01$) to .04 (N.S.) for happiness, and from .11 ($p < .01$) to .07 ($p < .05$) for being unhappy to leave.

[18] This interpretation, that length of residence has little direct effect, is consistent with Hunter's (1975) finding that length of residence was un- or negatively related to

Summary. Feelings of affection for a place, like social involvement, can be best understood as the outcome of the structure of opportunities and constraints people face. Perhaps two findings deserve special note. First, all else being equal, high-status people are not any less happy with their neighborhoods (which does not mean that the quality of the neighborhood is unimportant; see below), but they are more often willing to leave their neighborhoods. This we attribute to their greater opportunities. Second, length of residence alone is of minor importance; it is largely to the extent that time in a place has allowed people to build local, personal networks that it fosters affection for the place.[19]

TYPES OF PLACES AND AFFECT

Most previous research cannot help much to disentangle the connection between features of the neighborhood and people's feelings about their places, because the studies have focused on the *perceived* qualities of neighborhoods (for example, Speare, 1974; Morgan and Murray, 1974; Marans and Rodgers, 1974; Zehner and Chapin, 1974; and Kasl and Harburg, 1972). It is hardly informative to find that, when people are dissatisfied with features of their homes and neighborhoods, they are more likely to want to leave them. Thus, we rely largely on our own analysis, in which we used objective measures of neighborhood attributes.

Although family characteristics were important in structuring respondents' local social involvements, they were less so in fostering feelings of attachment. Instead, features of the place, especially the dwelling unit,

---

local involvement in a neighborhood that was being upgraded. The oldtimers were increasingly isolated from their neighbors.

[19] Examination of Appendix Table 8.1 reveals some effects of religion worthy of comment. Respondents who labeled themselves as atheists or who reported no religion tended to be more disaffected from their neighborhoods than were religionists, whether or not other aspects of their lives are taken into account (partial $\beta = -.08$ with "happy" and $-.05$ with reluctance to leave). Jews and Catholics were generally just as emotionally attached to their neighborhoods as were other people. However, when the social differences they have with Protestants—including somewhat more local involvement (see note nine)—are controlled, it appears that Jews and Catholics were distinctive in being unhappy with their neighborhoods (partial $\beta s = -.10, -.06$), and Jews were also distinctive in being willing to move ($-.08$). We can only speculate that these findings reflect either minority discontent in Protestant settings, or some special inclination of Protestants to be satisfied with their locales.

Early in our preliminary analyses, we developed and tested measures of a neighborhood's religious composition and homogeneity, but the results were not particularly informative. We found that the greater the proportion of the local population that was of the respondents' religion, the more neighboring they did, the more likely they were to have neighborhood kin and friends, and the happier they were. Most of those effects disappear, however, when the respondent's religion is controlled for. Our earlier analysis also suggests that religion is not a proxy for size of city or regional differences between North and South (see Stueve et al., 1975).

seem more important for understanding satisfaction with the locality.[20] People who owned their homes and people who lived in valuable—that is, costly—dwellings (the two generally went together, $r = .41$) tended to be happier with their neighborhoods and less willing to leave them. (The partial βs with reluctance to leave were: ownership, .09, and value, .15.) When these results are added to the fact that, all else equal, people in neighborhoods of higher-quality housing were happier with their places (partial $\beta = .10$) and those in areas of newer housing were more reluctant to move (.07), we can see the fruits of higher income. Although higher social class by itself does not promote affective attachment (in fact, it tends to do the opposite), what it provides—valuable homes in new, attractive areas—does promote satisfaction with a place.

Happiness with the neighborhood was also influenced by two contextual features. One, in this exclusively white and predominantly Protestant sample, racial and religious heterogeneity, all else equal, reduced local satisfaction; the more Catholics in the neighborhood and the greater the presence of blacks, the less the average resident liked the place (partial $\beta = -.07$ for each). Two, a high crime rate, as one might expect, led to expressions of unhappiness (partial $\beta = -.06$).

LOCAL TIES AND AFFECTIVE ATTACHMENT

Previous studies have shown that local involvement itself promotes feeling attached to a place (Kasarda and Janowitz, 1974; Fried, 1973; Lansing, 1966; Hunter, 1975). The more involved people are, the more they feel "invested" in their neighborhoods. However, the relationship is probably mutually reinforcing: liking a place also leads to getting involved.

In the national survey, people who were socially involved in a neighborhood were generally happier with it and more reluctant to leave it than were relatively unattached people, although the differences were not as great as might have been expected.[21] Of all the forms of social involvement, having friends in the neighborhood most influences satisfaction (partial $\beta = .11$ with being happy; .14 with being unhappy to leave). Neighboring was also significant (.08, .06), but the other types of local involvement— nearby kin, institutional ties, and organizational involvement—were less so.

[20] In contrast to the results reported in footnote 14, the introduction of home and neighborhood variables increased the explained variance by 144 percent (happy with neighborhood) and 115 percent (reluctance to leave). This difference is all the more dramatic given the totally subjective nature of reports of affect.

[21] Adding the measures of social attachment to the equations increased the explained variance 29 percent over that explained by the other individual and contextual variables, for both "happy" and "unhappy to leave." Even without controls the associations were not very strong. The highest zero-order r of social ties with "happy" is .17 (neighboring) and with "unhappy to leave," .19 (local friends)—see also Table 8.1.

All else equal, people had more positive feelings about a place when they interacted with neighbors and had nearby friends; that is, when they had local networks. Yet, given what we might expect, the effect was not very powerful: about the same, for example, as having a nice home or not having the needs that accompany a growing family. Furthermore, neighboring and neighborhood friends may be, in part, a *consequence* of liking a place, not just a cause of it. People who found a place they like may actively seek out neighbors.

We have found that characteristics of individuals—their families, homes, neighborhoods, and social networks—each *separately* influence their feelings about their place of residence. Yet any given person may have characteristics that incline him or her in contradictory ways. For example, many parents dislike their neighborhoods but, because of their children, tend to be locally involved anyway, and that promotes feelings of attachment. Affluent people purchase nice homes in attractive locales which they therefore like but, at the same time, their affluence seems to allow them a feeling of freedom from the neighborhood. Our analysis attempts to isolate the consequences for attachment of each of many separate factors. However, any real individual faces a "package" of such factors to which he or she responds.[22]

Conclusion

Let us return to the theoretical perspectives on attachment presented at the opening of this chapter. Psychological perspectives see attachment to place as fulfilling psychic needs. Sociological perspectives focus on social relations. One version claims that attachment is necessary for communal social relations, another that it is instrumental for social organization. Economic perspectives focus on material rewards and costs. Our own *choice-constraint* perspective views attachment as a choice limited by constraints of family stage, economic resources, and place. We cannot, of course, "prove" any of these views to be more valid than the others.

[22] In attempting to understand attachment to place, we have argued that attributes of families, homes, and neighborhoods shape the type and degree of local involvement. There is one more aspect of people's relations to their places that we think is important but that we were unable to explore directly: the match or "fit" *between* people and their places. Local involvement may result not only from the separate characteristics of families and their neighborhoods, but also from the congruence between the two—for example, the number of people in the household in comparison with the space available; or the degree of ethnic or economic similarity between a family and its neighbors. The research literature confirms that such congruence is important in tying people to their homes and neighborhoods (see Michelson, 1970, 1973a). Although preliminary analysis suggests that our data are too crude to measure this notion of fit (see Stueve et al., 1975), we are convinced on theoretical grounds and on the basis of research such as Michelson's that the congruence between families and their residences plays an important role in attaching people to their places and is worthy of further study.

However, we can review our findings to assess the relative plausibility and utility of these views, as far as they can explain local involvement and neighborhood satisfaction.

Consider several key findings from our own and others' research:

1. Attachment to place is not holistic but multidimensional. There are different ways of being attached, ways that are not strongly related to one another. And different types of people are attached in different ways.
2. Being tied socially to a place's people and its institutions is associated, but not strongly, with feeling warmly about the place. Just being connected to people in a locality is not enough to produce satisfaction with the locality. Of the various forms of attachment, voluntary ties (neighboring, local friends) are most effective in promoting feelings of attachment; functional ties (institutions, kin) are less effective.
3. The most powerful single factor influencing local involvement and satisfaction appears to be life stage. In particular, children promote local ties, but also promote a desire to leave.
4. People with many resources and fewer drains upon them are more likely to maintain voluntary local ties, but are less likely to have intense relations with neighbors. They are also more likely to maintain a consistent set of ties (see note 3).
5. People who have lived a long time in a neighborhood are more likely to feel attached to it, but largely insofar as they are involved in local social relations (and not independently). Residing in a neighborhood a long time is not, by itself, enough to create affective attachment.
6. Features of the place—the home, the physical neighborhood, and the people there—also influence attachment. Just any place will not do; localities differ in their capacities to involve residents.

We found, in sum, that, at least for this sample of Americans, local involvements are important in fostering neighborhood satisfaction—but not predominantly so. Formal ties (organizations and institutions) are least important; voluntary ties (neighboring and local friends) are most important. And factors other than social ties—life stage, space, and so on—are more important still. In addition, these findings and others (especially Fried, 1973) imply that certain ties (neighboring, for example) are important to well-off people in determining feelings of attachment because these people have satisfied their basic residential and social needs, while other ties (for example, local kin) are important to those less well off precisely because they depend on those ties to satisfy their basic needs.[23]

[23] This conclusion is based in part on some further analysis we conducted (and reported in Stueve et al., 1975). We examined the associations between forms of social involvement and affective attachment within special subgroups. These groups

How does this picture of local attachment compare to the theoretical perspective presented earlier? Any approach that stresses unidimensional involvement clearly oversimplifies the case. Psychological perspectives tend to stress a psychic need for holistic attachment that grows over time and is largely independent of specific life circumstances and specific places. Such approaches cannot account for the rich variation in how the people we have studied use and feel about their places. Similarly, even though many sociological perspectives locate the source of attachment in corporate group membership rather than internal psychic states, "community" theorists also tend to emphasize the holistic nature of communal bonds. Our findings challenge the community approach as well: institutional and kinship ties are weakly related to voluntary social ties; the latter are in turn only modestly related to feelings (see also Hunter, 1975).

Although we found that local attachment is not all-encompassing (there are "localities of limited liability"), attachment to place still persists. Indeed, people continue to form important local attachments. However, because their needs and alternatives vary, so do their ties.

Our findings that attachment to place is multidimensional and varies across family types seem most congruent with a model that emphasizes choices within constraints. We have argued that in selecting places, becoming attached to them, or deciding to leave, people must juggle many factors and make trade-offs among them. Because people vary in life stage, resources, and location, they face different kinds of constraints, and some people are better able to meet their needs and minimize their trade-offs than others. For example, people vary in their degree of local dependency. Whereas some people, such as the elderly, the poor, and housewives with children, need local ties to procure important services and social contacts, others are freer to choose when and how to become involved. Ultimately,

---

varied in the degree of choice and constraint they faced and we expected that which local ties mattered most for satisfaction would vary accordingly. We looked at two groups that were relatively mobile and had a wide range of choices (relatively affluent, childless, young respondents and similar but middle-aged respondents) and a few groups that were more constrained (low-income elderly, low-income families with children, low-income families with children and working mothers, and female-headed households): we regressed the affect measure on only the social ties variables. Although the results are complex, a few general conclusions are possible: Having friends in the neighborhood and, to a lesser extent, casual neighboring, promoted affective attachment for all groups, but were relatively more important for low-constraint groups. Other kinds of ties were independently associated with affect only among high-constraint groups (institutional ties for low-income families with working wives), while institutional ties and neighborhood kin were associated with affect for the low-income elderly (see Stueve et al., 1975). Further investigation may support what these findings hint: that low-constraint, high-choice people can be more responsive to—in the sense of more satisfied as a result of—opportunities for voluntary sociability found in different neighborhoods, while highly constrained families may be more responsive to formal ties, ascribed relations, and similar factors. (Ties tended to explain slightly more variance in affect among low-constraint than among high-constraint groups.)

people vary greatly in how they are attached to their neighborhoods.

Throughout our analysis, we have inferred needs, preferences, and alternatives on the basis of critical life-cycle and economic characteristics. Now we need studies that measure needs, preferences, and alternatives more directly. Researchers should examine directly the factors that structure the trade-offs and limit the choices people make. Only then can we fully understand attachment to place.

Appendix: Description of Scales Used in Chapter 8

1. *Institutional Ties*

Our measure of local institutional ties is an additive scale consisting of the following items:

ITEM	*R scored 1 Point if:*
a. Could you tell me the name of the church or temple which members of your family attend? Is (*name*) within walking distance? 1. IF NO: How long does it take to get there?	Family attended church within walking distance or within a ten-minute drive of home.
b. What are the names of the schools which your children attend? Is that in this neighborhood?	Respondent's children attended a local public elementary and/or high school.
c. How long does it take (head of household) to get to work? What kind of transportation does (head of household) normally take?	Workplace of household head was within walking distance or within a ten-minute drive of home.
d. How long does it take (name of wife) to get to work? What kind of transportation does (wife) normally take?	Workplace of wife was within walking distance or within a ten-minute drive of home.

The following item was included in the institutional scale used in the section on the nature of attachment to place, but was *not* included in the regression analyses.

e. Do you or your (husband/   Either husband or wife belonged
   wife) belong to the PTA   to the PTA.
   of (your child's) school?

2. *Sociable Neighboring*
   This is an additive scale consisting of the following items:
   Which of these things has anyone in your family done in the past few months with members of families who live in the neighborhood?
   CODE "YES" OR "NO" FOR EACH ITEM ASKED.

   a. Stopped and talked when we met.
   b. Had an informal chat together in their home or our home.
   c. Had dinner or a party together at their home or our home.
   d. Went out together for dinner or a movie.
   e. We got together on other occasions.
      (EXPLAIN)

   Respondents scored 1 point each for answering "yes" to items a,b,c or d,e. Items c and d were collapsed because they are virtually interchangeable. This is a quasi-Guttman scale; for example, families that dine with neighbors are almost certain to socialize in more informal ways. This scale was collapsed into four categories for the crosstabular analysis in Section I.

3. *Organizational Involvement*
   This scale consists of the following two items:
   a. Has anyone in your family attended the meeting of a neighborhood organization or group together in the past few months with members of families who live in the neighborhood?

   CODE YES OR NO FOR EACH ITEM ASKED.

   b. What neighborhood organizations do you or your family belong to? (OMIT CHURCH AND SCHOOL GROUPS.) IF NOT MENTIONED: Do you belong to any organized groups of renters or homeowners?

   Respondents scored 1 point if they attended local meetings or reported membership in at least one organization. For crosstabular analysis, respondents who reported any organizational membership were scored 1; others scored 0.

4. *Kin in Neighborhood*
   Based on the item below, this measure counts the number of types of

kin (parents, parents-in-law, siblings, siblings-in-law, and others) reported living in the neighborhood.

Do your parents live in this neighborhood, in another neighborhood in this metropolitan area/county, or do they live somewhere else? How about your husband's/wife's parents? How about your brothers and sisters? Your husband's/wife's brothers and sisters?

For the crosstabular analysis, respondents with any kin in the neighborhood were scored 1; others scored 0.

5. *Friends in Neighborhood*

Neighborhood friendships were measured by the following item:

Do most of your friends live in the neighborhood or do most of them live farther away?

Most in neighborhood . . .
Some do, some don't . . .
Most live farther away . . .

Respondents with at least some neighborhood friends scored 1; others scored 0.

6. *Happy with Neighborhood*

On the whole, how happy are you with living here in (name of neighborhood)? Would you say you're very happy, pretty happy, or not too happy with this neighborhood?

Very happy . . . 3
Pretty happy . . 2
Not too happy . 1

7. *Unhappy to Leave*

If, for any reasons, you had to move from here to some other neighborhood, would you be very unhappy, a little unhappy, or would you be happy to move—or wouldn't it make a difference?

Very unhappy 4
A little unhappy 3
Wouldn't make any difference . . 2
Happy to move 1

TABLE 8–A.1 Regressions of Attachment Dimensions on Individual and Contextual Predictors (National Survey)[a]

		SOCIAL ACTIVITY		INTIMATES		AFFECT	
	Institutional Ties[b]	Neighboring	Organizational Involvement	Neighborhood Kin	Neighborhood Friends	Happy Here	Sad to Move
Individual Traits[c]							
Prechildren Life Stage	05	08		13	08		−06
Children	35	13	10	18	10	−13	−16
Male Respondent				−06	05	−06	
SES of Household	24	17	16		−10		−08
Woman Works		−04	−07		−08		
Catholic			07	14		−06	
Jewish				05	06	−10	−08
Other or Atheist	−32	−05				−08	−05
Length of Residence	11	07	13	12	18		07
Home Traits:							
Owns Home							09
Monthly Cost			08			11	15
Neighborhood Traits:							
Presence of Blacks	06	−09				−07	
Percent Catholic	05					−07	
Proportion Newcomers							
Crime	−05	−06	06	−15		−06	
Activism			07	07	07		
Quality				−08	−06	10	
Age of Housing				−07	−06		
Suburb		06	08				−07
Local Involvement:							
Institutional Ties						08	06
Neighboring						05	
Organizational Involvement						05	
Neighborhood Kin							14
Neighborhood Friends						11	13
R^2	32	12	12	11	06	13	13

[a] Entries are standardized partial regression coefficients significant at $p < .05$; decimal points omitted.
[b] Definition of Dependent Variables—See Appendix to this chapter
[c] Definition of Independent Variables—See notes to Table 7.1, "National Survey"

9. "Authentic Community": The Role of Place in Modern Life

Claude S. Fischer
C. Ann Stueve

TURN-OF-THE-CENTURY social reformer Jacob Riis once proclaimed that his goal was "to arouse neighborhood interest . . . to link [neighbors] to one spot that will hold them long enough to take root and stop them from moving. Something of the kind must be done or we perish" (quoted by Chudacoff, 1975: 84). In this chapter, we are concerned with an argument about local "communities" that lies behind Riis's fear and ones similar to it: that people must be attached to a locality in order to have a supportive social network and to experience psychological well-being. We focus on two propositions: (1) local social relations are more intimate and supportive than social relations with people outside one's locality; and (2) residential mobility, because it involves disconnection from place, has long-term negative consequences. In the previous chapter, we evaluated theories of local attachment by how well they helped us to understand the *causes* of being attached or not; here we shall evaluate them by how well they help us to understand the *consequences* of being attached or not. We are especially interested in those theories that stress the need for attachment and the harm that presumably befalls the unattached.

In the first section, we restate more fully the theories that argue that the only "authentic community" (to use Vance Packard's phrase) is a local one, stressing in particular the analysis drawn from the "decline-of-community" tradition. In the second section, we use the Detroit data to compare the quality of local and extralocal relations. In the third section

163

we review what is known about the personal consequences of residential mobility.

The Authentic Community

At the beginning of Chapter 8, we briefly outlined several theoretical approaches to the topic of attachment to place. A few of these, particularly the psychological ones, were labeled "functional." These theories presume that there are certain basic "needs"—for territory, cognitive orientation, and the like—which attachment to place, and that alone, satisfies. From this perspective, place ties and a "sense of place" are "natural." As with most notions of intrinsic needs or natural conditions, their denial is thought to result in pathological consequences. In this case, the conclusion is that the absence of local roots, especially through residential mobility, produces alienation, loneliness, mental illness, and the like (see, for example, P. Berger et al., 1973; Toffler, 1970; Fromm, 1955).

Although this argument appears often in the psychological literature and in popular thought, the analysis derived from the classical decline-of-community theories is more powerful and more critical to the concerns of this book. Examination of those classical theories (see Chapter 1) suggests that they can be fairly summarized as follows: Communal social relations—those involving intimacy and mutual support—develop largely within traditional corporate groups, groups in which individual will is subordinate to that of the collectivity (and membership in which is usually based on ascribed traits, such as family, tribe, and birthplace). This combination—corporate groups producing communal ties—is a *community*. People are constrained from forming relations outside the group by physical impediments, social barriers (such as language), and their material dependence on the group. These constraints mean that members' relations are exclusively with one another, are based on interdependence, and involve frequent and many-faceted interaction over a lifetime. The communal qualities of social ties, intimacy and commitment, develop from such relations. The decline of community occurs when barriers are lowered and market institutions arise to satisfy material needs. People then can, and do, form specialized, instrumental, and dispersed relations outside the corporate group; and corporate groups wane. But, according to the theories, these new relations cannot provide the communal qualities found in intense, corporate relations. Thus, community has been lost, and so have communal ties.

The "decline-of-*local*-community" argument is a specific instance of this more general analysis. The neighborhood or village is held to be *fundamentally* (although in actuality decreasingly) a corporate group, a "*Gemeinschaft* of locality . . . a community of physical life" (Tönnies,

1887: 42; see also Durkheim, 1893; Park, 1916; Stein, 1960; Nisbet, 1969; and Alexander, 1967). Because of the isolation of premodern localities, people must turn to one another for economic and emotional relations. Out of these multiplex and frequent interactions, and dense networks, come the communal qualities of social bonds, or true community. Modern life has weakened the *Gemeinschaft* of locality by providing individuals both the incentives to reach beyond their localities and the technological means to do so. Given the option, most people take it: to work outside the village, travel, change residences, associate with outlanders, and so on. (Once this process is underway, it is increasingly difficult for those who do want intense local involvement to find it, since their neighbors are distracted.) Durkheim (1893) describes this turning-away process as he explains increases in anomie:

> Separated from the rest of society by barriers more or less difficult to clear, nothing turns us from local life, and, therefore, all our action is concentrated there. But as the fusion of segments becomes more complete . . . even the inhabitant of the small city lives the life of the little group immediately surrounding him less exclusively. He joins in relations with distant localities . . . his more frequent journeys . . . correspondence . . . the affairs occupying him outside, etc., turn his attention from what is passing around him . . . he is then less interested in his neighbors, since they take a smaller part in his life. . . . For all these reasons, local public opinion weighs less heavily on each of us . . . the common conscience loses its authority. . . . For the common conscience to be maintained, society must be divided into rather small compartments completely enclosing the individual (p. 300).

Both the common conscience and communal relations are weakened, so that people have "thousands of contacts, but the contacts are empty and unsatisfying" (Alexander, 1967: 239).

We do not, and cannot, address in this chapter the historical argument that the decline of the locality has sped a decline in communal bonds (see Chapter 10; also, Suttles, 1972). But we are interested in extracting a social-psychological proposition from it, one that can be examined in a single historical period. The proposition is that local social relations are more likely to be communal (intimate and supportive) than are social relations with people outside the locality. The proposition is based on the belief that local associates are more frequently seen, are known in multiple ways, know one another, and so on. Place-based networks thus more closely approximate the traditional community than do other networks. One derivation from this proposition is that people who cannot build strong local relations because they have recently moved are also likely to lack communal relations and, consequently, to suffer psychologically because of their isolation.

The proposition as stated here is largely implicit in most sociological writings (for example, Nisbet, 1969). However, it is stated quite straight-forwardly by popularizers of sociology. Urban designer Christopher Alexander (1967) asserts that true intimacy with someone requires seeing him or her daily and informally; the neighborhood is essentially the only context that offers this kind of contact.[1] Vance Packard (1972) describes the authentic community as

> a social network of people of various kinds, ranks, and ages who encounter each other on the streets, in the stores, at sports parks, at communal gatherings. A good deal of personal interaction occurs [and there is a recognition of the network as a distinct] place with an ongoing character (p. 16).

According to Packard, it is because people are becoming less and less involved in such local life that they are forfeiting deep social bonds and that we are becoming a "nation of strangers."

In contrast to these lines of analysis is an argument that "community without propinquity" is possible (Webber, 1968, 1970). People can maintain meaningful and supportive social relations without common residence and even without frequent face-to-face contact, by using modern means of communication and transportation. For such people, orientations to the neighborhood[2] may be friendly but not particularly committed; the locality is a "community of limited liability" (Janowitz, 1967). Pursued further, this argument suggests that the ties involved in local groups are probably not more communal than extralocal ties. In fact, the reverse may be true: local ties may be less communal. Local relations may be largely a product of propinquity, convenience, or the lack of an alternative (see Keller, 1968; Freeman, 1970), while the extralocal ties may be more often the products of personal affinity. Distant associates may also be more intimate because they must be particularly rewarding in order to be kept as associates. If people can find social support outside the locality, then disconnection from place need not have the dire consequences attributed to it by decline-of-local-community theorists. (From either point of view, disconnection from social relations altogether has dire effects.)

From these contrasting arguments, we draw two questions for empirical examination: (1) What are the qualitative differences between local and extralocal social relations? (2) What are the consequences of residential mobility? People who have moved have cut or loosened their bonds to associates in the places they have left behind and are unfamiliar to the people in the places they have come to. According to authentic community theories, they should be relatively isolated and vulnerable. According to

[1] Alexander sees the workplace as a context for formal and restricted interaction.

[2] The traditional neighborhood is implicitly and often explicitly the urban equivalent of the rural "community" in community theories (see Tönnies, 1887; Durkheim, 1893).

psychological theories of attachment to place, the "rootlessness" of movers should leave them disoriented and stressed. But according to community-without-propinquity views, there need not be such effects at all.[3]

Local Versus Extralocal Relations

One-third of the Detroit men interviewed in 1965–66 reported that *none* of the three male friends to whom they felt closest and saw most often lived in the neighborhood (within ten minutes); roughly another third reported that only one of their friends was nearby; and fewer than half reported that their closest brother lived nearby. In the largely female national sample, about two-thirds of the respondents stated that most of their friends lived outside the neighborhood; 60 percent reported no relatives nearby.

One approach which researchers have used to evaluate the consequences of such local attachment or its absence has been to compare the relations people have with their neighbors to those they have with kin, friends, and coworkers. Generally, people report that their neighbors are relatively low in intimacy, support, and importance (see, for example, Wellman, 1976; Bell and Boat, 1957; Axelrod, 1956; Zehner and Chapin, 1974; and Litwak and Szlenyi, 1969). However, this is not quite the proper comparison for our purposes, because it confounds how far apart two people reside with the role relations they share. We want to isolate the consequences of distance for each kind of role relation (for example, kin or coworker). Therefore, we examined differences between local and extralocal best friends in the Detroit sample and reviewed published research in which similar comparisons were made separately for friends, kin, or other "intimates." Although this procedure also has its limitations,[4] it does permit us to see whether local relations of a given kind are more communal than extralocal relations of that same kind.

---

[3] The other side of mobility is the people left behind. Although we do not deal extensively with this group, they might best be compared to forced movers—their social ties are broken against their will (see, for example, Ginsberg, 1975).

[4] First, we are somewhat limited in the extent to which we can logically generalize from differences between local and extralocal best friend, kin, and so on, to differences between local and extralocal associates in general. It may be that distance does not affect the quality of friendships and other major bonds, but does affect the nature of acquaintanceships, casual associates, and so on. Still, it seems that the quality of significant ties is the issue under debate here: Can people find intimacy and support outside the locality? Second, with reference to the classical theories of community, we are not comparing local multiplex relations to extralocal singleplex ties (for example, business contacts). In this chapter, we are simply looking at the differences between local and extralocal bonds. See Chapter 3 for a comparison of multiplex to singleplex friendships.

FREQUENCY OF CONTACT

The farther apart two people live, the less often they get together (for Detroit respondents and their friends, $\gamma = .39$; see also Klatzky, 1971; Firth et al., 1969; Litwak, 1960; and Adams, 1966). This effect appears over short distances as well as long distances. The Detroit men saw 58 percent of their best friends who lived in the neighborhood at least weekly outside of work, compared to 35 percent of their friends who resided elsewhere in the Detroit area and 25 percent of those living outside the area. Similarly, in the national survey, respondents were less likely to see their kin, the further away those kin lived.

The Detroit data suggest, however, that residential location is not the only locus of interaction. Work was a major alternative as a place of contact, even if the actual "getting together" took place outside of work (it might, for example, occur right after work). A man saw his *nonwork* friends much more often if they lived in his neighborhood than if they did not ($\gamma = .61$). But how often a man saw his *work* friends (outside of work hours) depended much less on where they lived; being neighbors helped, but only modestly ($\gamma = .16$). If we can generalize from the instance of the workplace, it would seem that the greater the number of places an individual and his real or potential friends regularly use (work, clubs, and so on), the less significant is the neighborhood as a locus of interaction.

Nevertheless, people see their local friends much more often than other friends. The next question is: How vital is face-to-face contact for other features of a relation? The proposition that local relations are more communal than extralocal ones assumes that frequent, casual, face-to-face interaction is critical for forming and sustaining communal ties. To be sure, intimacy cannot *develop* without frequent interaction between two people. But the evidence which we reviewed in Chapter 3 casts doubt on the assumption that frequent interaction is critical for *sustaining* intimacy. For one, the association between reported frequency and reported intimacy is real but not overwhelming ($\gamma = .14$).[5] More important, it is likely (as we argued in Chapter 3) that frequency is usually a consequence of intimacy, not a cause of it. We can point to further evidence in support of that argument: When the Detroit men had easy access to their friends—when those friends lived in the neighborhood or were coworkers—the respondents got

[5] We employed another measure of intimacy as well: which of three personal problems (marital relations, job difficulties, or a health problem) the respondent said he would discuss with his friends. Men who saw their friends relatively frequently said they would consult their friends on significantly more problems than did those who saw their friends infrequently. However, the difference was small (an average of 1.1 to 0.9). Wellman et al. (1973) report a firm association between frequency of contact with and the availability of support from an "intimate" ($\gamma = .35$). However, their measure of contact includes phone calls and letters, and the latter seem to be more important (Wellman, 1976: Table 9).

together with their most intimate friends more often than with their less intimate ones (among neighbors, $\gamma = .20$ between intimacy and frequency; among coworkers, $\gamma = .22$). In other cases, when access to friends was more problematic—that is, constraints of distance and time could intervene between desire for contact and actual contact—the men saw their less intimate friends almost as often as their more intimate ones (among non-neighbor friends, $\gamma = .05$; nonwork friends, $\gamma = .06$). If frequent contact created intimacy, then the association should hold equally in various logistical circumstances. If, as is the case, intimacy, along with other factors, determines frequency, then we should indeed observe a weaker association between the two when the other factors intervene.[6] Other studies point to the same conclusion: Frequent interaction—except perhaps early in getting to know someone—does not cause or sustain intimacy or commitment (see Adams, 1966; Klatzky, 1971).[7]

In addition, several studies have shown that networks can be mobilized for support even in the absence of face-to-face contact. Studies of kinship, in particular, indicate that rights and responsibilities—for material aid, for example—are exercised even after long separations (see Firth et al., 1969; Litwak, 1960; Litwak and Szelenyi, 1969; and Wellman et al., 1973). As J. C. Mitchell put it, "Face-to-face interaction is not a necessary condition for the obligations entailed in a relationship to be honored" (1969: 28). In sum, local associates are more frequently seen than extralocal ones, but that does not mean that their relations are more "communal" in quality.

[6] See also Chapter 3, note 16. We could have reported these results in a way more compatible with the "authentic community" thesis: Frequently seen friends were more likely to be intimate than infrequently seen friends, among neighbors and coworkers (thus suggesting that frequency *plus* proximity creates intimacy). However, that interpretation yields a couple of incongruities. It puts the workplace on an equal footing with the neighborhood as a locus of community. And it implies, without clear explanation, that frequency does *not* promote intimacy among non-coworkers or non-neighbors. It also predicts that frequently seen neighbor friends should have been the most intimate kind of friends; they were not. (Neighbor friends seen weekly or more were likely to be "very close" equally as often as non-neighbor friends seen as often—56 percent—and were *less* likely to be considered "very close" than outside-Detroit friends seen *less* than weekly, 62 percent of whom were so evaluated.)

[7] Wellman (1976) found no correlation between frequency of in-person contact and perceived closeness. Adams (1966) found that there was no association between how close a sample of men felt to their parents and how often they saw their parents when those parents lived either quite near or quite far away. In the first case, contact was obligatory, attitudes notwithstanding; in the second, personal contact was very inconvenient, attitudes notwithstanding. Only for those whose parents lived at intermediate distances, where contact could be a function of preference, was there an association between the frequency and feeling. Klatzky (1971: Ch. 2) found in a national male sample that the association between the genealogical proximity of a relative and the frequency with which that relative was seen was strong for relatives who lived nearby. At far distances, the effect of genealogical connection washed out, as all contact tended to be rare. (This is not Klatzky's interpretation of the data, but it is simpler than her own.)

SUPPORTIVENESS

Are local friends and relatives more supportive than extralocal ones? Not much. Wellman et al. (1973) asked a sample of working-class people in Toronto to name which of their intimates they could call upon for everyday assistance and for emergency aid. Whether people felt that an intimate was ready to assist them or not was only weakly associated with the intimate's location. Twenty-six percent of the intimates who lived in the same neighborhood were reported as available for everyday support; 23 percent of those living *outside* Toronto were reported as similarly supportive. The figures were 36 percent and 32 percent, respectively, for emergency aid.[8] In later analysis, Wellman (1976) concluded that there was no difference in availability for aid between intimates living in the neighborhood and those living elsewhere in the Toronto area. This finding is replicated by the studies mentioned above on the availability of support in the absence of face-to-face contact. (Of course, this does not deny that neighbors are more available for casual loans and services than are friends across town.)

INTIMACY

Are neighborhood friends considered more intimate than those outside the neighborhood? No. We saw in Chapter 3 that the Detroit men viewed the friends they drew from their current neighborhoods (neighborhood "source") as *less* intimate than their other friends. And, in general, they were slightly *less* likely to label friends living inside the neighborhood as "very close" (52 percent, $\gamma = -.10$; similarly, they were slightly less likely to have known friends inside the neighborhood 13 or more years than those outside, $\gamma = -.08$). Overall, the Detroit men were more likely to feel that their friends living outside the metropolitan area were "very close" (60 percent) than either neighborhood friends (52 percent) or those living elsewhere in the Detroit area (53 percent).

Details of this finding are worth exploring. First, the extent of the difference in reported intimacy between local and nonlocal friends varied with the class level of the respondents. Respondents with low incomes considered their neighborhood friends as *more* intimate than their non-neighborhood friends (income under $7,000, $\gamma = .13$); middle-income men rated the two types of friends about equal on intimacy ($7,000–$10,000, $\gamma = -.06$); and affluent men considered their friends living in

---

[8] Excluding kin from the list of intimates increased the effect of location. Wellman et al. (1973) report an overall association of $\gamma = .07$ between *either* kind of support and geographic proximity (six levels) from all "intimates," but a $\gamma = .17$ between *everyday* support and promixity to "friends." (They do not report the remaining figure: the association between distance and availability for *emergency* aid from "friends.")

the neighborhood as *less* intimate than those outside (over $15,000, $\gamma = -.18$). Consistent with our arguments about resource and choice, it appears that money enables people to reach beyond their localities for their most intimate ties, while the lack of money makes proximity more important.[9]

Second, the relative intimacy of local friends also depended on whether or not the friends were seen at work. The Detroit respondents differentiated the local versus the nonlocal among their *coworker* friends only slightly: those coworkers who were also neighbors were seen as a bit more intimate on the average than those coworker friends who were not neighbors ($\gamma = .07$). However, there was a notable difference by location among the *non-coworker* friends: the ones who were neighbors were rated as less intimate than the ones who were not neighbors ($\gamma = -.17$). Similarly, respondents considered the friends they *made* at work (source) as more intimate when they also lived nearby ($\gamma = .14$), their childhood or kin friends as equally intimate, location notwithstanding ($\gamma = .06, .05$), and their other friends as *less* intimate if they *were* neighbors ($\gamma = -.19$).[10] Being a neighbor promoted intimacy only when it was added to being a coworker (both generally low-intimacy relations, see Chapter 3); otherwise, it was not an ingredient for communal relations. Although these patterns are complex, it seems clear that in general local friends were not seen as more intimate than nonlocal ones.

The Detroit study provided another measure of intimacy, as well. Respondents were asked whether they would ordinarily discuss various problems with their friends (friends in general).[11] We examined the responses to three personal problems: "troubles between you and your wife," "difficulties at work with your boss," and "a serious medical problem." Respondents all of whose three friends lived *inside* the neighborhood said, on the average, that they would discuss one of these problems; respondents all of whose three friends lived *outside* the neighborhood *also* averaged one problem (that is, no difference). Finally, men who had most of their friends nearby were *not* notably more likely than other men to assert

---

[9] The income difference was strongest when only friends in the Detroit area are considered; for all income groups, friends outside the *area* were considered the most intimate. For the inside-the-area friends, neighborhood residence was *positively* associated with intimacy among the low-income respondents ($\gamma = .20$) and *negatively* among the high-income men ($\gamma = -.17$). Wellman's (1976) results are somewhat different. For his working-class Torontonians, there was no association between an intimate living outside the area and perceived closeness ($r = .03$). Nevertheless, his findings also challenge the localism-intimacy hypothesis.

[10] We cannot subdivide this last category of friends by source because of definitional problems. The "other" category is composed either solely of neighbors (neighbor source) or solely of non-neighbors (vountary associations, and no known role), so obviously we cannot compare neighbors to non-neighbors in each. See Chapter 3.

[11] The question did not specify *which* friend(s) would be consulted.

that "I become very attached to my friends" ($\gamma = .12$, N.S.) or "I keep in close touch with my friends" ($\gamma = .04$, N.S.). Again, there is little evidence to support the assertion that local friends are more intimate than extralocal friends.

RETHINKING LOCALISM AND INTIMACY

We found that men see neighborhood friends (and kin) more frequently than others, although workplace proximity seems to be an alternative to residential proximity. Frequent face-to-face contact does not seem, however, critical for maintaining the communal qualities of a bond. Certainly most relations cannot develop without frequent interaction, and many exchanges—borrowing tools, playing cards, for example—will not happen without physical meetings. But, given a network of close associates, intimacy and support seem largely independent of frequent contact (at least according to these and other survey respondents). And the conclusion must be that local associates are not more intimate and supportive than similar but extralocal intimates, and, in fact, they may be considered slightly less intimate. How might we explain this finding?

One answer is community without propinquity (Webber, 1970): modern transport and communications permit interaction over a long distance to be coupled with occasional visits. Since affluent people have more resources to take advantage of this technology, it is not surprising that they report slightly more physical dispersion of friends than do the less well off.[12] Another answer is that close relations have latent rights and responsibilities which need not be exercised regularly—for example, kinship obligations between relatives who have never even met (Firth et al., 1969). These two answers suffice to challenge strongly the authentic community proposition. Yet we shall forward an additional explanation that involves a still more fundamental rethinking of the issue.

The theories of natural connections to place are essentially functional (that is, attachment meets critical needs). The authentic community thesis is essentially mechanistic: being locally attached or not determines social

---

[12] In the Detroit data, the higher the occupational status of the respondent, the less likely it was that all three of his friends lived in the neighborhood ($\gamma = -.16$; and, vice-versa, the higher the average status of the friends, the less likely it was that they all lived in the respondent's neighborhood, $\gamma = -.27$). In general, there was a small, independent, negative relation between class and having one's friends nearby (partia $\beta = -.10$; see also Verbrugge [1973: 482]). In the national survey, respondents of higher social class were less likely than others to have kin or most of their friends in the neighborhood ($r = -.09$; $-.07$), a difference that withstood many controls (see Appendix Table 8.1). Fried (1973) also reports that class status was negatively related to having intimates nearby. (In his lowest status groups, the outside contacts were disproportionately kin—which was not true for the higher-status persons.) However, Wellman et al. (1973) report no class differences in the association between proximity and availability of an associate for support. In general, though, higher-status people are less "localized."

interactions, which in turn determine the communal qualities of those ties. Let us instead assume our decision-making analysis (Chapters 3 and 8): people consciously nurture and maintain those social relations that are materially and psychically "profitable" to them. That is, in the course of normal meetings and remeetings, people develop those relations that appear rewarding and let wither those that do not seem worth the effort—given the alternatives they have and the constraints to their social activities. As people move about, some ties are maintained and others let go. One of the important constraints—or, more accurately, costs—in this tacit social accounting is *distance*. We discussed the effect of distance on networks in Chapter 3 and briefly in Chapter 7. Now we will pursue the topic in somewhat greater detail.

Distance, as we have noted earlier, poses various costs to a relationship: the monetary price of travel and phone calls, the time involved in journeying, the bother of writing letters, and a reduction in the ease and speed with which an associate can come to one's assistance. These costs of distance enter people's "calculations" to produce the following result: for any two associates found equally rewarding, a person will be more likely to maintain contact with the closer by; and, ties will be maintained with relatively distant associates only to the extent to which their "rewardingness" outweighs the cost posed by their distance.[13] Thibaut and Kelley (1959) put it this way:

> A relationship voluntarily maintained over great distances would have to provide some sort of compensation for the high cost [of maintaining it]. Thus, we might expect that . . . the reward provided would be higher as compared with relationships maintained over short distances. If we assume that similarity with regard to values operates to heighten rewards, then relationships maintained over great distances would be expected to show relatively high value similarity (p. 41).

The conclusion of this argument is that, among a set of associates, the distant ones will, as a result of selection over time, be the more rewarding. If ratings of intimacy index rewardingness, then farther associates will be considered more intimate than nearer ones—the *opposite* of what the authentic community thesis predicts.

There is a problem with this logic, however: There is no reason why people cannot have, by accident or by mobility, their most intimate friends nearest them. Instead, the argument suggests a more complex association between distance and intimacy (as displayed in Figure 9.1). Friends who live nearby may either be very intimate or not; but the farther away the potential friend, the more intimate he or she must be in order to be selected and for the relation to be maintained.

[13] The exchanges involved in extralocal ties differ, of course, from those in local ties: for example, visiting on ritual occasions versus casual borrowing. But distance remains a cost in both sorts. If it were not, we would still each have our full complement of earlier friends, instead of having "lost" some along the way.

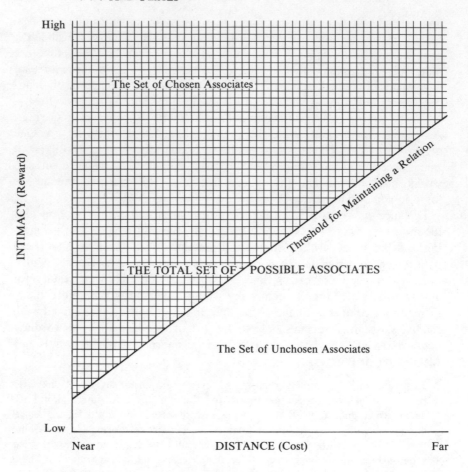

High

The Set of Chosen Associates

INTIMACY (Reward)

Threshold for Maintaining a Relation

THE TOTAL SET OF POSSIBLE ASSOCIATES

The Set of Unchosen Associates

Low

Near   DISTANCE (Cost)   Far

Figure 9.1 Hypothesized Relationship Between Distance and Intimacy

This model leads to certain empirical predictions. One is the prediction by Thibaut and Kelley that distant friends should be more similar to one another in their values than friends who live closer to each other. In support of this proposition, Thibaut and Kelley cite a survey study which found that respondents in a suburban development held values more similar to those of their friends who lived outside the development than to those of their friends who lived inside it. We do not have measures of value similarity in the Detroit survey,[14] but we do have measures of similarities in social position (see Chapter 4), which are usually related to similarities in values. Non-neighborhood friends were slightly more similar to the respondent in education and occupational status than were

[14] Actually, respondents were asked about their own and their friends' political affiliations. However, the latter reports tended to be unreliable (Laumann, 1973: Ch. 2).

his neighborhood friends ($\gamma = -.10$ between a friend being a neighbor and being similar in education to the respondent; $-.09$ for occupational status).[15] Similarly, a study of residents in a housing development found that the farther apart two friends lived, the more similar they were in background traits (Athanasiou and Yoshioka, 1973).

A second empirical prediction is that, in general, the greater the distance between two friends, the more intimate they should be. And the more affluent the individuals involved, the more this should be the case, for two reasons: In general, affluent people have more resources to search for and maintain "optimal" friendships (the most rewarding for the least cost) and are thus most likely to build "efficient" networks (ones following the principle reflected in Figure 9.1). Furthermore, because of their resources, affluent people can afford to move away from intimates but still maintain relations with them. They can optimize both housing preferences and social preferences (see Chapter 8 and the following discussion on mobility.) As we reported earlier, extralocal friends were indeed considered more intimate than local ones. (Those friends *most* likely to be called "very close, personal" lived outside the neighborhood, elsewhere in the Detroit area, and were not seen at work—59 percent were so labeled —or, better still, lived outside the metropolitan area—66 percent, versus 49 percent of all the others.) And, also reported earlier, the pattern was strongest among the most affluent.

Third, the model suggests that the relationship between distance and intimacy should be weakest for the most intimate types of friends. (Note in Figure 9.1 that there is no association between distance and intimacy in the top third of the chart.) This, too, we found. The association between distance and intimacy was essentially nil among kin and childhood friends; these intimate types of friendships (see Chapter 3) tended to be equally close regardless of distance. (The relationship was different— nearer friends, more intimate—among coworker friends, but why it was is unclear.)

Finally, the model suggests that, *for any given individual*, his or her distant friends will generally be more intimate than the nearer ones. To this point in the analysis of the Detroit survey, we have compared all the local friendships among the thousand men of the sample to all their extralocal friendships. We have not confronted the possibility that the results might be explained, not by types of *friendships*, but by types of *people*; that is, that "locals" might for some reason be less generally intimate than the more "cosmopolitan" (Merton, 1968: 441–74). Yet the argument we are making refers to each *individual's* weighing of relative

---

[15] In Verbrugge's (1973) analysis of this data, she also found that neighborhood friends were less similar in occupational prestige, age, and education than non-neighborhood friends. However, this was reversed in her analysis of a German small-town sample.

costs and rewards. We must compare among the friendships of each man. We tested this prediction by assigning each friendship of each respondent a rank on intimacy—less intimate than the other two friendships reported by the same respondent, as intimate, or more intimate than the other two —and a similar rank on distance.[16] Overall, there was a tendency for the *nearest* of a man's friends also to be the *least* intimate ($\gamma = -.11$).

As in our earlier comparison, the relative intimacy of a man's local friends as against his extralocal ones varied by both the class of the respondent and the origin of the friendship. However, the groups which in the previous tests showed the atypical pattern—local friends being more intimate—no longer did so in this analysis. First, low-income men considered their nearer friends just as intimate as their farther ones ($\gamma = -.01$); middle-income men thought the nearer ones were less intimate ($\gamma = -.11$); and high-income men thought likewise ($\gamma = -.13$). Second, among work friends, nearer friends were thought as intimate as farther ones ($\gamma = .02$), while among nonwork friends—the set that best exhibits the effects of residential distances—farther friends were clearly more intimate than nearer ones ($\gamma = -.19$).

In sum, these four pieces of evidence support the model presented earlier: that neighborhood friends may be very intimate or not, but the farther away a friend lives (that is, the higher the cost), the more rewarding that friendship must be in order to be maintained. This model interprets the role of place in social networks in a manner quite distinct from that of the authentic community model. What is important about places in this respect is not that they circumscribe social life, in turn fostering intimacy but, instead, that they separate people more or less from other places and people, and thus present costs in the maintenance of social ties, with the net effect that distant ties tend to be more intimate than nearer ones because if they were not more rewarding, they would not be kept.[17]

---

[16] More specifically, each friend was ranked 1 if less intimate than the other two friends, or equal to one and less intimate than the other, 2 if equal to the other two, or in between the other two, and 3 if more intimate than one or both of the other two friends. Similarly, with distance.

[17] We have so far not presented a test of the entire causal chain postulated by the "local community" thesis: that local relations are multiplex, dense, and frequently activated, all of which in turn promotes intimacy. Our present findings challenge the conclusion of the argument (that local relations are more intimate than extralocal ones), and the findings reported in Chapter 3 challenge the postulated causal connection of multiplexity, and so on, to intimacy. Nevertheless, for purposes of completion, the accompanying illustration shows the set of statistical associations.

At the *link* level:

LOCAL (friend outside Detroit/Detroit/neighborhood) — ($\gamma = -.06$) —— CLOSENESS
LOCAL ——— ($-.00$) —— MULTIPLEXITY*——— ($-.06$) —— CLOSENESS
LOCAL ——— ($.38$) —— FREQUENCY ——— ($.14$) —— CLOSENESS
LOCAL ——— ($.10$) —— DENSITY ——— ($.13$) —— CLOSENESS
LOCAL ——— ($-.06$) —— DURATION ——— ($.35$) —— CLOSENESS

Note that this model and the authentic community model both consider distance important; neither refers to a "non-place" realm (Webber, 1968). However, the "local community" thesis assumes that distance is a mechanical, *causal* factor that vitiates bonds; the present model assumes that it is a *cost* that people consider when deciding whether or not to pursue a given relation. The structure of results appears to support our model better. Near relations are not more communal than far ones, but distance is a factor in forming and maintaining relations.

So far in this chapter, we have examined the authentic community argument by comparing local social relations to extralocal ones. There is a very different approach to testing that argument: to examine the consequences to people of moving from their locales.

The Consequences of Residential Mobility

This section addresses the question of whether residential mobility, by loosening individuals' local ties, has social and psychological ill effects. Our answer is essentially negative. Research indicates that people generally tend to be neither psychologically harmed nor socially isolated by their moves, and, indeed, that they largely benefit from their moves. This answer is, however, conditional: The extent to which moves help or harm people partly depends on the degree of choice and the resources they have; people with little of each are harmed. Our discussion relies primarily on published research, supplemented at a few points by our own data. In the first part of our review, we consider who moves, why they move, and where. An inventory of basic facts about mobility is a necessary background for the analysis. In the second part, we present the many kinds of consequences that result from mobility. And, in part three, we consider the social distribution of gains and losses resulting from mobility.

WHO MOVES, WHY, AND WHERE

Approximately 20 percent of the American population moves each year, a rate that has remained relatively constant for over a quarter-century (Bureau of the Census, 1971; L. Long, 1976). Within a decade,

---

At the *network* level:

NUMBER of best friends in neighborhood ————($r = .01$)—— TOTAL CLOSENESS
NUMBER —— (.10) —— DENSITY ———————— (.09) —— TOTAL CLOSENESS
NUMBER —— (.29) —— TOTAL FREQUENCY — (.13) —— TOTAL CLOSENESS

* Measure here excludes neighbor role.

These statistics indicate either very small associations, or a structure of associations that is incompatible with the postulated causal order (see Blalock, 1964).

an estimated 75 percent of the population has moved at least once (Abu-Lughod and Foley, 1960). Many of the annual moves are made by a small number of frequent movers (Morrison, 1972; Lansing and Mueller, 1967). Most moves cover only a short distance. In one survey of metropolitan households, approximately 85 percent of the families' most recent moves were within the same metropolitan area, 60 percent within five miles, and 25 percent within the neighborhood (Butler et al., 1969: 9; see also Bureau of the Census, 1971; Zimmer, 1973; and Simmons, 1968).

An examination of the characteristics of persons who move and the reasons they move suggests the following generalization: The people who are most likely to move are those who anticipate benefits from their moves and are best able to profit from them. (In some cases, research reports permit us to distinguish between *migrants*—those who move long distances —and *local movers*. In other cases, the two are combined or there are no differences. We make the distinction where possible and appropriate.) More specifically, the characteristics of those who most often move can be summarized as follows:

Skills. In the United States and abroad, migrants tend to be better skilled and generally more competent than stay-at-homes (Bradfield, 1973; Bastide and Girard, 1974a; Tilly, 1970). In the United States, better-educated and white-collar workers are more likely to migrate than others (although they may be less likely to move locally—Morrison, 1972; L. Long, 1973; Bureau of the Census, 1971, 1974).[18]

Life-Cycle. Both local and long-distance moves are most likely for persons in their twenties as they leave home, leave school, seek jobs, are discharged from the armed forces, get married, or have their first children (Morrison, 1972; Simmons, 1968; Bastide and Girard, 1974a, 1974b). Thus, it is persons who are most flexible and as yet unrooted who are most likely to move.

Race. Non-whites appear to be less likely to migrate than whites but more likely to move locally—often as a result of coercion (for example, urban renewal—Lansing and Mueller, 1967; Bureau of the Census, 1971, 1974).

Residential History. As mentioned earlier, the more people have moved, the more likely it is that they will move again.[19]

Local Ties. Families with no kin or friends in the area are more likely

[18] An exception should be noted: local and long-distance moves tend to be high for unemployed males. However, the unemployed who migrate far tend to be younger, better-educated, and more skilled than the rest of the unemployed (Lansing and Mueller, 1967).

[19] This repeated mobility can be interpreted in several ways: (1) white-collar occupations necessitate frequent mobility; (2) changes in family size require repeated moves; (3) recent arrivals are less bound to the neighborhood and thus more likely to move again; (4) past mobility gives people the confidence to undertake new moves; and (5) some persons are dispositionally "rootless." Only the latter group would seem to be especially vulnerable to "pathologies."

to prefer moving from it and to do so than are other families (Lansing and Mueller, 1967; see also Chapter 8).

In short, people with the most to gain, the least to lose, and the most resources to use in making a move are the most likely to move. This is especially true for the minority who migrate. (See Ritchey [1976] for a recent review of the literature on migration.)

The motivations for mobility are usually simple and reasonable. Economic considerations underlie most long-distance migrations, as persons seek work or report to a new job. This is particularly true of young, college-educated, and skilled males.[20] A notable minority of migrants report family reasons (24 percent in one study, half of whom gave only family reasons). These motivations include setting up households upon marriage, moving to be with kin who have left for economic reasons, moving to get away from kin, or choosing a town because of relatives who live there. These motivations are especially common for older migrants. (On these points, see Morrison, 1972; Lansing and Mueller, 1967; Bastide and Girard, 1974b; and Drass and Shulman, 1975.)

The primary reason for local moves is dissatisfaction with housing, a dissatisfaction which usually arises from increases in family size: marriage and the arrival of children. Births produce a cluster of moves in the early years of family formation. Other reasons which are less frequently given include the social composition of the neighborhood, the cost of housing, and accessibility. In a minority of cases, people are forced to move because of fire, demolition, eviction, and other nonvoluntary causes (Abu-Lughod and Foley, 1960; Simmons, 1968; Zimmer, 1973).

Where people move will, of course, also affect the outcome of the move. Most migrants select a destination on the basis of jobs and the location of their kin and friends, usually after having considered only a few places (Lansing and Mueller, 1967; Gulick et al., 1962). People migrate predominantly to cities where they have associates who provide material aid, emotional support, information, and social introductions (see, for example, Tilly and Brown, 1974; Girard et al., 1970; Poucher, 1970; Choldin, 1973; and MacDonald and MacDonald, 1964). People who have blue-collar jobs, who are quite young or quite old, or who are less educated tend to move to places where they have kin. White-collar people are more likely to select a place on the basis of employment and to depend on various contacts, new work associates, or "mobility specialists" (professionals who assist movers) once they arrive (Tilly and Brown, 1974; Rose and Warshay, 1957; our analysis of the national survey).

In making local moves, families tend to select neighborhoods where they "fit" in terms of social class, family stage, and life-style (Simmons,

---

[20] Specific economic motivations vary by class. Transfers and desire for higher pay are the predominant motives for people in higher-status occupations, while simply finding work and a steady job are more often the motivations for blue-collar workers (Lansing and Mueller, 1967).

1968; Michelson et al., 1973; Gans, 1967). This choice maximizes the opportunities for finding compatible associates and pursuing a desired life-style. Consequently, movers are usually able to reestablish their preferred styles of casual social interaction (McAllister et al., 1973, although the evidence is not unanimous—Key, 1967), and eventually to develop close friendships, although it may take longer for older migrants (Gulick et al., 1962).

THE MULTIPLICITY OF CONSEQUENCES

Moves bring both rewards and costs, and movers vary in the extent to which they gain or lose on balance. The authentic community thesis leads us to expect that most movers lose, at least in the long run, and personally if not materially, because they have torn up their community "roots." We can consider three types of consequences: feelings of satisfaction with the move, changes in social relations and life-styles, and alterations of psychological states. (An important analytical issue should be noted: Even if an association, positive or negative, between mobility and these conditions should be discovered, it would be necessary—but difficult—to determine whether mobility caused the conditions, whether the conditions predisposed people to move, or whether a third factor, say, poverty in the place of origin or hostility to migrants in the place of destination, caused the correlation.)

Research on people's feelings about moving indicates that they are gen-erally quite willing to move and that they feel satisfied with the move. A national survey, for example, found that over 80 percent of recently mobile urbanites were satisfied with their new housing situations and over 70 percent considered the new neighborhoods *at least* as "nice" as the old (Butler et al., 1969: 42; see also Gans, 1967; Michelson, 1973a, 1973b; Key, 1967; B. Berger, 1960; Lansing, 1966; and Poucher, 1970).[21]

Social relations are frequently affected by mobility, especially in the case of long-distance migration. Several studies have indicated that the straining or sundering of bonds to old associates can be an important sacrifice, a major adjustment problem, and a significant source of dis-satisfaction in residential change (see Gulick et al.. 1962; Fried, 1963; Young and Willmott, 1957). However, most persons appear to reduce this disruption by moving near kin and friends or relocating in compatible neighborhoods where replacements for lost ties are available. (And there are cases in which movers actually wish to sunder inhibiting social ties: Little, 1973; Gans, 1963.)

Even for those who encounter difficulties in their moves, there is one factor that usually facilitates the transition: *time*. In general, the longer people reside in a neighborhood, the more involved they are with indi-

---

[21] Drass and Shulman (1975) found that the most glowing reports of satisfaction with a new job and house following a move tended to moderate after six months.

viduals and institutions there (see Chapter 8; Kasarda and Janowitz, 1974; Gulick et al., 1962; Drass and Shulman, 1975).[22] Note carefully that time in a place connects people to the social milieu of *that* place. There is no evidence that it is required or even important for other social ties.[23] Time allows processes to develop (for example, meeting neighbors, investing in a house) that *localize* individuals' networks.

We were able to bring more evidence to bear on the association between mobility and local ties by analyzing the national survey; specifically the measures it provides of respondents' involvements with people in their localities. (In the last chapter, we reported that length of residence in a neighborhood promoted local ties. Here the concern is with individuals' histories of mobility.) Overall, there was little association between the number of different homes in which the respondent had lived (since marriage or, if single, since leaving home) and local ties such as neighboring and organizational involvement. The one noteworthy exception was that frequent movers were less likely to have kin in the neighborhood than were other respondents $(\gamma = -.22)$. Similarly, people who had moved long distances (from outside the county rather than elsewhere in the same county or elsewhere in the same neighborhood) were less likely to have kin in the neighborhood $(\gamma = -.26)$ but just as likely to neighbor $(\gamma = .09)$ or to be otherwise tied into their localities. These results seem to challenge a critical assumption in the argument about mobility: other than removing people from their kin, frequent and distant moves do not seem to hinder individuals' capacities for making local social connections (given some time to do so).

With regard to psychological states and behavioral patterns, the research evidence indicates that mobile persons are no more vulnerable to psychological or adaptive problems than are the non-mobile, whether one measures those conditions in terms of verbal reports or by "deviant" behavior. Butler et al. (1973) made a longitudinal study that found virtually no associations between mobility and reports of psychic well-being. Studies of migration and rates of hospitalization for mental disorders suggest that American migrants may show a higher incidence of mental disorder than non-migrants, but the results are complex, contradictory, and sometimes negligible (Kantor, 1965, 1969).[24] And migration appears not to be cor-

---

[22] Simple neighboring is an exception; it seems to emerge almost immediately and then to level off (McAllister et al., 1973; Gulick et al., 1962; our analysis of the national survey; although this may not be so for families forced to relocate— Key, 1967).

[23] In the Detroit survey, years of residence in the neighborhood was correlated essentially only with attributes of relations which either indicated localization or the effects of age (itself correlated at $r = .32$ with years of residence). Number of friends correlated $r = .06$ with years in the neighborhood; controlling for age reduced it to .03. Average reported intimacy of friends correlated .03 with years in the neighborhood; controlling for education raised it to .05 (N.S.).

[24] Kantor (1969) contends that there is a relationship between mobility and mental illness, but that it varies with the social characteristics of the migrants, social-

related with alienation (according to studies in developing nations—Nelson, 1969; Cornelius, 1971), participation in civil disorders (Kerner Commission, 1968; Nelson, 1969), or consistently with crime (Kinman and Lee, 1960).

We examined the connections between measures of mobility and self-reports of happiness, worrying, enjoyment of life, sociability, and sense of efficacy among the national survey respondents. Again, the overall effects were small, although movers were slightly less positive. People who had moved often reported slightly less happiness ($\gamma = -.08$) and a slightly lower sense of efficacy ($\gamma = -.06$) than did other respondents; those were the largest associations. People who had moved far the previous time differed little from other respondents, but tended to have more *positive* reports about themselves (of happiness, $\gamma = .06$; not worrying, .07; feeling efficacious, .08).

In sum, most people appear able to maintain their mental balance and their preferred life-styles either by maintaining contact with previous friends and services (see Jacobson, 1973), or by quickly finding substitutes. In general, people continue their prior ways of life, and when they do change, it is usually a desired and planned change: for example, in the case of the house purchaser who wishes to garden (Gans, 1963, 1967; Michelson, 1973; B. Berger, 1960). Of course, some people do suffer from mobility; we shall consider them immediately. The main point, however, is that for the bulk of movers, the predictions of the authentic community thesis are not confirmed.

The evidence is consistent, however, with the picture of local attachment drawn in the last chapter: that different people, depending on their wants and resources, are attached in different ways to localities of "limited liability." Once attachment is seen as a connection of pragmatic concerns rather than of natural bonds, it is not surprising that mobility fails to be a source of major disruption for most people.

THE DISTRIBUTION OF BENEFITS AND LOSSES

If there is a single characteristic that distinguishes those who benefit from mobility from those who lose from it, it is the degree of choice they have. People who benefit are those who, because of their resources and knowledge, can choose whether to move or not, and where to move. Such choices affect how easily movers are able to maintain ties with the people left behind and how easily they are able to forge new ties. Access to communications and transportation also affects people's ability to sustain old relations. Those who are constrained to stay near home in unwanted

psychological aspects of the situation, characteristics of the sending and receiving communities, and indices of mental illness which are used.

or unfamiliar new places are vulnerable to loneliness, especially when they are socially distinct from their neighbors: for example, being ethnically different (Gans, 1967; Michelson, 1973a; Young and Willmott, 1957).

Being forced to move, because of fire or eviction, will often produce "grieving for an old home" and problems of adjustment (Fried, 1963; Key, 1967). The poor are especially likely to be forced out of their homes by events beyond their control; so are blacks. According to one survey, such forced relocation was the single most important reason for moving among blacks and the least important reason among whites (McCallister et al., 1971). Similarly, the opportunity to select an appropriate destination is not distributed equally to all. Class and race are barriers to many places. Lack of adequate information when picking a destination can also lead to unfortunate consequences: when, for example, problems of access to old associates are underestimated (Michelson, 1973a; Clark, 1966). Finally, the social distribution of access to prior friends follows the same patterns; the poor, the elderly, and the minorities are generally least able to travel about.

One notable group, married women, tends to suffer from all three handicaps: relatively little choice in deciding whether and where to move, and physical constraint upon arrival. As suggested by our discussion of suburbs (Chapter 7), wives are frequently moved to suit a husband's job or housing preferences, more likely than men to be torn from important social ties or at least to be upset by those separations, sometimes forced to give up their jobs (Long, 1974; Duncan and Perruci, 1976) and, if they are housewives, often relegated to staying pretty much in the house, suffering loneliness, boredom, and unhappiness. (On these points see Michelson, 1973a; Gans, 1967; Berger, 1960; Komarovsky, 1967; and Young and Willmott, 1957.) The only psychological effect of moving which Butler and his associates (1973) found was among women: female movers reported slightly more "mental disorder" than did female non-movers (see also Campbell et al., 1976: 204–205). We are not saying that *most* wives suffer from residential moves; the opposite seems true. However, wives are more vulnerable than others to such harm. (Perhaps still more vulnerable are young children and the elderly; however, we do not have much data to address that issue. Long [1975] reports that children who move tend to fall behind in school.)

There is an important group, people who have moved frequently, that does not fall among the "vulnerable," even though one would have expected that they would suffer most. Our analysis of the national survey indicated, for example, that among respondents who had moved recently, those who had previously resided in five or more homes were just about as likely to report neighboring, local organizational involvement, interest in the neighborhood, and reluctance to move as were recently moved respondents with little or no relocation experience. (Among those with little education, repeated mobility may have retarded local integration a bit, while among those with much education, repeated moves may have facilitated local involvement. Perhaps the latter developed the social skills needed for rapid integration.)

In addition, there is an important group of people who suffer because they want to move but cannot. Over half the people who report that they would like to move are found in the same location a year later (Speare, 1974; Lansing, 1966). Among these people are the "trapped" elderly caught in changing neighborhoods which they cannot leave because they cannot afford to move or do not know how to leave (see, for example, Ginsberg, 1975).

SUMMARY

Residential mobility does not usually create long-term psychic or social difficulties. Why are the predictions wrong? Some of the findings we have reviewed suggest both why most persons are not harmed and why certain minorities are:

—Most moves are quite short
—Many, if not most, persons' ties to their places are limited and replaceable with ties elsewhere
—Those who move most and farthest are usually those best capable of handling the adjustment and of maintaining old ties
—People generally choose destinations which have populations and services most conducive to the mover's integration
—People usually move voluntarily when they have good reason to believe that the move will improve their circumstances

Moves that do result in negative consequences are usually those which violate one of the last three conditions: the movers are unskilled, have picked unreceptive destinations, or have been forced to move.

The explanation for our findings involves, once again, choice and resources. In most cases, people have *chosen* whether and where to move on the basis of their needs, resources, and alternatives. Skilled and affluent people tend to move relatively long distances and to places without pre-existing contacts. They have a greater range of (known) alternatives and greater ability to preserve old ties. Less advantaged persons, with fewer alternatives, tend more often to move to where they have associates. In either case, people tend to choose in ways that maintain their supportive social networks as well as advance them materially.

One might argue that this analysis implies that no one suffers from mobility. Quite the contrary, it points to those who would be most vulnerable: those with few alternatives on when or where to move—the evicted or, often, wives; those with few resources to maintain old ties; and those who have misunderstood their alternatives. Or a critic might argue that there is a more pervasive sort of misperception occurring: movers may be maximizing their short-term, material, and even social gains but sacrificing their long-term well-being by diffusing and draining their social relations. Although this thesis may be true, there is to date little evidence to support it. (For example, respondents to the national survey who had lived a long time in one place did not appear to be better adjusted than those who were relatively new to their neighborhoods.) [25] We assume that people generally judge their options correctly and know what is best for themselves.[26]

In sum, moving in itself does not lead to long-term social or psychological problems. The real issue seems to be whether people can choose to move and where to move, and whether they have enough resources to cope with the move. Indeed, the characteristics of those who suffer from mobility—lack of alternatives, resources, or skills—are also characteristic of many who suffer from immobility, including elderly people stuck in deteriorating neighborhoods, jobless people unaware of opportunities outside their town, and ambitious youth confined to a restricting small town. The problems associated with mobility are largely not problems of the mobility itself but of the decisions and adjustments people can make with regard to it.

Conclusion

In this chapter, we have examined the proposition that local social relations are generally more communal than extralocal ones, and the

[25] Years of residence in the current *neighborhood* had low correlations with self-reports of sociability, efficacy, or worry. It was correlated $r = -.10$ with happiness, but controls for age and education reduced all the correlations to below .02. In other analyses, we examined the association of years in the current *home* with these variables. The interesting result was that the associations, low as they were, tended to be slightly higher among those with less than a high school education (for example, with efficacy, $\gamma = .09$). This is consistent with our argument that mobility is more of a problem for people with less choice and and fewer resources. (The opposite was true with regard to getting involved in the neighborhood: higher-education people responded much more to their tenure in a home. For example, the association of length of residence with being interested in neighborhood problems was $\gamma = .48$ for the college-educated and $-.01$ for those with less than a high school diploma.)

[26] At the beginning of this chapter, we mentioned another and more fundamental argument about long-term consequences which we should consider, although it takes us somewhat afield of our social-psychological analysis: that, as a result of rational mobility on the part of individuals, a collectively irrational situation has arisen. There no longer exist in modern life any places in which "communal" relations can be found. (Consequently, there is no reason *not* to move since the moving of everyone else has eliminated the possibility of finding or creating community.) This argument is difficult to deal with in a historically bound analysis such as ours. We will make only two observations here. One, the historical assumptions in this "lost community" thesis are questionable (see Chapter 10). Two, there still remains in modern life, as the classical theorists suggested, some range from more to less

derivative proposition that residential mobility has deleterious social and psychological consequences because it weakens individuals' integration into the neighborhood. There is little support for either proposition in our data or in published research.

Combined with the findings in Chapter 8 that attachment to place is multidimensional and that people are attached in various and specific ways, these results severely challenge theories about local social life that consider local roots as natural or psychologically necessary. Combined as well with the findings in Chapter 3 that multiplexity, frequency, and density are *not* substantial sources of intimacy, the present findings challenge the authentic community thesis that social relations turned inward to a locality are richer and deeper than specialized relations with people outside of it. (To repeat our earlier qualification, these findings do not suffice to dismiss the classic decline-of-community theory. There may be no more true communities, so that all our modern-day comparisons are irrelevant to the historical argument. Instead, we have addressed a social-psychological corollary.)

Notions that modern life can provide community without propinquity come closer to describing the actual role of place today than do ideas of natural or authentic community. But perhaps these ideas go too far in the other direction. Technology has lowered the barriers posed by distance, but it has not eliminated them. Places are still distinguished by the distances that separate them from other places (as well as by their attractiveness, climate, and so on). These distances pose costs to individuals in developing and maintaining social relations. We argued that one effect of these costs is to lead people to prune their distant associates to those who are most intimate. Thus, it is the more geographically stretched social relations that tend to be most communal. (Although the specific statistical findings in support of our argument were usually not very strong, we are persuaded by the pattern of results.)

In the final analysis, the critical issue is not how place and distance *determine* social relations, but how people make *decisions* about different places and cope with space as a *constraint,* or cost, in their social lives. To the extent that people have adequate information, a range of options, and the resources to implement their decisions, they make choices that improve their lives, whether the choice is to move to a new home or to ignore their neighbors in favor of friends on the other side of town. Problems arise to the degree to which those conditions are not met, and as usual it is people without money, skills, or power who are especially vulnerable. Rootlessness is far less a problem in modern life than is powerlessness to decide where to plant one's roots.

---

stable places, but little evidence to indicate that this range is notably associated with social or psychic well-being.

PART 3

CONCLUSION

THERE HAVE BEEN two general levels to this book: one, a set of specific studies of social networks in urban settings; the other, more general, an exploration of the nature of "community" in modern life. Our primary purpose has been to present empirical research on the characteristics of social networks, how networks are shaped by social structure, and how they interact with urban ecology. As investigations of separate topics—life-cycle variations in networks, the effects of suburbia, and so on—the substantive chapters can each stand alone; there is no need to repeat their conclusions here. We will concentrate instead on the second level, the continuing theoretical issues that run through the separate chapters.

Some of the issues we have treated are significant because they arise from important theories about the historical development of modern society. Yet, nowhere have we discussed history *per se*. The first part of the concluding chapter is a brief review of the historical evidence on the "decline-of-community" thesis. The second section returns to the distinction we drew in Chapter 1 and frequently thereafter between "mechanistic" causal models of how social and ecological factors affect people and an approach which explains those effects in terms of individual choices made within social constraints. The last section returns to the social-psychological assumption that we argued in Chapter 1 was inherent in the decline-of-community thesis: that constraints on the choice of social relations promotes communal social bonds.

10. Comments on the History and Study of "Community"

Claude S. Fischer

Community and Place in Historical Perspective

MOST OF THE TOPICS dealt with in the previous chapters emerged from our general interest in the decline-of-community thesis. We analyzed those issues by abstracting sociological propositions from the historical argument and then testing those propositions against contemporary research and data drawn from contemporary populations. As we cautioned at a few points, this abstraction limits our ability to draw inferences about the historical process from our conclusions about the sociological propositions. In this section, we shall address the decline-of-community thesis in its own terms. Our treatment must necessarily be quite limited. We are not historians and are not writing history. Nevertheless, even a cursory review of secondary sources strongly suggests that the decline-of-community theory can be questioned on historical, as well as on sociological, grounds.

THE "DECLINE OF ATTACHMENT TO PLACE"

We have been specifically interested in two elements of the "decline" theory: the decline of place and the decline of communal networks. The first part of the argument is that people's attachments to place—most significantly, to place-based social groups—have declined historically. Modern historiography indicates that this assertion is only a partial truth. We will see that rootlessness has not supplanted attachment to place, but instead that freedom from place has supplanted constraint to place. In the following review, residential stability will be taken as the key measure of attachment to place.

189

The first observation is probably a cliché to historians, if not to sociologists: Western social history does not give evidence of any simple linear trend, either "progress" or decline, in this regard or in most others. Residential patterns fluctuate from time to time and place to place as a consequence of economic and other social circumstances. When land is plentiful and labor is needed, people stay put; when demographic or technological changes alter the situation, people are mobile (see Bloch, 1966; Stone, 1966; Berkner, 1973; M. Anderson, 1973; Greven, 1970; and Braudel, 1967). Looking back over our shoulders, we see that history is not a landscape of even slope but one of jagged hills and valleys—formations corresponding to families, wars, technological innovations, and other discontinuities of human life. Nevertheless, perhaps there is still some general direction to Western history and some secular change in the role of place in people's lives.

But if we intend to map that abstract slope, drawing a line from our time backward, where do we mark the origin? Where is the "once upon a time" of the decline theory? Shall it be a hill or a valley? Robert Nisbet (1969) selects the Middle Ages, which happens to be a peak of relative stability—although not of personal security—rising from centuries of chaos (Bloch, 1961). Even then, given how far back the twelfth and thirteenth centuries lie, it is extremely difficult to say just how place-centered life was for the average European. Probably, the constrictive institutions of feudal serfdom did indeed guarantee more continuity in place than the West has known since, but one cannot be certain.

We can be somewhat surer of our conclusions when we look nearer, say to rural England in the sixteenth and seventeenth centuries. There we can discern, despite frequent fluctuations, rates of residential stability *about equal to those of the modern era*. Roughly half the men living in these English towns in a given year were not to be found there ten years later (Laslett, 1971: 156; Stone, 1966). The same was true across the Atlantic, in New England. Although the early Puritan villages were very stable as long as land was plentiful (for example, Lockridge, 1970: 63–64), within about two generations mobility increased sharply. Farms became too small to support all of a man's sons, and the younger ones had to leave (see Rutman, 1975; Lockridge, 1971; Bumstead and Lemon, 1968; Demos, 1970). For example, 40 percent of the men in the third generation of Andover, Massachusetts, emigrated (Greven, 1970). Boston reached the level of a 50-percent-per-decade departure rate before 1700.[1] And these Puritan villages were the most cohesive and stable in New England (P. Smith, 1968).

This pattern continues to the modern day, albeit with many variations

[1] Actually, 47 percent in eight years; calculated from Henretta (1965), text and Table 1.

from one place to another and one decade to another. Thernstrom's is probably the most complete summary of the research on geographical mobility in America (1973: 221–32). Reviewing studies of many towns through the period from 1800 to 1968, he concludes:

> Over the span of a century and two-thirds, there was no long-term trend toward either increased or decreased population mobility in the United States (p. 224).
>
> The probability that only between 40 and 60 percent of the adult males to be found in an American community at one point in time could still be located there a decade later held not only for most cities throughout the nineteenth and twentieth centuries; it applied in farming communities untouched by urbanization as well. . . .
>
> The only marked deviation from this pattern appeared in the earliest years of settlement on the frontier, in which population turnover was exceptionally rapid (pp. 225–27).

There are even some reasons to suspect that residential mobility has *decreased* since the nineteenth century.[2]

These conclusions about long-term changes in residential stability are based on sound but nevertheless crude reconstruction. The census provides us with much more exact data for the post–World War II period. Between 1948 and 1970, *opportunities* for mobility expanded substantially in the United States. In addition to general economic growth, the number of available homes increased (12 percent on a per capita basis), and transportation facilities grew enormously (92 percent in automobiles per capita; 1,250 percent in passenger-miles flown per capita).[3] Yet, *rates* of mobility and migration remained essentially constant throughout the period: each year, about one out of five families moved (Bureau of the Census, 1971; Simmons, 1968). The trend, such as it is, may actually be of a decline in mobility (L. H. Long, 1976).

What can we conclude from this review? Attachment to place, at least as indicated by rates of emigration, cannot be shown to have declined in the centuries for which mass data are available. Either modern society is not especially rootless and transient, or this is a rootlessness that has lasted over 12 generations. This conclusion is, however, somewhat difficult to accept: Has nothing changed in people's relations to their places? Actually, there are some signs of significant changes. Consider three:

First, it seems that *who* it is that moves has changed somewhat. Although

---

[2] For one, Knights (1969) studied residential mobility of all kinds (that is, not just leaving town) in Boston from 1830 to 1860 and concluded: "A rule of thumb would be that ante-bellum Bostonians were at least twice as mobile residentially as are Americans of today" (p. 268: see also Simmons, 1968: 624). For another, moves across city lines today probably mean less than they did then. To a great extent, contemporary moves of this kind are from city to suburb, after which movers usually maintain the jobs and most of the closest associates they had before.

[3] Calculated from U.S. Statistical Abstracts.

the evidence is only suggestive, it appears that before this century the mobile population was relatively disadvantaged: farmers' younger sons without inheritances (in, for example, both old and New England), refugees, drought-stricken peasants, and other unfortunates. But today migrants tend to be better off than those who do not move (see Chapter 9). In Thernstrom's (1973) research, 1920 seems to be an important turning point. Before then, movers were largely blue-collar; after then, largely white-collar.

Second, people today are better able to construct and maintain social ties with persons outside their localities. We hardly need statistics to confirm the point; advertisements by the telephone, automobile, and airline industries stress it repeatedly. Nevertheless, there are statistics. For example, during the past several generations, the likelihood of marrying someone from one's own village has declined (D. S. Smith, 1973; while the likelihood of marrying someone of the same age has increased; Shorter, 1975: 153–54). Over the past generation in the United States, the probability of marrying someone living within the same census tract has declined (while the chance of marrying someone of the same social class has increased; Dinitz et al., 1960). People seem increasingly to choose associates on the basis of similarity and compatibility rather than proximity.

Third, it also appears that, for better or worse, the influence of one's neighbors has declined. Gradually, in stages, and at different rates in different places, local social control—whether vested in feudal lord, parish, clergy, or village elders—has weakened. Both neighbors' moral authority and their ability to coerce have waned, the former probably as a result of the latter (for Europe, see Shorter, 1975; rural France, Bloch, 1966; rural Germany, Heberle, 1960; colonial New England, Bushman, 1967). It is this change that caused most concern to the classical sociologists.

These changes indicate that there has been a decline not in *attachment* (that is, voluntary commitment) to place but in *constraint*—involuntary limitation—to a place. Put another way, choice has increased with respect to place.[4] Relatively fewer people are forced to move; more are able to move. In terms of net migration, these two trends seem to have roughly balanced out. People can increasingly choose to stay in their localities while forming ties outside of them. That they *can* do so does not mean they *must* or *do*. Couples who marry are still disproportionately likely to be neighbors, as are people who become friends. And people still have some need, although less, to attend to the opinions of neighbors.

The "decline-of-local-community" argument must therefore be restated in terms of constraint. It is precisely constraint on social choice that, as we

---

[4] Of course, some choices have been reduced. One cannot easily choose to live in a feudal manor, or in an isolated village (although rural communes are a possibility). Nevertheless, it seems safe to assert a net increase in choice of places.

argued in Chapter 1, the community theory assumes is necessary for communal social relations. In step with this logic, we turn next to consider the historical argument that there has been a decline in communal relations.

THE "DECLINE OF COMMUNAL RELATIONS"?

The decline in the control of local groups over the individual has, according to the general thesis, resulted in a decline in the communal quality of social ties. Personal relations in the modern age are said to be shallow, transient, unreliable, "morally empty and psychologically baffling" (Nisbet, 1969: 52). Has such a decline occurred? As difficult as it is to measure historical trends in attachment to place, it is well nigh impossible to assess historical changes in the nature of intimate ties (especially since we should not expect any simple linear trends). Nevertheless, we proceed.

We can begin with the feudal manor. As described by French historian Marc Bloch (1961, 1966), the manor was certainly a corporate society. Social ties were constrained within the group. Serfs, for example, could not marry outside the manor, and exceptions to this rule were made only for a price (1966: 88). Although people could under certain circumstances leave the group, they did so at the risk of forfeiting protection in a very dangerous world (1961: 139). What was the character of personal relations in this local, dense, and multiplex society? While we can assume that people were committed to their kindred (enough to avenge blood debts, for example), we can only speculate about the emotional quality of these ties. Bloch quotes as "characteristic" the comment of one baron who, threatened with the execution of his son, responded, "What recks it me of the child? Have I not still the anvils and hammers wherewith to forge finer ones?" (1961: 135). Marriages were, of course, largely ones of convenience. And beyond the kin there seem to have been few, if any, intimate ties:

> In France, in speaking of kinfolk, one commonly called them simply "friends" (*amis*) and in Germany, *Freunde*. . . . The general assumption seems to have been that there was no real friendship save between persons united by blood (1961: 123–24).

Centuries later in rural Europe, the lord's authority was assumed by the village's rich and powerful elders, and the local society remained corporate (Bloch, 1966; Shorter, 1975). What of social relations there? Kinship was certainly important but was not necessarily intimate. In fact, historian Edward Shorter (1975) insists that kin ties were not intimate. In eighteenth-century Austria, for example, parents typically made formal contracts with their sons in order to guarantee support in their old age (Berkner, 1972)—a formalism somewhat shocking to modern sensibilities.[5] Aside from kin, social relations appear to have been a mixture of mutual interdependence and mutual suspicion. Neighbors, as Rudolf Heberle (1960: 9) points out, "did things for one another, whether they liked each other or not." Indeed, some social distance between neighbors was preferred.

It is difficult to reconstruct the personal lives of long-deceased peasants, but it is possible to gain some insight into their lives by looking at studies of relatively modern European villages. Studies of rural villages in Ireland (Arensberg, 1968), France (Wylie, 1964), Italy (Banfield, 1958), and Spain (Freeman, 1970), for example, show a similar pattern: strong commitments to kin interdependence but social distance (and frequently suspicion and hostility) among neighbors.

The early Puritan towns were perhaps the classic "corporate communities" (see, for example, Lockridge, 1970). They were intentional communities, in many ways not dissimilar to modern rural communes. They were literally corporate: they were chartered, land was held in common and collectively divided, and one had to apply for admission to the church and town (which were the same). The Puritans rigorously enforced commitment to the group (for example, members who moved too far from the church to attend it regularly were pressured to move back) and resisted incursions from outside. Leaders enforced a rigid orthodoxy on members' public and private lives. It was "in a very real sense, a totalitarianism of true believers. . . . Difference inevitably implied deviation and deviation in a community of saints was indefensible" (Zuckerman, 1970: 6).

> In each community the agencies of law and authority merged so that the individual felt himself confined within a unified governing structure. . . . Social institutions, conscience, and the forces of nature meshed in the communal experience to restrain rebellious dispositions (Bushman, 1967: 16–17; see also P. Smith, 1968).

What of personal ties in these corporate towns? Kin relations were strict and authoritarian. Fathers had strong economic, as well as moral, control over sons. As in Austria, filial duties were formally stipulated (for example, Greven, 1970). Although we can assume that there was affection as well (Demos, 1970), we cannot assume there was more affection than there is among kin in modern New England. As to non-kin ties, again one

---

[5] This non-romantic feature of kinship appears in many contexts, especially in what we might call premodern "survivals." For example, in his autobiographical description of Southern share-cropper families early in the twentieth century, "Nate Shaw" tells of the specific, monetary accounting husbands and wives and parents and children made of their exchanges. Buying was a common form of distribution within the family (Rosengarten, 1974).

can only speculate. The founding families were probably bound up in an intensely "communal" experience. On the other hand, casual personal friendships would seem to be a sinful indulgence, and it was common for people to watch and report one another's activities (see Zuckerman, 1970). In any case, no matter how communal Puritan towns were at their peaks, those peaks were quickly descended. Within two generations or so, the pressures of growing populations on limited land and the lures of the outside world had broken down the isolation and unity of the Puritan town (Bushman, 1967; Greven, 1970; Boyer and Nissenbaum, 1974).

Given the skimpiness of the historical evidence, might not a contemporary comparison between rural and urban places substitute for a comparison between premodern and modern? The analogy is a precarious one. But if we proceed nevertheless to make the comparison, we find that the evidence here as well does not support the decline theory. All in all, social science research has failed to confirm differences between urban and rural populations in the quantity or quality of personal ties (see Fischer, 1976).[6]

Some may object to this line of argument with a common complaint (it has been common for ages): Is it not obvious from all the signs around us that personal ties have disintegrated? Look at the climbing rates of divorce, crime, suicide, political conflict, and the like. There are two answers: (1) These indicators may be signs of distress, but they are not necessarily signs of weakened personal ties. For example higher divorce rates may reflect increased opportunities for people to escape unhappy relations and to find happier ones; conflict may be a result, not of disintegration, but of greater cohesion among deprived peoples (see Tilly et al., 1975). (2) As we warned earlier, history is not linear; contemporary trends may be misleading. Since World War II, and especially since 1960, many signals of "distress" have zoomed upward: violent crime, suicide among young people, political disaffection, expressions of unhappiness, and so on. But many of these indicators were *declining* (for example, crime rates) or *steady* (for example, suicides) from the turn of the century until about 1960. Recent events—whether or not they indicate decline of community—can hardly be taken as representative of modern society.

Some conclude from the historical and anthropological evidence that modern society has brought *more*, not less, communal relations. Shorter (1975) argues vigorously that the weakening of the local corporate group has been associated with the rise of true intimacy and love in the family. Anthropologist Oscar Lewis, student of peasants in both village and city, once asserted (1965: 498):

---

[6] In other respects as well, there are intriguing parallels between the historical and the locational comparison. Urban relations are probably more often singleplex and geographically dispersed than rural ones.

> I suspect that there are deeper, more mature human relationships among cosmopolitan individuals who have chosen each other in friendship than are possible among . . . peasants who are thrown together because of kinship or residential proximity.

And there is Simmel (1922: 189):

> We have observed the progress from a differentiation and combination [of individuals] according to external, schematic criteria to a differentiation and combination in terms of their real solidarity and affinity.

We are not quite so daring as these authors and will conclude only that the historical evidence does not support the theory of the decline of communal relations. The closed corporate groups of the past are waning and new sources of personal networks are supplementing traditional ones, but there are few signs that intimate and supportive relations are in decline.

THE ARCADIAN MYTH REVISITED

Although our conclusion may strike some sociologists as novel, it is probably tediously familiar to most historians. Why, then, is there such persistence in sociological (and popular) thought—implicitly, if not explicitly—of the idea that people were once upon a time more stable with social relations more communal than today? There are, no doubt, several reasons, the most innocent being simple and charming nostalgia. But there are probably a few significant sources of systematic bias as well.

One is the nature of the historical evidence sociologists have usually relied upon. History until recently has been the story of the prominent and well-to-do. It is they who write memoirs, collect souvenirs, and store memorabilia in attics of family homes. The mass of the populace leaves no diaries, is compelled to sell heirlooms, and suffers its homes to be burned or torn down. No wonder, then, that our picture of an earlier time has been one of comfortable people sedately chatting with their neighbors on the verandas of stately homes. Those are virtually the only pictures we have been left; and, in them, the poor and the transient are invisible. (Isaac Asimov is reputed to have remarked, in reference to the bromide about "the good old days when everyone had servants," "Ah, yes, but *we* would have been the servants!") [7]

This bias is related to another: the point of view of the commentator. As cultural critic Raymond Williams (1973: 38) put it in his major study of the Arcadian myth: "There is only one real question. Where do we stand, with whom do we identify" as we read of serfs and lords, cottagers and gentry? Historians and sociologists have usually identified with the

---

[7] Gretchen Swidler, personal communication, 1975.

people who benefited most from the corporate societies of the past rather than with the masses in those societies.

And this bias relates to yet another: the *wish* to see an Arcadian past in order to make a statement about the present. The historical facts are stark. As Williams says, "Nobody, by any exercise of sentiment, can convert the eighteenth century rural village into a 'rural democracy' or, absurdly, a commune" (p. 102), and "when we moved back in time, consistently directed to an earlier and happier rural England, we could find no place, no period, in which we could seriously rest" (p. 35). And yet the pastoral image remains strong and even grows in power, because it serves some people as a means of rebuking the present. It is used, logically enough, by reactionaries in their complaints about the decline of authority and tradition and the rise of license and "mobocracy." Ironically, the myth of the Golden Age is also used by many radicals who justify any efforts to forge a new order by claiming that it is not new at all but the restoration of a bygone and lamented past. It is a powerful idea indeed that can join the fervent right and left under its banner, and it is all the stronger for that strange alliance. The myth of the Arcadian past is certainly more powerful than our effort to debunk it. And so it shall no doubt survive us all.

A Sociological Perspective

As the decline-of-community thesis can be seriously questioned on historical grounds, so it can be questioned on sociological grounds—that is, in terms of its implicit social psychology. One set of such questions concerns its general model of, or perspective on, the way social and ecological structures affect individuals.

In Chapter 1, we distinguished (as others have done before us) two orientations to the study of human behavior: one, which we labeled "mechanistic," interprets social action as the effect of external forces; the other, which we developed into a "choice-constraint" perspective, interprets behavior as the result of actors deciding among structured sets of alternatives. We argued for the latter view, in a tone not unlike Raymond Boudon's (1976: 1180): "To pursue [a theoretical analysis] requires that men not be considered as punch cards, as a set of juxtaposed variables, but that they be seen as actors, able and willing to take decisions depending on their resources and on the context." Some of the arguments in the decline-of-community school appear to assume a mechanistic perspective.

Several specific analyses have supported our conviction that seeing people as actors is generally more useful than seeing them as acted upon. We suggested, for example, that network analysis, itself a useful approach to urban studies, is particularly congruent with an emphasis on socially structured choice (Chapter 2); the interrelations of network attributes are better understood as reflecting the contexts and contents of choices people face than as "impacts" of structural features (Chapter 3); people seem to "trade off" certain aspects of social relations for other attributes, as in trading off ethnic versus economics similarity (Chapter 4); and the consequences of residential mobility are best understood in terms of whether and why people *choose* to move (Chapter 9).

A specific instance of the mechanistic perspective is the way some researchers have looked at ecological variables such as location, density, and size. Implicitly at least, the model they hold is one in which these particular structural factors "impinge" on individuals and trigger responses. We suggest instead a model in which, to quote Louis Wirth (1945: 177), "physical factors . . . are at best conditioning factors offering the possibilities and setting the limits for social and psychological existence and development. In other words, they set the stage for man, the actor."

The latter approach seems to have proven fruitful here. Population density is commonly seen as "impacting on" people. Our research indicates that it probably does not impact; instead, it sets up certain opportunities and constraints for individual choice (Chapter 6). For example, density brings more potential associates within range, but it can also bring more competitors for resources into an area. The distinctiveness of social life in suburbia is not a direct consequence of its ecology but is instead the result of choice—the choice of some people to move there and of others not to, and the choices people must face once they are there (Chapter 7). We found that the patterns of attachments people had to their neighborhoods were quite selective and seemingly best explained by a "decision-making" model (Chapter 8). Similarly, we could explain the consequences of relative attachment or lack thereof in terms of the choices open to people in various places (Chapter 9).

The idea that one should look at ecological factors as the "stage" for an "actor" seems obvious upon serious reflection. Yet the mechanistic approach comes almost naturally to many. For example, psychologists have recently become interested in the personal consequences of the urban environment. Most of the analyses they have presented ask what the environment *does to* people—a mechanistic approach that is likely to prove disappointing.[8]

These and similar conclusions we drew are, of course, only suggestive. It is certain neither that further research would confirm them nor that a mechanistic analysis would fail to work just as well. Yet we are struck by the clarity which a "choice" perspective provides. Now it must be

---

[8] For critiques of environmental psychology's applicability to urban studies, see Baldassare and Fischer (1977) and Fischer (1977).

once more admitted that we draw this distinction between mechanical and choice models much too sharply. Most of those whom we label mechanistic no doubt acknowledge that in the final analysis structural conditions affect people through their choices or lack thereof. It is "obvious" that individuals are decision-makers. Well, as George Casper Homans once wrote, "One can get pretty obvious if one tries, and in a good cause I believe in trying" (1967: 45). The good cause here is to emphasize the priority in sociological analysis of stipulating that "units of analysis" are choosing actors.

Choice is important in other respects as well. In our analyses *degree of choice* was usually the most critical determinant of whether people would be affected negatively or not by conditions many assume to be universally detrimental. Geographic separation from friends, population density, suburban residence, residential mobility—these and similar ecological factors are problems largely to the extent that people lack *choice* (in, for example, deciding to move) or *resources* to make the most of their choice (for example, to travel to visit kin). We found at points, for example, that high income provdes both relative freedom *to* (meet people from diverse settings, select similars as friends, and so on) and freedom *from* (the neighborhood, the loss of ties after moving, and so on).

CHOICE AND STATISTICAL ASSOCIATIONS

Choice may be quite important in yet another respect: in weakening the associations we can observe between social structure and social networks.

In much of our data analysis we discovered weak statistical relationships between structural variables—for instance, those measuring attributes of places—and aspects of people's networks. This was not always so—for example, life-cycle had substantial effects on friendships. The weak associations often had meaningful substantive implications. And as we argued earlier, it is the *pattern* of associations, not the *size,* that matters most in the evaluation of theories. Nevertheless, there was a tendency toward weak associations. To some extent, this trend can be attributed to problems of reliability and validity in our measures.[9] But the low

[9] It is no doubt true that the measures we had as indicators for key concepts were on occasion of limited reliability, and perhaps of limited validity as well. In part, this is inevitable in reanalyzing data that was collected by other researchers for other purposes. But, in part, this is also the inevitable result of pioneer research. Systematic efforts to measure attributes of people's personal networks by mass survey are relatively recent. The Detroit Area Study, in spite of its limitations, has provided a few significant first steps in this direction. And the same problems of new research apply with respect to measuring people's relations with the places they live. We remain confident of the general pattern of results and of their substantive meanings, but concede that weak measures probably reduced their size.

We are more aware than anyone else of these sorts of limitations in our evidence

associations can also be explained in another way, one with broader implications.

Even if sociologists had perfect measures, they might still typically discover small associations between structural factors and network characteristics, because people *anticipate and adjust*. (This discussion generalizes from the cne in Chapter 7 on anticipations and adjustments to suburban residence.) As argued throughout this book, people are active constructors and protectors of their social networks. Individuals probably try to maintain networks with certain characteristics suited to each one's preferences—in number of friends, style of interaction, time spent with kin, and so on. Using roughly accurate popular understandings of the world, people can anticipate the effects of certain changes and act accordingly to protect their networks (for example, refusing a job promotion that might estrange them from coworker friends). And, once some effect has occurred, they can adjust so as to restore the network structure (for example, letting some prior friendships lapse after having made some new friends). To the extent to which people can anticipate, adjust, decide, and act in these protective ways, their networks are resilient to outside forces and will "bounce back" to their original shapes. (The ability to do this depends, of course, on the opportunities and constraints each individual faces.) And to the extent that people in a society share common preferences for social relations, personal networks will therefore tend to vary within a much narrower range than is theoretically possible.

For the empirical study of networks, these anticipations and adjustments mean that, although it may be in principle true that structural factors have great effects on networks (hypothetically, it could be demonstrated by experiment), those effects would not be seen in a cross-sectional study of the general population, because, at any given moment, most people are maintaining networks within the narrow, common range. For example, if we could move people randomly to city or suburb and prevent their adjustments, such as purchases of new cars, we might well see strong

---

and in our analysis. But this project began as exploratory research, directed toward learning how best to study social networks and their connections to place. To that end, we have searched the published literature and closely analyzed two major surveys. Out of this work, we have learned both substantively and methodologically. And we are taking our methodological lessons to heart in our current research. One lesson of this sort may be of general interest; it applies to the study of networks. Although it is possible to study social networks using survey techniques by asking respondents to name people within general categories—for example, "friends," or "people you feel closest to"—we have found that this has severe limits. Such categories tend to seduce us into what has been called *verbal realism*—mistaking a set of disparate objects as similar because they are given the same name. People do not mean the same thing when they say "friend"; that term covers a heterogeneous set of associates: casual acquaintances for some, only life-long intimates for others, non-kin only for yet others, and so on. We are presently using, with some success, an alternative method of eliciting the names of respondents' associates: asking about specific activities and relations (for example, "whom did you last see socially?" or "whom would you turn to for advice about jobs?").

differences in the networks of the two groups, differences that we cannot see in real populations. One way around this problem is to study people's networks extensively over time, watching the adjustments they make to changes in their lives. Even this technique fails to indicate their anticipations and the changes they *avoid* making. Another technique, which we have used on occasion in this book, is to look at groups of people who are limited in their ability to anticipate, choose, or adjust for strong effects of structure on networks. (For example, we found that low-income migrants tend to integrate themselves more slowly into new neighborhoods.) Nevertheless, the problem—if we have indeed touched on a real phenomenon—is a significant and difficult one. Not only might it explain low correlations here, it raises a major issue in the study of the individual and social structure generally: There may be real effects of social structure on individual lives—real in that we could create them experimentally, real in that people make decisions based on anticipating them, and real in that people must adapt in order to neutralize them—but that we can observe only dimly with our usual techniques.

Constraint and the Fate of Community

Once the decline-of-community thesis is seen from this choice-constraint perspective, one can also see in it a basic social-psychological proposition: that communal (intimate and supportive) relations emerge only or primarily from relations within corporate groups (see pp. 6–14). Upon further examination, the key to this belief turned out to be, in turn, the assumption that relations constrained within a group or place become dense, multiplex, frequent, and functionally important, and thereby become more communal than others. What modern life has supposedly brought is a loosening of these constraints, a reaching out from the group or place, and a subsequent decline in communal bonds. Benjamin Zablocki (1971) states this assumption in an unusually explicit way:

> With the automobile and the telephone, it is probably easier for people of common interests to find one another, and spend time together, than ever before in history. Such communities of interest are a kind of intentional community, but they fall short of satisfying the human need for communal relationships. For one thing, an individual characteristically belongs, not to one, but to a number of different communities of interest. Since relationships between members of such interest groups tend to be segmental and transitory, their members tend to avoid becoming deeply dependent on one another. . . . Another problem stems from the fact that communities of interest often have no physical center or boundaries. Spread out all over a city or region, this sort of community lacks any sense of permanence beyond the motivations of individual members (pp. 293–94).

Zablocki goes on to note that this problem is one aspect of the "dilemma of freedom versus community." The traditional corporate groups were indeed "stultifying" he states, but they provided communal ties that modern people lack. There is, however, an alternative view to all this: that modern, freely chosen ties are actually *more* communal; that they are, as Simmel put it, ties of "real solidarity and affinity."

The question is, then: Does restriction on people's social relations—particularly spatial restriction—promote more communal relations? We cannot answer this question; but we can contribute to an answer.

Our own research and the research reported by others on social networks would suggest "no." In Chapter 3 we found that role multiplexity and frequency of face-to-face contact were probably not sources of intimacy. Network density was somewhat related to intimacy but still problematic. Its associations with other *Gemeinschaft* qualities were weak. Dense networks were not particularly likely to come out of the ascribed social contexts Tönnies emphasized—kinship and locality—any more than out of more freely chosen ones—work and voluntary associations. Dense networks were not particularly homogeneous or longlasting and only slightly more intimate than others. How should we understand network density? People select rewarding social relations out of the contexts in which they live. Sometimes their constraints (or their tastes) cause people to choose many of their closest relations from the same settings, resulting in a high density. Network density is thus a possible *result* of the search for communal bonds, not a *cause* of it.

Neither our data nor those of others seem to support critical tests of the constraint and community propositions. In Chapters 8 and 9, we looked at the role of place in forming communal ties. Neither in examining why people are attached to their places nor in assessing the consequences of attachment did we find reason to believe that the absence of "a physical center or boundaries" in people's "communities of interest" debilitates their social ties. At a few points, we found the workplace as likely a source of close ties as the home place. Other kinds of evidence as well—the historical and anthropological research cited earlier in this chapter—challenge the thesis. Indeed, except perhaps for studies of "intentional communities" (according to classical theory, a contradiction in terms), little if any empirical evidence has ever been forwarded in support of the decline thesis or its underlying social psychology.

We suggest that the lowering of social and spatial barriers and the consequent increase in the freedom to choose social relations have not led to less communal social ties. And it may just have led to the opposite. The disintegration of the monolithic community has perhaps led to the proliferation of many personal communities, each more compatible and more supportive to the individual than ascribed corporate groups.

This strain of thought brings us to yet more global concerns: assumptions about the nature of the individual and the nature of society. We have suggested that the expansion of choice in social relations at least sustains the quality of individuals' ties. This does *not* necessarily mean that the increase in individual choice—or, conversely, the decline of the corporate group—is *in toto* "good." We have *not* been addressing the issue of whether Western society is progressing or declining. That is a separate (not to mention colossal) issue.

Most of us wishfully believe in "packages" of good or evil, that good causes have good effects, evil effects have evil causes, and changes are consistent in one way or the other (see, for example, Kelley, 1971). Well, life is not like that. For example, expanding choice may bring unhappiness. Kenneth Kenniston (1965) writes:

> The actual extent of choice in American society—and in democratic technological societies everywhere—has increased enormously in the past centuries. But . . . many Americans have come to experience this freedom as at best a mixed blessing and at worst an acute problem; the demand that one choose and make commitments in the face of an enormous variety of socially available options is increasingly felt as a heavy demand (p. 261).

People may indeed seek to "escape from freedom" (Fromm, 1941).

Similarly, increased choice may mean increased risk for many people. Latter-day corporate groups may not have provided optimal relations, but they have at least guaranteed *some* relations. (Even so, we should remember the instability many people faced in traditional societies.) Modern life may thus be more of a gamble in which many hit the social jackpot and others go stone broke.[10]

Increased choice may be rewarding to *individuals,* the above qualifications notwithstanding, but still be a net loss for *society.* As is at least implicit in the classic theories about the individual and society, what is good for one is not always good for the other. With the decline of tradition and authority, people pursue their rational individual interests, but the result can be collectively irrational. For example, people seek individual wealth and prestige, resulting in a "rat race" for all; or, people try to satisfy individual needs, neglecting collective needs. As individual rewards grow, society crumbles and in the end everyone loses.

These and other warnings about the increase of choice in modern life (see Nisbet, 1969, for example) are serious, plausible, and worthy of attention. We have dealt with only one such warning, and with that one only partially. One last comment about these warnings: The decline-of-community theory (and theories similar to it: for example, mass-society theory) assumes that when average individuals, members of the mass, choose freely, they are likely to choose in ways that harm them, if not in the short run, then in the long run. Indeed, one ought to be neither

---

[10] This point was suggested by Ann Swidler.

romantic nor sanguine about people's abilities to use freedom well, even in their own interest. Each of us occasionally commits errors of judgement, indulgences, evasions of responsibility, and the like. But, in the absence of clear evidence supporting or contradicting that assumption, we are prejudiced in favor of the alternative: that people generally know what is good for them. We opt for assuming the dignity and sensibility of the individual.

Bibliography

ABU-LUGHOD, J. 1968. "The city is dead—long live the city." In *Urbanism in World Perspective,* edited by S.F. Fava. New York: Crowell.

ABU-LUGHOD, J., AND M.M. Foley. 1960. "The consumer votes by moving," and "Consumer preferences: The city versus the suburb." In *Choices and Housing Constraints,* edited by N.N. Foote et al., pp. 134–214. New York: McGraw-Hill.

ADAMS, B. 1966. *Kinship in an Urban Setting.* Chicago: Markham.

AIELLO, J.R.; Y. EPSTEIN; AND R.A. KARLIN. 1975. "Effects of crowding on electrodermal activities." *Sociological Symposium* 14 (Fall): 43–57.

ALEXANDER, C. 1967 (1973). "The city as a mechanism for sustaining human contact." In *Urbanman,* edited by J. Helmer and N.A. Eddington, pp. 239–74. New York: Free Press.

ANDERSON, E.N., JR. 1972. "Some Chinese methods of dealing with crowding." *Urban Anthropology* 1 (Fall): 141–50.

ANDERSON, M. 1973 (1975). "Family, household, and the industrial revolution." In *The American Family in Historical Perspective,* edited by M. Gordon, pp. 34–58. New York: St. Martin's Press.

ANDERSON, T.R., AND J.A. EGELAND. 1961. "Spatial aspects of social area analysis." *American Sociological Review* 26 (June): 392–99.

ARDREY, R. 1966. *The Territorial Imperative.* New York: Atheneum.

ARENSBERG, C.M. 1968. *The Irish Countryman.* Revised edition. Garden City, N.Y.: Natural History Press.

ARIES, P. 1962. *Centuries of Childhood.* New York: Knopf.

ARONSON, D.R., ed. 1970. "Special issue: Social networks." *Canadian Review of Sociology and Anthropology* 7 (4).

ASCH, S. 1956. "Studies in independence and conformity." *Psychological Monographs* 70 (9).

ATHANASIOU, R., AND G.A. YOSHIOKA. 1973. "The spatial character of friendship formation." *Environment and Behavior* 5 (March): 43–66.

AXELROD, M. 1956. "Urban structure and social participation." *American Sociological Review* 21 (February): 14–18.

BABCHUCK, N. AND A.P. BATES. 1963. "The primary relations of middle-class couples." *American Sociological Review* 28 (5): 377–84.

BANFIELD, E.C. 1958. *The Moral Basis of a Backward Society.* New York: Free Press.

BALDASSARE, M. 1975a. "The effects of density on social behavior and attitudes." *American Behavioral Scientist* 18 (July-August): 815–25.

———. 1975b. "Residential density, local ties, and neighborhood attitudes. *Sociological Symposium* 14 (Fall): 93–102.

———. 1976. "Residential Crowding in Urban America." Ph.D. dissertation, University of California, Berkeley.

BALDASSARE, M., AND S. FELLER. 1976. "Cultural variation in personal space: theory, methods, and evidence." *Ethos* 3 (Winter): 481–503.

BALDASSARE, M., AND C.S. FISCHER. 1975. "Suburban life: Powerlessness and need for affiliation." *Urban Affairs Quarterly* 10 (March): 314–26.

———. 1977. "The relevance of crowding experiments to urban studies." In *Psychological Perspectives on Environment and Behavior,* edited by D. Stokols. New York: Plenum Press.

BARNES, J.A. 1954. "Class and committees in a Norwegian island parish." *Human Relations* 7 (1): 39–58.

———. 1969. "Networks and political process." In *Social Networks in Urban Situations,* edited by J.C. Mitchell. Manchester, Eng.: University of Manchester Press.

———. 1972. "Social networks." Addison-Wesley Module in Anthropology 26: 1–29.

BASTIDE, H., AND A. GIRARD. 1974a. "Mobilité de la population et motivations des personnes." *Population* 29 (mai-juin): 579–607.

———. 1974b. "Mobilité de la population et motivations des personnes, II: Les motifs de la mobilité." *Population* 29 (juillet): 743–69.

BECKER, M. 1970. "Sociometric location and innovativeness." *American Sociological Review* 35: 267–82.

BELL, C., AND H. NEWBY. 1974. "Introduction." In *The Sociology of Community,* pp. xliii–li. London: Cass.

BELL, W. 1959. "Social choice, life styles, and suburban residence." In *The Suburban Community,* edited by W.M. Dobriner, pp. 225–47. New York: Putnam.

BELL, W., AND M. BOAT. 1957. "Urban neighborhoods and informal social relations." *American Journal of Sociology* 62 (January): 391–98.

BERELSON, B.; P.F. LAZARSFELD; AND W.N. McPHEE. 1954. *Voting.* Chicago: University of Chicago Press.

BERGER, B. 1960. *Working-Class Suburb.* Berkeley: University of California Press.

BERGER, P.; B. BERGER; AND H. KELLNER. 1973. *The Homeless Mind.* New York: Vintage.

BERKNER, L.K. 1972 (1975). "The stem family and the developmental cycle of the peasant household." In *The American Family in Historical Perspective,* edited by M. Gordon, pp. 34–58. New York: St. Martin's Press.

———. 1973. "Recent research on the history of the family in Western Europe." *Journal of Marriage and the Family* 35 (August): 393–406.

BIDERMAN, A.; M. LOURIA; AND J. BACCHUS. 1963. *Historical Incidents of Extreme Overcrowding.* Washington: Bureau of Social Science Research.

BLALOCK, H.M., JR. 1964. *Causal Inferences in Nonexperimental Research.* Chapel Hill: University of North Carolina Press.

BLAU, P. 1963. *The Dynamics of Bureaucracy.* Revised edition. Chicago: University of Chicago Press.

――――. 1964. *Exchange and Power in Social Life.* New York: Wiley.

BLAU, P., AND O.D. DUNCAN. 1967. *The American Occupational Structure.* New York: Wiley.

BLOCH, M. 1961. *Feudal Society,* Vol. 1. Translated by L.A. Manyon. Chicago: University of Chicago Press.

――――. 1966. *French Rural History.* Translated by J. Sandheimer. Berkeley: University of California Press.

BLUMER, H. 1969. *Symbolic Interactionism.* Englewood Cliffs, N.J.: Prentice-Hall.

BOISSEVAIN, J. 1973. "Preface." In *Network Analysis,* edited by J. Boissevain and J.C. Mitchell, pp. vii–xiii. The Hague: Mouton.

――――. 1974. *Friends of Friends.* London: Blackwell.

BOISSEVAIN, J., AND J.C. MITCHELL, eds. 1973. *Network Analysis: Studies in Human Interaction.* The Hague: Mouton.

BOOTH, A. 1975a. "Final report: Urban crowding project." Mimeo. Canadian Ministry of State for Urban Affairs.

――――. 1975b. "The effect of crowding on child health and development." *American Behavioral Scientist* 18 (6): 736–49.

BOTT, E. 1955 (1971). *Family and Social Network.* Second edition. New York: Free Press.

BOUDON, R. 1976. "Comment on Hauser's review." *American Journal of Sociology* 81 (March): 1175–86.

BOURG, C.J. 1975. "Elderly in a southern metropolitan area." *The Gerontologist* 15 (February): 15–22.

BOYER, P., AND S. NISSENBAUM. 1974. *Salem Possessed.* Cambridge, Mass.: Harvard University Press.

BRADBURN, N.M.; S. SUDMAN; AND G. GLOCKEL. 1970. *Racial Integration in American Neighborhoods.* Chicago: National Opinion Research Center.

BRADFIELD, S. 1973. "Selectivity in rural-urban migration: The case of Huaylas, Peru." In *Urban Anthropology,* edited by A. Southall, pp. 351–72. New York: Oxford University Press.

BRAUDEL, F. 1967. *Capitalism and Material Life.* Translated by M. Kochan. New York: Harper and Row.

BREIGER, R.L. 1974 "The quality of persons and groups." *Social Forces* 53 (December): 181–89.

――――. 1976. "Career attributes and network structure." *American Sociological Review* 41 (February): 117–36.

BRETON, R. 1964. "Institutional completeness of ethnic communities and the personal relations of immigrants." *American Journal of Sociology* 70 (September): 193–205.

BRUNER, E.M. 1973. "Kin and non-kin." In *Urban Anthropology,* edited by A. Southall. New York: Oxford University Press.

BUCKLEY, W. 1967. *Sociology and Modern Systems Theory.* Englewood Cliffs, N.J.: Prentice-Hall.

BUMSTED, J.M., AND J.T. LEMON. 1968. "New approaches in early American studies: The local community in New England." *Historie Sociale* 2: 98–112.

Bureau of the Census. 1971. "Household and family characteristics: March 1970." *Current Population Reports,* Series P-20, No. 218. Washington: U.S. Government Printing Office.

———. 1974. "Mobility of the population of the United States, March 1970 to March 1973." *Current Population Reports,* Series P-20, No. 262. Washington: U.S. Government Printing Office.

BURSTEIN, P. 1976. "Social networks and voting: Some Israeli data." *Social Forces* 54 (June): 833–47.

BURT, R.S. 1973. "The differential impact of social integration on participation in the diffusion of innovations." *Social Science Research* 2 (August): 125–44.

BUSHMAN, F.L. 1967. *From Puritan to Yankee.* Cambridge, Mass.: Harvard University Press.

BUTLER, E.W. et al. 1969. *Moving Behavior and Residential Choice.* Chapel Hill, N. C.: Center for Urban and Regional Studies.

BUTLER, E.W.; R.J. MCALLISTER; AND E.J. KAISER. 1973. "The effects of voluntary and involuntary residential mobility on females and males." *Journal of Marriage and the Family* 35 (May): 219–27.

BUTTERWORTH, D.S. 1962 (1970). "A study of the urbanization process among Mixtec migrants from Tilantongo to Mexico City." In *Peasants in Cities,* edited by W. Magnin, pp. 93–113. Boston: Houghton Mifflin.

CALHOUN, J.B. 1962. "Population density and social pathology." *Scientific American* 206: 139–48.

CAMPBELL, A.; P.E. CONVERSE; AND E. W. RODGERS. 1976. *The Quality of American Life.* New York: Russell Sage Foundation.

CANTOR, M.H. 1975. "Life space and the social support system of the inner city elderly of New York." *The Gerontologist* 15 (February): 23–26.

CAPLOW, T. 1955. "The definition and measurement of ambiences." *Social Forces* 34: 28–33.

CARP, F.M. 1975. "Life-style and location within the city." *The Gerontologist* 15 (February): 27–33.

CARROTHERS, G.A. 1956. "An historical review of the gravity and potential concepts of human interaction." *Journal of the American Institute of Planners* 22 (Spring): 94–102.

CATTON, W.J., AND R.J. SMIRCHICH. 1964. "A comparison of mathematical models for the effect of residential propinquity on mate selection." *American Sociological Review* 29: 522–29.

CHOLDIN, H.M. 1973. "Kinship networks in the migration process." *International Migration Review* 7: 163–75.

CHOMBART DE LAUWE, P-H. 1961. "The sociology of housing methods and prospects of research." *International Journal of Comparative Sociology* 2 (1): 23–41.

CHUDACOFF, H.P. 1975. *The Evolution of American Urban Society.* Englewood Cliffs, N.J.: Prentice-Hall.

CLARK, R.W. 1971. *Einstein: The Life and Times.* New York: World.

CLARK, S.D. 1966. *The Suburban Society.* Toronto: University of Toronto Press.

CLARK, W.A.V. 1976. "Migration in Milwaukee." *Economic Geography* 52 (January): 48–60.

CLAUSEN, J., AND S. CLAUSEN. 1973. "The effects of family size on parents and children." In *Psychological Perspectives on Population,* edited by J. Fawcett, pp. 185–208. New York: Basic Books.

COLEMAN, J.S. 1957. *Community Conflict.* New York: Free Press.

———. 1974. *The Mathematics of Collective Action.* Chicago: Aldine.

———. 1975. "Social structure and a theory of action." In *Approaches to the Study of Social Structure,* edited by P. Blau, pp. 76–93. New York: Free Press.

COLEMAN, J.S.; E. KATZ; AND H. MENZEL. 1966. *Medical Innovation.* Indianapolis: Bobbs-Merrill.

COLES, R. 1975. "Survival drill in the suburbs: The cold, tough world of the affluent family." *Psychology Today* (November): 67 ff.

COOPER, C.C. 1972. "Resident dissatisfaction in multi-family housing." In *Behavior, Design, and Policy Aspects,* edited by W.M. Smith, pp. 119–45. Green Bay, Wisc.: University of Wisconsin Press.

CORNELIUS, W.A., JR. 1971. "The political sociology of cityward migration in Latin America: Toward empirical theory." In *Latin American Urban Research,* Vol. 1, edited by F.F. Rabinovitz and F.M. Trueblood, pp. 95–147. Beverly Hills, Calif.: Sage.

COSER, L.A. 1974. *Greedy Institutions.* New York: Free Press.

———. 1976. "Sociological theory from Chicago dominance to 1965." In *Annual Review of Sociology* 2, edited by A. Inkeles. Palo Alto, Calif.: Annual Reviews, Inc.: 145–60.

COURGEAU, D. 1975. "Les réseaux de relations entre personnes." *Population* 30 (mars-avril): 271–83.

CRANE, D. 1972. *Invisible Colleges.* Chicago: University of Chicago Press.

CRAVEN, S., AND B. WELLMAN. 1973. "The network city." *Sociological Inquiry* 43: 57–88.

DAHL, R.A. 1967. "The city in the future of democracy." *American Political Science Review* 61 (December): 953–70.

DAVIS, D.L. 1975. "The shadow scale." *Sociological Review* 23: 143–50.

DAVIS, D.L.; K. BERGIN; AND G. MAZIN. 1974. "When the neighbors get noisy we bang on the walls: A critical exploration of density and crowding." Paper presented to American Sociological Association (August), Montreal.

DEMOS, J. 1970. *A Little Commonwealth.* New York: Oxford University Press.

DEUTSCH, K. 1961. "On social communication and the metropolis." *Daedalus* 90 (Winter).

DEUTSCH, M., AND R. KRAUSS. 1965. *Theories in Social Psychology.* New York: Basic Books.

DINITZ, S.; F. BANKS; AND B. PASAMANICK. 1960. "Mate selection and social class: Changes during the past quarter century." *Marriage and Family Living* 22 (November): 348–51.

DONALDSON, S. 1969. *The Suburban Myth.* New York: Columbia University Press.

DRAPER, D. 1973. "Crowding among hunter-gatherers: The !Kung Bushmen." *Science* 177: 301–302.

DRASS, R., AND N. SHULMAN. 1975. "Migrant relocation study." Mimeo. Department of Sociology, McMaster University, Hamilton, Canada.

DUNCAN, R.P., AND C.C. PERRUCI. 1976. "Dual occupation families and migration." *American Sociological Review* 41 (April): 252–61.

DURKHEIM, E. 1889 (1976). "Review of Ferdinand Tönnies' *Gemeinschaft und Gesellschat.*" *Revue Philosophique* 27: 416–22. Translated by M. Traugott. Manuscript. University of California, Santa Cruz.

———. 1893 (1933). *The Division of Labor in Society.* Translated by G. Simpson. New York: Free Press.

———. 1897 (1951). *Suicide.* New York: Free Press.

———. 1914 (1973). "The dualism of human nature and its social conditions." In *Emile Durkheim on Morality and Society,* edited by R. Bellah, pp. 149–63. Chicago: University of Chicago Press.

EASTON, D. 1965. *A Framework for Political Analysis.* Englewood Cliffs, N.J.: Prentice-Hall.

EINSENSTADT, S.N. 1956. *From Generation to Generation.* New York: Free Press.

EMERSON, R. M. 1976. "Social exchange theory." *Annual Review of Sociology* 2 : 335–62.

ERICKSEN, E.P., AND W.L. YANCEY. 1976. "Networks and status: Alternative hypotheses." Paper presented to the American Sociological Association (August), New York City.

EVANS, A.W. 1973. *The Economics of Residential Location.* London: Macmillan.

FAVA, S.F. 1959. "Contrasts in neighboring: New York City and a suburban county." In *The Suburban Community,* edited by W.M. Dobriner, pp. 122–30. New York: Putnam.

———. 1975. "Beyond suburbia." *Annals of the American Academy* 422 (November): 10–24.

FELLIN, P., AND E. LITWAK. 1963. "Neighborhood cohesion under conditions of mobility." *American Sociological Review* 28 (June): 364–76.

FELSON, M., AND M. SOLAUN. 1975. "The fertility-inhibiting effect of crowded apartment living in a tight housing market." *American Journal of Sociology* 80 (6): 1410–27.

FESTINGER, L.; S. SCHACHTER; AND K.W. BACK. 1950. *Social Pressures in Informal Groups.* Stanford, Calif.: Stanford University Press.

FINIFTER, A.W. 1974. "The friendship group as a protective environment for political deviants." *American Political Science Review* 68 (June): 607–25.

FIRTH, R.; J. HUBERT; AND A. FORGE. 1969. *Families and Their Relatives.* London: Routledge and Kegan Paul.

FISCHER, C.S. 1972. " 'Urbanism as a way of life': A review and an agenda." *Sociological Methods and Research* 1 (November): 187–242.

———. 1973. "On urban alienations and anomie." *American Sociological Review* 38 (June): 311–26.

———. 1975. "The study of urban community and personality." *Annual Review of Sociology* 1: 67–89.

———. 1976. *The Urban Experience.* New York: Harcourt Brace Jovanovich.

———. 1977 (forthcoming). "Sociological comments on psychological ap-

proaches to urban life." In *Advances in Environmental Research,* edited by
A. Baum and S. Valins. Norwood, N.J.: Lawrence Erlbaum Association.

FISCHER, C.S.; M. BALDASSARE; AND R.J. OFSHE. 1975. "Crowding studies and
urban life: A critical review." *Journal of American Institute of Planners*
(November): 406–18.

FISCHER, C.S., AND R.M. JACKSON. 1976. "Suburbs, networks, and attitudes."
In *The Changing Face of the Suburbs,* edited by B. Schwartz, pp. 279–308.
Chicago: University of Chicago Press.

FOLEY, D. 1975. "Accessibility for residents in the metropolitan environment."
In *Metropolitan American in Contemporary Perspective,* edited by A. Hawley and V. Rock. New York: Halstead Press.

FRANKENBURG, R. 1965. *Communities in Britain: Social Life in Town and
Country.* Baltimore: Penguin.

FREEDMAN, J.L. 1975. *Crowding and Behavior.* San Francisco: Freeman.

FREEDMAN, J.L.; S. KLEVANSKY; AND P. EHRLICH. 1971. "The effects of
crowding on human task performance." *Journal of Applied Social Psychology* 1: 7–25.

FREEDMAN, J.L.; A. LEVY; R. BUCHANAN; AND J. PRICE. 1972. "Crowding and
human aggressiveness." *Journal of Personality and Social Psychology* 8:
528–48.

FREEDMAN, S.T. 1970. *Neighbors: The Social Contract in a Castilian Hamlet.*
Chicago: University of Chicago Press.

FRIED, M. 1963. "Grieving for a lost home." In *The Urban Condition,* edited
by L.J. Duhl, pp. 151–71. New York: Basic Books.

———. 1973. *The World of the Urban Working Class.* Cambridge, Mass.:
Harvard University Press.

FROMM, E. 1941. *Escape from Freedom.* New York: Rinehart.

———. 1955. *The Sane Society.* New York: Holt, Rinehart and Winston.

GALLE, O.; W. GOVE; AND J. MCPHERSON. 1972. "Population density and
pathology: What are the relations for man?" *Science* 176: 23–30.

GANS, H.J. 1962a. "Urbanism and suburbanism as ways of life: A reevaluation of definitions." In *Human Behavior and Social Processes,* edited by
A.M. Rose, pp. 625–48. Boston: Houghton Mifflin.

———. 1962b. *The Urban Villagers.* New York: Free Press.

———. 1963. "Effects of the move from city to suburb." In *The Urban Condition,* edited by L.J. Duhl, pp. 184–98. New York: Basic Books.

———. 1967. *The Levittowners.* New York: Vintage.

GASPARINI, A. 1973. "Influence of the dwelling on family." *Ekistics* 216: 344–48.

GATES, A.S.; H. STEVENS; AND B. WELLMAN. 1973. "What makes a good
neighbor?" Paper presented to American Sociological Association (August),
New York.

GEERTZ, C. 1963. "The integrative revolution." In *Old Societies and New
States,* pp. 105–57. New York: Free Press.

GERGEN, K.J. 1972. "Multiple identity." *Psychology Today* (May): 31 ff.

GILLESPIE, D.L. 1971. "Who has the power? The marital struggle." *Journal
of Marriage and the Family* 33 (August): 445–58.

GINSBERG, Y. 1975. *Jews in a Changing Neighborhood.* New York: Free Press.

GIRARD, A.; H. BASTIDE; AND G. POURCHER. 1970. "Geographic mobility and urban concentration in France." In *Readings in the Sociology of Migration,* edited by C.J. Jansen, pp. 179–202. Oxford, Eng.: Pergamon.

GLICK, P.C. 1975. "A demographer looks at American families." *Journal of Marriage and the Family* (February): 15–26.

GOODE, W.J. 1959. "The theoretical importance of love." *American Sociological Review* 24: 38–47.

———. 1963. *World Revolution and Family Patterns.* Glencoe, Ill.: Free Press.

———. 1972. "Presidential address: The place of force in human society." *American Sociological Review* 37: 507–19.

———. 1973. "Violence between intimates." In *Exploration in Social Theory,* edited by Goode, pp. 145–97. London: Oxford University Press.

GRANOVETTER, M. 1973. "The strength of weak ties." *American Journal of Sociology* 78 (May): 1360–80.

———. 1974. *Getting a Job.* Cambridge, Mass.: Harvard University Press.

GREENFIELD, R.J., AND J.F. LEWIS. 1969. "An alternative to a density function of overcrowding." *Land Economics* 45: 282–85.

GREER, S. 1967. "Postscripts: Communication and community." In *The Community Press in an Urban Setting,* edited by M. Janowitz, pp. 245–70. Second edition. Chicago: University of Chicago Press.

———. 1972. *The Urbane View.* New York: Oxford University Press.

GREER, S., AND E. KUBE. 1959 (1972). "Urbanism and social structure: A Los Angeles study." In *The Urbane View,* by Greer, pp. 34–54. New York: Oxford University Press.

GREVEN, P.J. 1970. *Four Generations.* Ithaca, N.Y.: Cornell University Press.

GRIFFITT, W., AND R. VEITCH. 1971. "Hot and crowded: Influences of population density and temperature on interpersonal affective behavior." *Journal of Personality and Social Psychology* 17: 92–98.

GRUENBERG, B. 1974. "How free is time?" Unpublished doctoral dissertation, University of Michigan, Ann Arbor, Michigan.

GUEST, A.M. 1972. "Patterns of family location." *Demography* 9 (February): 159–71.

GULICK, J. 1973. "Urban anthropology." In *Handbook of Social and Cultural Anthropology,* edited by J.J. Honigman, pp. 979–1029. Chicago: Rand McNally.

GULICK, J; C.E. BOWERMAN; AND K.W. BACK. 1962. "Newcomer enculturation in the city." In *Urban Growth Dynamics,* edited by F.S. Chapin, Jr., and S. Weiss, pp. 315–58. New York: Wiley.

GUTKIND, P.C.W. 1965 (1969). "African urbanism, mobility and social network." In *The City in Newly Developing Countries,* edited by G. Breese, pp. 389–400. Englewood Cliffs, N.J.: Prentice-Hall.

HALL, E.T. 1966. *The Hidden Dimension.* New York: Random House.

HAWLEY, A.H. 1971. *Urban Society.* New York: Ronald Press.

———. 1972. "Population density and the city." *Demography* 9: 521–29.

HAWLEY, A.H., AND B. ZIMMER. 1971. *The Metropolitan Community.* Beverly Hills, Calif.: Sage.

HEBERLE, R. 1960. "The normative element in neighborhood relations." *Pacific Sociological Review* 3 (Spring): 3–11.

HENRETTA, J. 1965. "Economic development and social structure in colonial Boston." *William and Mary Quarterly*, 3rd Series, 22: 75–92.

HENRY, J. 1958. "The personal community and its invariant properties." *American Anthropologist* 60: 827–31.

HESS, B. 1972. "Friendship." In *Aging and Society*, Vol. 3, edited by M.W. Riley et al., pp. 357–93. New York: Russell Sage Foundation.

HILLERY, G.A. 1955. "Definitions of community: Areas of agreement." *Rural Sociology* 20 (June): 111–23.

HOCHSCHILD, A. 1975. "Toward a sociology of emotions and feelings." In *Another Voice*, edited by M. Millman and R. Kanter. Garden City, N.Y.: Doubleday Anchor.

HOMANS, G.C. 1950. *The Human Group.* New York: Harcourt, Brace and World.

———. 1967. *The Nature of Social Science.* New York: Harcourt Brace Jovanovich.

———. 1974. *Social Behavior.* Second edition. New York: Harcourt Brace Jovanovich.

HOUSTON, M.J., AND S. SUDMAN. 1975. "A methodological assessment of the use of key informants." *Social Science Research* 4: 151–64.

HOYT, H. 1969. "Growth and structure of twenty-one great world cities." In *The City in Newly Developing Countries*, edited by G. Breese, pp. 205–18. Englewood Cliffs, N.J.: Prentice-Hall.

HUME, D. 1748 (1955). *An Inquiry Concerning Human Understanding.* Indianapolis: Liberal Arts Press (Bobbs-Merrill).

HUNTER, A. 1974. *Symbolic Communities.* Chicago: University of Chicago Press.

———. 1975. "The loss of community." *American Sociological Review* 40 (October): 537–52.

HUTT, C., AND M. VAIZEY. 1966. "Differential effects of group density on social behavior." *Nature* 209: 1371–72.

JACOBS, J. 1961. *The Death and Life of Great American Cities.* New York: Random House.

JACOBSON, D. 1973. *Itinerant Townsmen: Friendship and Social Order in Urban Uganda.* Menlo Park, Calif.: Cummings.

JANOWITZ, M. 1967. *The Community Press in an Urban Setting.* Second edition. Chicago: University of Chicago Press.

KADUSHIN, C. 1966. "Friends and supporters of psychotherapy: On social circles in urban life." *American Sociological Review* 31: 786–802.

KAIN, J.F. 1968. "Urban travel behavior." In *Social Science and the City*, edited by L.F. Schnore, pp. 161–94. New York: Praeger.

KANTER, R.M. 1972. *Commitment and Community.* Cambridge, Mass.: Harvard University Press.

KANTOR, M.B. 1965. *Mobility and Mental Health.* Springfield, Ill.: Thomas.

———. 1969. "Internal migration and mental illness." In *Changing Perspectives in Mental Health*, edited by S.C. Plog and R.B. Edgerton, pp. 364–94. New York: Holt, Rinehart and Winston.

KASARDA, J.D. 1976. "The changing structure of metropolitan America." In *The Changing Face of the Suburbs*, edited by B. Schwartz, pp. 113–36. Chicago: University of Chicago Press.

KASARDA, J.D., AND M. JANOWITZ. 1974. "Community attachment in mass society." *American Sociological Review* 39 (June): 328–39.

KASL, S.V., AND E. HARBURG. 1972. "Perceptions of the neighborhood and the desire to move out." *Journal of American Institute of Planners* 38 (September): 318–22.

KATZ, E. 1966. "Occupational contact networks." *Social Forces* 37 (1): 52–55.

KATZ, E., AND P. LAZARSFELD. 1955. *Personal Influence.* New York: Free Press.

KELLER, S. 1968. *The Urban Neighborhood.* New York: Random House.

KELLEY, H.H. 1968. "Interpersonal accommodation." *American Psychologist* 23 (June): 399–410.

———. 1971. "Moral evaluation." *American Psychologist* 26 (March): 293–300.

KENNISTON, K. 1965. *The Uncommitted.* New York: Dell.

———. 1971. "Prologue: Youth as a stage of life." In *Youth and Dissent*, pp. 3–21. New York: Harcourt Brace Jovanovich.

KERCKHOFF, A.C. 1974. "The social context of interpersonal attraction." In *Foundations of Interpersonal Attraction,* edited by T.L. Huston, pp. 61–78. New York: Academic Press.

Kerner Commission. 1968. *Report of the National Advisory Commission on Civil Disorders.* Washington: U.S. Government Printing Office.

KEY, W. 1967. *When People Are Forced to Move.* Social Security Administration. Washington: U.S. Government Printing Office.

KINMAN, J. L., AND E.S. LEE. 1966. "Migration and crime." *International Migration Digest* 3: 7–14.

KLATZKY, S.R. 1971. *Patterns of Contact with Relatives.* Washington: American Sociological Association.

KLEINER, R.J., AND S. PARKER. 1976. "Network participation and psychological impairment in an urban environment" In *Urbanism, Urbanization, and Change,* edited by P. Meadows and E.H. Mizruchi, pp. 322–36. Second edition. Reading, Mass.: Addison-Wesley.

KNIGHTS, P. 1969. *The Plain People of Boston.* New York: Oxford University Press.

KOHN, M.L. 1963. "Social class and parent-child relationships: An interpretation." *American Journal of Sociology* 68: 471–80.

KOMAROVSKY, M. 1967. *Blue-Collar Marriage.* New York: Vintage.

KORNBLUM, W. 1974. *Blue-Collar Community.* Chicago: University of Chicago Press.

KRIESBERG, L. 1973. *The Sociology of Social Conflicts.* Englewood Cliffs, N.J.: Prentice-Hall.

LANSING, J.B. 1966. *Residential Relocation and Urban Mobility.* Ann Arbor, Mich.: Survey Research Center.

LANSING, J.B., AND G. HENDRICKS. 1967. *Living Patterns and Attitudes in the Detroit Region.* Detroit: Southeast Michigan Council of Governments.

LANSING, J.B., AND W. LADD. 1964. *The Propensity to Move.* Washington: U.S. Government Printing Office.

LANSING, J.B.; R. MARANS; AND R. ZEHNER. 1970. *Planned Residential Environments.* Ann Arbor, Mich.: Institute for Social Research.

LANSING, J.B., AND E. MUELLER. 1967. *The Geographic Mobility of Labor.* Ann Arbor, Mich.: Institute for Social Research.

LASLETT, P. 1971. *The World We Have Lost.* Revised edition. New York: Scribner's.

LAUMANN, E.O. 1966. *Prestige and Association in an Urban Community.* Indianapolis: Bobbs-Merrill.

———. 1973. *Bonds of Pluralism.* New York: Wiley.

LAUMANN, E.O.; L.M. VERBRUGGE; AND F.V. PAPPI. 1974. "A causal modelling approach to the study of a community elite's influence structure." *American Sociological Review* 39 (April): 162–74.

LAWRENCE, J.E. 1974. "Science and sentiment: Overview of research on crowding and human behavior." *Psychological Bulletin* 81 (10): 712–20.

LAZARSFELD, P., AND R.K. MERTON. 1954. "Friendship as a social process." In *Freedom and Control in Modern Society,* edited by M. Berger et al., pp. 18–66. New York: Van Nostrand.

LEEDS, A. 1973. "Locality power in relation to supralocal power institutions." In *Urban Anthropology,* edited by A. Southall, pp. 15–42. New York: Oxford University Press.

LEVINE, D.N., ed. 1971. *Georg Simmel on Individuality and Social Forms.* Chicago: University of Chicago Press.

LEVINE, J. 1972. "The sphere of influence." *American Sociological Review* 37: 14–27.

LEVY, L., AND A.N. HERZOG. 1974. "Effects of population density and crowding on health and social adaptation in the Netherlands." *Journal of Health and Social Behavior* 15 (3): 228–40.

LEWIS, O. 1961. *The Children of Sanchez: Autobiography of a Mexican Family.* New York: Random House.

———. 1965. "Further observations on the folk-urban continuum and urbanization." In *The Study of Urbanization,* edited by P.H. Hauser and L. Schnore, pp. 491–503. New York: Wiley.

LINDZEY, G., AND D. BYRNE. 1968. "Measurement of social choice and interpersonal attraction." In *Handbook of Social Psychology,* Vol. 2, edited by G. Lindzey. Reading, Mass.: Addison-Wesley.

LIONBERGER, H.F., AND G.D. COPUS. 1972. "Structuring influence of social cliques . . ." *Rural Sociology* 37 (March): 73–85.

LIPSET, S.M.; M. TROW; AND J.S. COLEMAN. 1962. *Union Democracy.* Garden City, N.Y.: Doubleday Anchor.

LITTLE, K.L. 1973. *African Women in Towns.* London: Cambridge University Press.

LITWAK, E. 1960. "Geographical mobility and extended family cohesion." *American Sociological Review* 25 (June): 385–94.

LITWAK, E., AND A. SZELENYI. 1969. "Primary group structures and their functions: Kin, neighbors, and friends." *American Sociological Review* 34 (August): 465–81.

LOCKRIDGE, K.A. 1970. *A New England Town: The First Hundred Years.* New York: Norton.

———. 1971. "Land, population, and the evolution of New England society,

1630–1790; and an afterthought." In *Colonial America*, edited by S.M. Katz, pp. 466–91. Boston: Little, Brown.

LONG, L.H. 1972. "The influence of number and ages on children on residential mobility." *Demography* 9 (August): 371–82.

———. 1973. "Migration differentials by education and occupation." *Demography* 10 (May): 243–58.

———. 1974. "Women's labor force participation and the residential mobility of families." *Social Forces* 52 (March): 342–48.

———. 1975. "Does migration interfere with children's progress in school?" *Sociology of Education* 48 (Summer): 369–81.

———. 1976. *The Geographical Mobility of Americans.* Current Population Reports: Special Studies, Series P-23, No. 64. Washington: U.S. Government Printing Office.

LONG, N. 1958. "The local community as an ecology of games." *American Journal of Sociology* 64 (November): 251–61.

LOO, C. 1972. "The effects of spatial density on social behavior of children." *Journal of Applied Social Psychology* 2: 372–81.

LOPATA, H.Z. 1972. *Occupation: Housewife.* New York: Oxford University Press.

LOWENTHAL, M.F. et al. 1975. "Life-course perspectives on friendship." In *Four Stages of Life,* by M. Lowenthal et al., pp. 48–61. San Francisco: Jossey-Bass.

MACDONALD, J.S., AND L.D. MACDONALD. 1974. "Chain migration, ethnic neighborhood formation, and social networks." Reprinted in *An Urban World,* edited by C. Tilly, pp. 226–35. Boston: Little, Brown.

MAISONNEUVE, J. 1966. *Psycho-Sociologie des Affinités.* Paris: Presses Universitaires.

MARANS, R.W., AND W. RODGERS. 1975. "Toward an understanding of community satisfaction." In *Metropolitan America in Contemporary Perspective,* edited by A. Hawley and V. Rock, pp. 299–354. New York: Halstead Press.

MARTIN, R.D. 1972. "Concepts of human territoriality." In *Man, Settlement and Urbanism,* edited by P.J. Ucko, R. Tringham, and G.W. Dimbelby, pp. 427–45. Cambridge, Mass.: Schenkman.

MARX, K. 1846 (1973). "The materialist basis of society." In *Karl Marx on Society and Social Change,* edited by N.J. Smelser, pp. 3–6. Chicago: University of Chicago Press.

MATZA, D. 1969. *Becoming Deviant.* Englewood Cliffs, N.J.: Prentice-Hall.

MAUSS, M. 1925 (1954). *The Gift.* Translated by I.G. Cannison. Glencoe, Ill.: Free Press.

MCALLISTER, R.J.; E.W. BUTLER; AND E.J. KAISER. 1973. "The adaptation of women to residential mobility." *Journal of Marriage and the Family* 35 (May): 197–204.

MCALLISTER, R.J.; E.J. KAISER; AND E.W. BUTLER. 1971. "Residential mobility of blacks and whites: A longitudinal survey." *American Journal of Sociology* 77: 445–46.

MCGAHAN, P. 1972. "The neighbor role and neighboring in a highly urban area." *Sociological Quarterly* 13 (Summer): 937–408.

MᶜPHERSON, J.M. 1975. "Population density and social pathology: A reexamination." *Sociological Symposium* 14 (Fall): 77–90.

MEAD, G.H. 1934. *Mind, Self, and Society*. Chicago: University of Chicago Press.

MEIER, R.L. 1962. *A Communication Theory of Urban Growth*. Cambridge, Mass.: M.I.T. Press.

MERTON, R.K. 1957. "The role-set: Problems in sociological theory." *British Journal of Sociology* 8 (2): 106–20.

———. 1975. "Structural analysis in sociology." In *Approaches to the Study of Social Structure,* edited by P.M. Blau, pp. 21–52. New York: Free Press.

MICHELSON, W. 1970. *Man and His Urban Environment*. Reading, Mass.: Addison-Wesley.

———. 1973a. "Environmental change." Research Paper No. 60. Centre for Urban and Community Studies, University of Toronto.

———. 1973b. "The reconciliation of 'subjective' and 'objective' data on physical environment in the community." *Sociological Inquiry* 43: 147–73.

MICHELSON, W.; D. BELGUE; AND J. STEWART. 1973. "Intentions and expectations in differential residential selection." *Journal of Marriage and the Family* 35 (July): 189–96.

MICHELSON, W., AND K. GARLAND. 1974. "The differential role of crowded homes and dense residential areas in the incidence of selected symptoms of human pathology." Research Paper No. 67. Centre for Urban and Community Studies, University of Toronto.

MILGRAM, S. 1965. "Some conditions of obedience and disobedience to authority." *Human Relations* 18: 57–75.

———. 1970. "The experience of living in cities." *Science* 167: 1461–68.

MILLS, C.W. 1956. *The Power Elite*. New York: Oxford University Press.

MINAR, D.W., AND S. GREER. 1969. *The Concept of Community*. Chicago: Aldine-Atherton.

MITCHELL, J.C., ed. 1969. *Social Networks in Urban Situations*. Manchester, Eng.: University of Manchester Press.

———. 1973. "Networks, norms, and institutions." In *Network Analysis,* edited by J. Boissevain and J.C. Mitchell, pp. 15–36. The Hague: Mouton.

MITCHELL, R.E. 1971. "Some social implications of high density housing." *American Sociological Review* 36 (February): 18–29.

———. 1975. "Ethnographic and historical perspectives on relationships between physical and socio-spatial environments." *Sociological Symposium* 14 (Fall): 25–40.

MONTAGU, A., ed. 1973. *Man and Aggression*. Second edition. New York: Oxford University Press.

MORGAN, D.J., AND J.R. MURRAY. 1974. "A potential population distribution and its dynamics." Manuscript. National Opinion Research Center, Chicago.

MORRIS, D. 1969. *The Human Zoo*. New York: McGraw-Hill.

MORRIS, E.W., AND M. WINTER. 1975. "A theory of family housing adjustment." *Journal of Marriage and the Family* 37 (1): 79–88.

MORRISON, P. 1972. "Population movements and the shape of urban growth: Implications for public policy." In *Population, Distribution and Policy,* Vol.

5, Research Reports, Commission on Popuation Growth and the American Future, edited by S.M. Mazie, pp. 281–322. Washington: U.S. Government Printing Office.

NATHANSON, C.A. 1974. "Moving preferences and plans among urban black families." *Journal of the American Institute of Planners* 40: 353–59.

NELSON, J.M. 1969. "Migrants, urban poverty, and instability in developing nations." Center for International Affairs, Harvard University, Cambridge, Mass.: Occasional Paper No. 22.

NEUGARTEN, B.L., AND J.W. MOORE. 1969. "The changing age-status system." In *Middle Age and Aging,* edited by Neugarten. Chicago: University of Chicago Press.

NEWCOMB, T. 1961. *The Acquaintance Process.* New York: Holt, Rinehart.

NISBET, R.A. 1966. *The Sociological Tradition.* New York: Basic Books.

———. 1969. *The Quest for Community.* 1969 edition. New York: Oxford University Press.

———. 1973. *The Social Philosophers.* New York: Crowell.

O'BRIEN, D.J., AND R.S. STERNE. 1974. "Toward a sociology of choice: An exploration of the paradigm crisis." Paper presented to American Sociological Association (August), Montreal.

OGBURN, W.F. 1954 (1964). "Why the family is changing." In *William F. Ogburn on Culture and Social Change,* edited by O.D. Duncan, Chicago: University of Chicago Press.

PACKARD, V. 1972. *A Nation of Strangers.* New York: McKay.

PARK, R.E. 1916 (1969). "The city: Suggestions for investigation of human behavior in the urban environment." In *Classic Essays on the Culture of Cities,* edited by R. Sennet, pp. 91–130. New York: Appleton-Century-Crofts.

PARSONS, T. 1942 (1949). "Age and sex in the social structure of the United States." In *Essays in Sociological Theory,* edited by Parsons, pp. 89–103. New York: Free Press.

———. 1951. *The Social System.* New York: Free Press.

———. 1968. *The Structure of Social Action,* volume 1. New York: Free Press.

PARSONS, T., AND R.F. BALES. 1955. *Family, Socialization, and Interaction Process.* Glencoe, Ill.: Free Press.

PERLMAN, J.E. 1975. *Myths of Marginality.* Berkeley: University of California Press.

PLANT, J.S. 1960 "Family living space and personality development." In *A Modern Introduction to the Family,* edited by N.W. Bell and E.F. Vogel, pp. 510–20. New York: Free Press.

PONS, V. 1969. *Stanleyville.* London: Oxford University Press.

POUCHER, G. 1970. "The growing population of Paris." In *Readings in the Sociology of Migration,* edited by C.J. Jansen, pp. 179–202. New York: Pergamon.

PUTNAM, R.D. 1966. "Political attitudes and the local community." *American Political Science Review* 60 (September): 640–54.

RAINWATER, L.; R.P. COLEMAN; AND E.G. HANDEL. 1959. *Working Man's Wife.* New York: McFadden.

REISS, A.J., JR. 1955. "An analysis of urban phenomena." In *The Metropolis in Modern Life,* edited by R.M. Fisher, pp. 41–51. New York: Doubleday.

RIECKEN, H.W., AND G.C. HOMANS. 1954. "Psychological aspects of social structure." In *Handbook of Social Psychology,* Vol. 2, edited by G. Lindzey. Reading, Mass.: Addison-Wesley.

RIESMAN, D. 1959. "The suburban sadness." In *The Suburban Community,* edited by W.M. Dobriner, pp. 375–408. New York: Putnam Press.

RILEY, M.W.; A. FONER, et al. 1968. *Aging and Society.* Vol. 1: *An Inventory of Research Findings.* New York: Russell Sage Foundation.

RITCHEY, P.N. 1976. "Explanations of migration." *Annual Review of Sociology* 2: 363–404.

ROBERTS, B. 1973. *Organizing Strangers.* Austin: University of Texas Press.

ROBINSON, J.P. 1976. "Interpersonal influence in election campaigns." *Public Opinion Quarterly* (Fall): 304–19.

ROETHLISBERGER, F.J., AND W.J. DICKSON. 1939. *Management and the Worker.* New York: Wiley.

ROGERS, E.M., AND F.F. SHOEMAKER. 1971. *Communication of Innovations.* New York: Free Press.

ROSE, A.M., AND L. WARSHAY. 1957. "The adjustment of migrants to cities." *Social Forces* 36: 72–76.

ROSENGARTEN, T. 1974. *All God's Dangers: The Life and Times of Nate Shaw.* New York: Avon.

ROSSI, P. 1956. *Why Families Move.* Glencoe, Ill.: Free Press.

RUBIN, Z. 1973. *Liking and Loving.* New York: Holt, Rinehart and Winston.

RUTMAN, D.B. 1975. "People in process: The New Hampshire town of the 18th century." *Journal of Urban History* 1 (May): 268–92.

SCHERER, K.R.; R.P. ABELES; AND C.S. FISCHER. 1975. *Human Aggression and Conflict.* Englewood Cliffs, N.J.: Prentice-Hall.

SCHMITT, R. 1957. "Density, delinquency and crime in Honolulu." *Sociology and Social Research* 41: 274–76.

———. 1966. "Density, health and social disorganization." *Journal of the American Institute of Planners* 32: 38–40.

SEGAL, M.W. 1974. "Alphabet and attraction." *Journal of Personality and Social Psychology* 30 (November): 654–57.

SHIBUTANI, T. 1961. *Society and Personality.* Englewood Cliffs, N.J.: Prentice-Hall.

SHORTER, E. 1975. *The Making of the Modern Family.* New York: Basic Books.

SHULMAN, N. 1972. "Urban social networks." Ph.D. dissertation, University of Toronto.

———. 1975. "Life cycle variations in patterns of close relationships." *Journal of Marriage and the Family* (November): 813–21.

SIEBER, S.D. 1974. "Toward a theory of role accumulation." *American Sociological Review* 39 (August): 567–78.

SIMMEL, G. 1905 (1969). "The metropolis and mental life." In *Classic Essays on the Culture of Cities,* edited by R. Sennet, pp. 47–60. New York: Appleton-Century-Crofts.

———. 1907 (1971). "Exchange." In *Georg Simmel on Individuality and Social Form,* edited by D.N. Levine, pp. 43–69. Chicago: University of Chicago Press.

———. 1908 (1971). "Group expansion and development of individuality." In *Georg Simmel on Individuality and Social Forms,* edited by D.N. Levine, pp. 251–93. Chicago: University of Chicago Press.

———. 1922 (1955). *Conflict and the Web of Group Affiliations.* Translated by K.H. Wolff and R.H. Bendix. New York: Free Press.

SIMMONS, J.W. 1968. "Changing residence in the city." *The Geographical Review* 58 (October): 622–51.

SIMON, H.A. 1957. *Models of Man.* New York: Wiley.

———. 1959. "Theories of decision-making in economics and behavioral science." *American Economic Review* 49 (June): 253–83.

SLATER, P.E. 1963. "On social regression." *American Sociological Review* 28 (June): 339–64.

SMITH, D. 1971. "Household space and family organization." In *Social Space: Canadian Perspectives,* edited by D. Davies and K. Herman, pp. 62–69. Toronto: New Press.

SMITH, D.S. 1973. "Parental power and marriage patterns: An analysis of historical trends in Higham, Massachusetts." *Journal of Marriage and the Family* 35 (August): 419–28.

SMITH, J.; W.H. FORM; AND G.P. STONE. 1954. "Local intimacy in a middle-sized city." *American Journal of Sociology* 60 (November): 276–84.

SMITH, P. 1968. *As a City upon a Hill.* New York: Knopf.

SMITH, T.S. 1976. "Inverse distance variation for the flow of crime in urban areas." *Social Forces* 54 (June): 802–15.

SOMMER, R. 1969. *Personal Space: The Behavioral Basis of Design.* Englewood Cliffs, N.J.: Prentice-Hall.

SOUTHALL, A. 1973. "The density of role-relationships as a universal index of urbanization." In *Urban Anthroprology,* edited by A. Southall, pp. 71–106. New York: Oxford University Press.

SPEARE, A., JR. 1974. "Residential satisfaction as an intervening variable in residential mobility." *Demography* 11 (May): 173–89.

SPEARE, A., JR.; S. GOLDSTEIN; W.H. FREY. 1975. *Residential Mobility, Migration, and Metropolitan Change.* Cambridge, Mass.: Ballinger.

SPENCER, H. 1895. *The Principles of Sociology.* New York: Appleton.

STACK, C. 1974. *All Our Kin.* New York: Harper and Row.

STEIN, M.R. 1960. *The Eclipse of Community.* New York: Harper and Row.

STEGMAN, M.A. 1969. "Accessibility models and residential location." *Journal of American Institute of Planners* 35 (January): 22–29.

STINCHCOMBE, A.L. 1959. "Bureaucratic and craft administration of production." *Administrative Science Quarterly* 4: 168–87.

———.1975. "Merton's theory of social structure." In *The Idea of Social Structure: Papers in Honor of Robert K. Merton,* edited by L. Coser, pp. 11–34. New York: Harcourt Brace Jovanovich.

STOKOLS, D. 1974. "The experience of crowding in primary and secondary environments." Paper presented to American Psychological Association (September), New Orleans.

———. 1977. *Human Crowding*. Monterey, Calif.: Brooks-Cole.

STONE, L. 1966. "Social mobility in England, 1500–1700." *Past and Present* 33: 16–55.

STOUFFER, S.A. 1940. "Intervening opportunities: A theory relating mobility and distance." *American Sociological Review* 5 (December): 845–57.

STUEVE, C.A.; K. GERSON; AND C.S. FISCHER. 1975. "The structure and determinants of attachment to place." Paper presented to American Sociological Association (August), San Francisco.

SUSSMAN, M.B. 1959 (1974). "The isolated nuclear family: Fact or fiction?" In *Sourcebook in Marriage and the Family,* edited by Sussman, pp. 25–30. Boston: Houghton Mifflin.

SUTCLIFFE, J.P., AND B.D. CRABBE. 1963. "Incidence and degrees of friendship in urban and rural areas." *Social Forces* 42 (October): 60–67.

SUTTLES, G.D. 1968. *The Social Order of the Slum: Ethnicity and Territory in the Inner City*. Chicago: University of Chicago Press.

———. 1972. *The Social Construction of Communities*. Chicago: University of Chicago Press.

SZALAI, A., ed. 1972. *The Use of Time*. The Hague: Mouton.

TALLMAN, I. 1969. "Working-class wives in suburbia: Fulfillment or crisis?" *Journal of Marriage and the Family* 31 (February): 65–72.

TALLMAN, I., AND R. MORGNER. 1970. "Life-style differences among urban and suburban blue collar families." *Social Forces* 48 (March): 334–48.

TARR, J.A. 1973. "From city to suburb: The 'moral' influence of transportation and technology." In *American Urban History*, edited by A.B. Callow, Jr., pp. 202–12. Second edition. New York: Oxford University Press.

THERNSTROM, S. 1973. *The Other Bostonians*. Cambridge, Mass.: Harvard University Press.

THIBAUT, J., AND H.H. KELLEY. 1959. *The Social Psychology of Groups*. New York: Wiley.

TILLY, C. 1970. "Race and migration to the American city." In *The Metropolitan Enigma*, edited by J.Q. Wilson, Jr., pp. 144–69. Garden City, N.Y.: Doubleday Anchor.

———. 1972. "An interactional scheme for analysis of communities, elites, and urbanization." Manuscript. Department of Sociology, University of Michigan, Ann Arbor, Michigan.

TILLY, C., AND C.H. BROWN. 1974. "On uprooting, kinship, and auspices of migration." In *An Urban World*, edited by Tilly, pp. 108–32. Boston: Little, Brown.

TILLY, C.; L. TILLY; AND R. TILLY. 1975. *The Rebellious Century*. Cambridge, Mass.: Harvard University Press.

TOFFLER, A. 1970. *Future Shock*. New York: Bantam.

TOMEH, A.K. 1964. "Informal group participation and residential pattern." *American Journal of Sociology* 70 (July): 28–35.

———. 1967. "Informal participation in a metropolitan community." *Sociological Quarterly* 8 (Winter): 85–102.

TONNIES, F. 1887 (1957). *Community and society*. Translated and edited by C.P. Loomis. New York: Harper Torchbook.

TREADWAY, R. 1969. "Social components of metropolitan population densities." *Demography* 6 (February): 55–74.

TUAN, Y. 1974. *Topophilia*. Englewood Cliffs, N.J.: Prentice-Hall.

VAN DEN BERGHE, P. 1974. "Bringing beasts back in: Toward a biosocial theory of aggression." *American Sociological Review* 39 (December): 777–88.

VERBRUGGE, L. 1973. "Adult friendship contact." Ph.D. dissertation, University of Michigan, Ann Arbor, Michigan.

VON ROSENBLADT, B. 1972. "The outdoor activity system in an urban environment." In *The Use of Time,* edited by A. Szalai, pp. 335–55. The Hague: Mouton.

WALLACE, W.L. 1975. "Structure and action in the theories of Coleman and Parsons." In *Approaches to the Study of Social Structure,* edited by P. Blau, pp. 121–34. New York: Free Press.

WALLDEN, M. 1975. "Activity patterns of urban residents: Part 2: The frequency of activities outside the home." *National Swedish Building Research Summaries* Rg.

WARD, S.K. 1974. "Overcrowding and social pathology: A re-examination of the implications for the human population." Paper presented to annual meeting of Population Association of America, New York.

WARNER, W.L. et al. 1963. *Yankee City*. Abridged edition. New Haven: Yale University Press.

WEBBER, M.M. 1968. "The post-city age." *Daedalus* 97 (Fall): 1091–1110.

———. 1970. "Order in diversity: Community without propinquity." In *Neighborhood, City, and Metropolis,* edited by R. Gutman and D. Popenoe, pp. 792–811. New York: Random House.

WEBER, M. 1947. *The Theory of Social and Economic Organization*. Translated by A.M. Henderson and T. Parsons. New York: Free Press.

WELLMAN, B. 1976. "Urban connections." Research Paper No. 84, Centre for Urban and Community Studies, University of Toronto.

WELLMAN, B. et al. 1973. "Community ties and support systems." In *The Form of Cities in Central Canada,* edited by L.S. Bourne, R.D. MacKinnon, and J.W. Simmons. Toronto: University of Toronto Press.

WHITE, H.C.; S.A. BOORMAN; AND R.L. BREIGER. 1976. "Social structure from multiple networks. I. Block-models of roles and positions." *American Journal of Sociology* 81 (January): 730–80.

WHITTEN, N.E., AND A.W. WOLFE. 1974. "Networks analysis." In *The Handbook of Social and Cultural Anthropology,* edited by J.J. Honigman, pp. 717–46. Chicago: Rand McNally.

WHYTE, W.F. 1955. *Street Corner Society*. Enlarged edition. Chicago: University of Chicago Press.

WHYTE, W.H. 1956. *The Organization Man*. New York: Simon and Schuster.

WILKINSON, R.K., AND E.M. SIGSWORTH. 1972. "Attitudes to the housing environment." *Urban Studies* 9 (June): 193–214.

WILLIAMS, R. 1973. *The Country and the City*. New York: Oxford University Press.

WILNER, R.; R. WALKEY; J. PINKERTON; AND M. TAYBACK. 1962. *The Housing Environment and Family Life*. Baltimore: Johns Hopkins Press.

WINCH, R.F. 1958. *Mate Selection: A Study of Complementary Needs.* New York: Harper and Row.

WINSBOROUGH, H. 1965. "The social consequences of high population density." *Law and Contemporary Problems* 30 120–26.

WIRTH, L. 1928 (1956). *The Ghetto.* Chicago: University of Chicago Press.

——. 1938. "Urbanism as a way of life." *American Journal of Sociology* 44 (July): 3–24.

——. 1945. "Human ecology." Reprinted in *Classic Essays on the Culture of Cities,* edited by R. Sennet, pp. 170–79. New York: Appleton-Century-Crofts.

WOLF, E.R. 1966. "Kinship, friendship, and patron-client relations." In *Social Anthropology of Complex Societies,* edited by M. Banton. ASA monograph No. 4. London: Tavistock.

WOLFE, A.W. 1970. "Social network analysis." Unpublished paper. Department of Anthropology, University of Wisconsin, Milwaukee.

WOLPERT, J. 1965. "Behavioral aspects of the decision to migrate." *Papers of the Regional Science Association* 15: 159–69.

WYLIE, L. 1964. *Village in the Vaucluse.* New York: Harper and Row.

YOUNG, M., AND P. WILLMOTT. 1957. *Family and Kinship in East London.* Baltimore: Penguin.

ZABLOCKI, B. 1971. *The Joyful Community.* Baltimore: Penguin.

ZEHNER, R.B., AND S.F. CHAPIN, JR. 1974. *Across the City Line.* Lexington, Mass.: Lexington Books.

ZEITLAN, M.; L.A. EWEN; AND R.E. RATCLIFF. 1974. " 'New princes' for old? The large corporation and the capitalist class in Chile." *American Journal of Sociology* 80 (July): 87–123.

ZELAN, J. 1968. "Does suburbia make a difference?" In *Urbanism in World Perspective,* edited by S.F. Fava, pp. 401–408. New York: Oxford University Press.

ZIMMER, B. 1973. "Residential mobility and housing." *Land Economics* 69 (3): 344–50.

——. 1975. "Urban centrifugal drift." In *Metropolitan America in Contemporary Perspective,* edited by A. Hawley and V. Rock, pp. 23–92. New York: Halstead Press.

ZUCKERMAN, M. 1970. *Peaceable Kingdoms: New England Towns in the Eighteenth Century.* New York: Knopf.

Index

Abu-Lughod, Janet, 5
Access, 120, 121, 124
Action, theory of, 6n
Adjustment, 123, 133, 200
Affective attachment: *see* Subjective feelings, attachment to place and
Age: *see also* Life-cycle
  friendship choice and, 59, 62, 68, 70–72, 74–78, 80–81, 91–97, 199
  segregation, 91–92
  -similar friendships, 91–97
  stratification, 91
Alexander, Christopher, 166
Anomie, 165
Anticipation, 123, 133, 200
Arcadian myth, 196–197
Attachment to place, 139–161; *see also* Authentic community
  decision-making models, 141, 142, 198
  "decline" of, 189–193
  definition of, 139
  economic perspective, 141, 142, 155
  forms of, 142–144
  functional perspective, 141
  institutional ties, 143, 144, 156, 158–159
  length of residence and, 148, 152, 156
  life-cycle and, 141–142, 147, 151, 156
  local intimates, 143, 144, 159–160
  measures of, 143–144, 145n
  mechanistic causal models, 141
  neighborhood features and, 150–151, 156
  psychological perspective, 140, 142, 155, 157, 164, 167

religion and, 153n, 154
  social involvement, 139, 143, 144–151, 154–155, 159
  socioeconomic status and, 141–142, 147–148, 150, 152, 154, 156
  sociological perspective, 140–141, 155, 157
  subjective feelings (affective attachment), 139, 142, 151–155, 156, 157n, 160–161
  women's employment and, 147, 152
Authentic community, 164–167
  local versus extralocal relations, 167–177
  residential mobility, 177–185
Authority, 11, 192

Baldassare, Mark, 101–115
Bloch, Marc, 193
Boissevain, J., 29, 33, 40n
Bott, E., 36, 37
Bottom-up process, 29
Boudon, Raymond, 197
Bounded rationality, 42, 43
Breiger, Ron, 29n

Calhoun, John, 101, 102
Chicago School, 4
Childhood friendships, 51–52, 55–56, 69, 70–71, 83–85, 89–90, 175
Choice-constraint model, 2, 3, 5, 10–14, 39–40, 42–43, 57–58, 77, 155, 157, 197–204
City-suburban differences, 126–127
Classical community theorists, 140, 157
Clustering, 36
Coleman, James, 3, 6n, 21
Commitment, 53, 61, 71, 87, 96

225